The External Implications of European Integration

The European Initiative

Series Editor: PROFESSOR DAVID G. MAYES
National Institute of Economic and Social Research, London, and
Co-ordinator of the Economic and Social Research Council (ESRC)
research project *The European Initiative.*

The late 1980s and early 1990s have produced major events and
changes in Europe which are set to produce fundamental shifts in the
economic, political and social changes throughout the continent. The
European Community's Single Market Programme due for completion
at the end of 1992 and the sweeping political reforms and revolution in
Eastern Europe have been the catalysts. This new series of books has
been established to publish the best research and scholarship on
European issues and to make an important contribution to the
advancement of knowledge on European issues.

Professor Mayes is Co-ordinator of a major research initiative on
European issues by the Economic and Social Research Council. The
Series, in addition to publishing the leading contributions made by that
initiative, will also publish other titles drawn from all disciplines in the
Social Sciences, including Economics, Political Science and Sociology.

Titles in the Series:

The European Challenge: Industry's Response to the 1992 programme
edited by David G. Mayes

The External Implications of European Integration
edited by David G. Mayes

The New Europe: Changing Economic Relations between East and West
by Susan Senior Nello

The External Implications of European Integration

Kym Anderson
David G. Mayes (editor)
Dermot McAleese
Jacques Pelkmans
Jon Stanford
John M. Stopford
Stephen Woolcock
George N. Yannopoulos

HARVESTER
WHEATSHEAF

New York   London   Toronto   Sydney   Tokyo   Singapore

First published 1993 by
Harvester Wheatsheaf
Campus 400, Maylands Avenue
Hemel Hempstead
Hertfordshire, HP2 7EZ
A division of
Simon & Schuster International Group

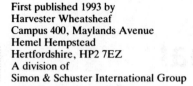

Typeset in 10/12 pt Times
by Keyset Composition, Colchester

Printed and bound in Great Britain by
BPCC Wheatons Ltd, Exeter

British Library Cataloguing in Publication Data

A catalogue record for this book is available from
the British Library

ISBN 0-7450-1422-4

---

1 2 3 4 5   97 96 95 94 93

Contents

Preface

This book was born out of a number of different concerns. The first stems from the 'Britain in Europe' research programme at the National Institute of Economic and Social Research (NIESR) in London, where it had become clear that a markedly different perception of what was being attempted by the completion of the European Single Market was held in third countries from the one that prevailed in the European Commission. Part of the debate was about the intentions of the European Community, and part of it about the possible impact that Community actions might have upon third countries. While it had become clear by early 1989 that the aspects of the Single Market that might originally have been achieved by an increase in the effectiveness of external barriers round the Community were being considerably diluted, there was no emerging consensus on the sign let alone the size of the potential impact on third countries. The Commission's own estimates had largely ignored this dimension, and other attempts to tackle the issues had been decidedly limited.

It was therefore decided to organise a small conference at NIESR on the impact of the Single Market on the major non-European countries. To give the conference both scope and focus the conference papers looked at the countries round the Pacific, as these include all the major non-European countries and a very considerable range of economic structures and cultures. Stephen Woolcock was invited to look at the United States, George Yannopoulos at Japan and Jacques Pelkmans at the Association of South East Asian Nations (ASEAN). David Mayes, who organised the conference, completed the picture by considering the impact on Australia and New Zealand. The authors also focused on different aspects of the impact, Woolcock looking principally at trade relations, Yannopoulos at direct investment, Mayes at trade and

Pelkmans at a range of further influences from other Community policies as well. These four papers (subject to limited revision) form chapters 5–8 of the present book; earlier versions were published in the November 1990 issue of the *National Institute Economic Review* and are reproduced here with permission.

These papers engendered considerable debate, particularly in Australia, and Jon Stanford, Alan Bollard and David Mayes put together a joint research proposal to consider in more detail the impact on Australia and New Zealand. As part of the project it was decided to hold a second conference in London, this time at Australia House. By then, although funding had not been forthcoming for any of the three authors, Stanford had been appointed Australian Public Service Fellow at the Sir Robert Menzies Centre in the Institute of Commonwealth Studies at the University of London for a year, and David Mayes had become co-ordinator of the Economic and Social Research Council's 'Single European Market' research initiative, *The Evolution of Rules for a Single European Market*. These two groups sponsored the second conference, which was held in late 1991.

The focus was decidedly on the future, and considered not just the Single Market, but economic and monetary union, the proposed expansion of the EC, and the challenge posed by the Central and East European countries' process of transition to a market economy. Although Australia was very clearly the third country of prime concern, and the Australian High Commissioner was kind enough to open the conference, the focus was deliberately cast wide. Dermot McAleese was invited to look at the framework of the EC's trade policy in this context. Following his work for the GATT, Kym Anderson was invited to take a broad look at the possible development of trade and production, while John Stopford, of the London Business School, was invited to extend the work he had earlier completed for the OECD on the role of the principal actors in achieving market change, the multinational companies.

The conference was completed by papers by Mayes and Stanford. The former extended the previous analysis to include the impact on third countries of the recent steps in European integration, while the latter considered the response that Australia should make in the field of industrial policy. Together, these give a very full picture of the potential impact on third countries of the process of European integration in the 1990s. The papers by McAleese, Stopford and Anderson form chapters 2–4 of the present book, and Stanford's chapter 9.

The book is completed by two new chapters (chapters 1 and 10), by David Mayes. Chapter 1 takes a broad look at the issues, and uses material from the 1990 and 1991 papers as well as presenting new sections; quantitative and qualitative results for third countries are suggested. Chapter 10 is new and presents a brief consideration of the response that third countries might make in the light of these possible impacts.

In inviting contributors we sought to ensure that there would be a good balance between those who believed that European integration over the last fifteen years of the twentieth century was likely to be generally beneficial to third countries, and those who were ambivalent. In fact, there was relatively little debate about the impact on third countries in the conferences, but much more debate about what third countries should do. Chapter 10 summarises some of that debate.

The papers were written independently and the authors are not responsible for each other's views. Furthermore, the views expressed here cannot be attributed to NIESR, the GATT, the ESRC or the Commonwealth of Australia. We are, however, very grateful to all the organisations, which over the years have enabled the research on which this work is based to take place. Special thanks is due to the NZ Institute of Economic Research and its Director Alan Bollard, who helped with much of the work on New Zealand, and to Andrew Britton who has commented throughout and who agreed to devote the resources of NIESR to the first conference.

It is with great regret that I have to report the death of George Yannopoulos while the book was in the copy-editing stage. I updated his chapter with his agreement when he was taken ill earlier in the year and the book is dedicated to his memory.

David G. Mayes

1

The implications of closer integration in Europe for third countries[1]

David G. Mayes

During the second half of the 1980s the countries of Europe set in train four steps in the process of integration, all of which will have marked effects not just on their own behaviour but on that of the world as a whole throughout the 1990s and beyond. The four steps began with the decision to create a 'Single European Market' in 1985 among the members of the European Community. In the second move, signed in 1992,[2] this market is to be extended to the members of EFTA through the European Economic Area Agreement. However, before either of these processes was completed the EC had agreed to conclude a new treaty on European Union, which would create an economic, political and monetary union, the terms of which are set out in the Maastricht Treaty. This treaty was in the process of ratification at the time of writing (1992). However, far more dramatic than these momentous events was the collapse of the political order in Eastern and Central Europe, with the ending of the communist regimes there, the moves towards a market-oriented system with closer integration with the West and the creation of new states out of the former Soviet Union and Yugoslavia.

How these changes came about, and the way they have developed, have largely been matters of internal concern for the European countries, but because of their sheer scale they have had to have regard for their consequences on others. In particular, the Single European Market was intended as a means of improving European competitive performance. This was especially in response to the challenge from Japan in many advanced products and to the slow growth, or 'Eurosclerosis', which had seemed to characterise performance after the first oil crisis of 1974. Since any improvement would inevitably be at the expense of third countries, these countries were concerned that any change should be fair in their eyes.

The Community has argued that, in so far as the Single Market will result in a substantial expansion of trade and economic activity in the world, it will be a clear source of advantage for everyone. Indeed, past evidence of the establishment or expansion of trading areas shows that, in total, the gains from expansion considerably outweigh the costs from diversion of trade (this is explored in more detail by Dermot McAleese in chapter 2).[3] However, the Single Market is no ordinary example of tariff reduction. The sources of gain and loss come from far more than trade alone, and they deserve further specific analysis.

The European Commission organised an extensive programme of studies to assess the consequences of the Single Market, and this resulted in the publication of the *Cecchini Report – 1992: The European Challenge* and *The Economics of 1992* by Michael Emerson and colleagues (1989) with seventeen volumes of background papers under the general title *The Costs of Non-Europe*. The focus of these papers is almost exclusively on the internal costs of non-tariff barriers, which the 1992 programme is designed to remove. The external implications are largely restricted to generalisation,[4] although an indication of the potential for external gain can be derived.[5] As Jacques Delors put it in the foreword to the *Cecchini Report*, 'This large market without frontiers . . . gives a unique opportunity to our industry to improve its competitivity' (Cecchini 1988, p. xi). His next sentence talks about the world as a whole, but is ingeniously ambiguous: 'It will also increase growth and employment and contribute to a *better balance* in the world economy' (emphasis added). He says neither what 'better' means in this context nor for whom it is 'better'.

Our concern here has been to form a clearer view of whether these changes are really as benign as they have been made out to be for third countries, particularly for countries like Australia and New Zealand, which already have considerable experience of the adverse effects of the EC's policies in agriculture, and the virtual impossibility of getting any adequate redress through the organisations of the world trading system.

Since any changes stemming from closer European integration are likely to lead not just to a uniform expansion of welfare across the world but to some redistribution of benefits, some countries and regions will gain more than others. Even relative movements will provoke controversy, but there is fear in some quarters that there will be actual losses in some cases. As Begg and Mayes (1991) and Hager *et al.* (1992) make clear, these losses are likely to be felt within the Community and not just in third countries. However, the opportunity exists for compensating payments within the Community, as is illustrated by the structural and cohesion funds. Third countries can only offset the potential impact by trying to persuade the EC to amend its legislation, by capitalising on the opportunities offered by the Single Market more effectively, or by retaliating. Retaliation can take either the traditional form of imposing restrictions on imports from the EC or by replicating some of the sources of gain by forming regional trading groupings which exclude the EC, like NAFTA (North American Free Trade Agreement), which is awaiting ratification.

It would be wrong to concentrate on just one of the current steps in integration; it is the overall impact which will be observed, not its components. However, economic and monetary union can be viewed largely as an extension of the same process of trying to improve competitive efficiency as the formation of the Single Market, although the increased importance of the ecu in transactions in world markets, particularly at the expense of the US dollar, may generate further concerns. Indeed, the Commission's initial assessment of the implications, as set out in *One Market, One Money*, in *European Economy* (1990, with background papers in a special edition the following year), suggests that the impact will be comparatively small, and that the possibility exists for a rather larger, favourable 'dynamic' effect, which had previously been neglected. We examine this aspect further, below.

However, the upheavals in Central and Eastern Europe have had a much more dramatic impact on behaviour, not just because of the implications for patterns of world trade and payments, but because of their security implications. With the relaxing of the threat from the former Soviet bloc has come a reappraisal in the West of defence capabilities and the need to maintain defence support industries on the same scale as in the past. This will result in substantial changes to the economic structure, even though these may be on nothing like the scale of the changes in Eastern and Central Europe itself. The process of transformation in the former Eastern bloc is imposing a series of strains. The need for a massive inflow of investment funds to realign industry towards the production of goods and services which will be competitive on the open market was always appreciated, although there was little consensus about the scale involved. However, the extent of the collapse of the economic system and the scale of help required in the short term was grossly underestimated, by the Eastern bloc countries themselves and by the West. In both the longer and shorter term these processes of change will have major implications for countries outside Europe.

We cannot hope to deal with all of these issues here and our focus is restricted in terms of time, with a concentration on the 1990s, and in terms of geographic area, as we concentrate on the industrialised and rapidly industrialising countries rather than with the developing world. (See *Journal of Common Market Studies* (1990) for much of the problem for developing countries.) Given the location of Europe's major competitors – the United States and Japan – our focus is primarily the countries of the Pacific Rim (excluding South and Central America), although there are some substantial difficulties in viewing the Pacific as a region (Bollard and Mayes 1992), because of its sheer size, whether measured by area, GDP or population.

Furthermore, we are faced with a moving target. European integration does not have a single, defined path, but a set of overlapping processes, which are determined by different groups. The picture changes even as we write. The Single Market is due to come into full operation on 1 January 1993, after what has been dubbed the 1992 Programme of 280 measures has been agreed and implemented. Only a few measures remained to be agreed in the last few months of 1992. However, implementation of many of these is now scheduled to take much longer. For example, systems for mutual recognition and Europe-wide certification of pharmaceutical products will not come into operation until 1995. In any case, the Single Market is likely to be an evolving system for many years to come, with considerable fragmentation remaining for the foreseeable future.

The Maastricht Treaty, due to come into force on 1 January 1993, had not been ratified at the end of September 1992. While ratification was not expected to be a formality, the EC members have been disturbed to find that the Danish electorate rejected it, albeit by a very small margin. Although all twelve member states have said that they do not intend to renegotiate the treaty, a way forward still has to be found which will be acceptable to the Danish electorate. Current thinking is that this can be achieved by a new protocol which, *inter alia*, emphasises the principle of 'subsidiarity'. That is to say, the role of the member state, rather than the Commission, will be emphasised in the execution of policy, where this is both efficient and does not lead to significant spillover effects on other member states. Nevertheless, the future of economic and monetary union has been thrown into some confusion, and the timetable for change, which was already complex, is now subject to further uncertainty. This has been amplified by the events of September 1992, when both sterling and the lira were forced out of the ERM by market pressures. The inability to negotiate a re-alignment weakens the credibility of the system considerably.

However, these uncertainties pale into insignificance compared with the difficulties in Eastern and Central Europe, even taking account of the fact that the EC is likely to begin negotiations in 1993 with a group of EFTA countries, including Austria, Finland, Sweden and possibly Norway, on full membership of the Community. The process of transition to market economies and closer integration with the West has proved much more complex and costly than most people had hoped. Even the former East Germany, which has had the easiest path to integration through union with West Germany, has encountered problems of unemployment and costs of investment in infrastructure and industry on such a scale that it is affecting the development of the entire European Community. The need to finance this investment has led to higher interest rates in Germany restricting growth elsewhere. (See Britton and Mayes (1992) and the sections on the world economy in recent issues of the *National Institute Economic Review*.)

Although difficult, it is possible to see a way forward in the case of Hungary, while Czechoslovakia seems likely to divide into two states, and Poland has yet to get its inflation under control. Other Eastern bloc countries are either far less advanced in the process of change (Bulgaria, Romania, Albania and the Baltic states, for example), or are still in the process of defining their borders (Yugoslavia, Russia and some other parts of the former Soviet Union). These internal problems are slowing down the pace of integration with the West, holding up both the signing of formal agreements and the conclusion of private sector trade and investment deals. Problems of establishing property rights and law and order add an element of high risk to what is already a difficult operation. The uncertainties and privations may mean that substantial backward steps will be taken in the process of development and European integration. Nevertheless there are already co-operation, aid and financing agreements with many of the states, and further steps in the integration process seem certain as the 1990s progress.

We can therefore observe a series of actual and potential impacts from European integration which radiate outwards from what might be described as the core, or at least a core, of the present EC. The Belgium and Luxembourg Economic Union is the furthest developed piece of integration between separate member states (especially since the Irish pound was unpegged from parity with sterling), followed by Benelux and the links between them, much of western Germany, eastern France and northern Italy.[6]

The other members of the EC are rather less integrated in a variety of respects, and hold differing views about the extent and speed of the further integration they would like to see. We have already noted the reservations in Denmark about some of the aspects of closer integration, while British reservations were already built into the Maastricht Treaty, with the option not to participate in the final stage of monetary union and the refusal to accept the social dimension of the agreement. This different treatment in the case of the United Kingdom also extends to its trading patterns. For while these concentrate more and more on the Community it still has a greater importance than other member states for external (i.e. non-EC) links. This is further emphasised by the strong pattern of international investment, both inwards and outwards.

The more important secondary ring, in economic terms, relates not to these higher income regions but to what are described as the less favoured regions of the Community. These include the whole of Ireland, Portugal and Greece, southern Italy and most of Spain. These have a per capita income of less than 75 per cent of the EC average and benefit within the Community from the structural funds, which will be increased considerably through the cohesion funds established by both the European Economic Area agreement and the Maastricht Treaty. This transfer of resources adds an extra dimension to the process of integration occurring in the rest of the EC, and hence also adds an extra dimension to the wider impact of integration. Establishing fair competition within the European Single Market has involved the banning of state aids, thus removing a range of non-tariff measures to support exports and import substitution without any requirement for third countries to take reciprocal action. (These support measures are still permitted on a regional basis, however.)

The EFTA countries represent a third ring round the core of the Community. However, the impact here may have to be subdivided if only some EFTA members opt to become full members of the EC.

Central and East European countries comprise a fourth ring – again, one which should probably be subdivided. The former East Germany is a case on its own, while Poland, Hungary and Czechoslovakia have the most advanced agreements. Other countries have varying degrees of linkage, down to Serbia, which is currently (1992) the subject of a trade embargo. Nevertheless, it is clear that these countries will form part of a favoured group, with increasing links with the EC and the rest of Western Europe.[7]

Two further rings can be identified. The first relates to what can be described as the Mediterranean countries, and the second to all the associated former colonies covered by the Lomé and similar agreements. Both of these have preferential agreements with the Community. The focus of this book is on what is left, what we have described as 'third' countries. These too can be grouped, and our focus is principally the countries of the Pacific.

Within the Pacific region we can distinguish four major groups of countries. The first are the major players, principally Japan and the United States, although Canada is a significant player in this group by virtue of its close economic ties with the United States. The major feature of this group is that it has real bargaining power with the EC. Because of their economic size and importance in the EC's trade flows,

these countries exercise a sufficiently credible threat through retaliation or other measures that the EC has to take heed of their views.
Furthermore, many other countries may follow them, so that Japan
and the United States can effectively act as spokesmen for world
opinion. The drawback of this representative role is that neither the
United States nor Japan is typical of many other countries' economic
position, so where their interests and those of United States/Japan do
not coincide, there is much less opportunity to express those views
effectively.[8] Second, this first group of countries contains most of the
world's major companies outside Europe, so that its influence is also
felt effectively through the market. Indeed, it is the success of those
companies rather than the success of the policies of their governments
which has been a major stimulus to increasing the pace of integration
and to establishing the pre-eminence of the market over the planned
system in practice.

The second group of Pacific countries discussed here are what can
be described as the major success stories of recent years. First, the
'dragons' or 'tigers': Hong Kong, Singapore, Taiwan and South Korea,
which have already made much of the transition from being developing
to being industrialised countries. Following in their footsteps are the
rest of the ASEAN countries: Malaysia, Indonesia, the Philippines,
Thailand and Brunei. These have had an influence on the EC through
their rapid growth rate and penetration of markets in particular
product areas. However, their bargaining power is relatively weak and
as yet largely untried, as their growth has been rather more constrained by internal factors than by difficulties of access to markets.

Third come Australia and New Zealand, which are a particular focus
of this book. Historically, they have had extensive trading links with
Europe, dominated by trade with the United Kingdom. The major
impact of economic integration in Europe since the 1960s has been to
drive them further into being 'Pacific' nations rather than 'European'
countries a long way from Europe. Both have experienced considerable economic difficulties in the transition, and have been going
through a process of reorientation the scale of which in some sectors
resembles that of Eastern rather than Western Europe. The next steps
in European integration could be crucial. At one extreme, the need to
address problems in Southern, Central and Eastern European countries could result in a further diversion of resources away from the
pattern of unfettered free trade, depressing Australasian prospects by
hitting their agricultural and resource markets. Alternatively, it could
provide a stimulus to growth as European demand rises more strongly
and investment flows in both directions develop the links between the
economies.

In the following chapters we look specifically at the impact of

European integration on the United States, Japan, ASEAN, Australia and New Zealand. However, this omits from detailed consideration a large proportion of both the land area and the population of the countries which border the Pacific in what makes up the residual and rather heterogeneous group of countries. This group includes China, the Russian federation, most of Indo-China as well as the host of small countries among the Pacific islands.[9] At present the links with these countries are weak; and even though the forthcoming reintegration of China and Hong Kong in 1997 is generating a considerable expansion in the role of China, by comparison, this group has relatively little contact with Europe. We have therefore excluded it from explicit treatment.

We begin, however, by assessing the routes and likely extent of the external implications of closer European integration in general terms in this chapter to provide a basis for the more detailed country-by-country analysis of the chapters to come, followed by an exploration of the EC's external trade policy (Chapter 2) and competitiveness across the world as a whole and its likely impact on the countries of the Pacific (Chapter 3). The book concludes with two chapters which discuss the implications for policy of these changes and suggest how the various countries might best respond, first, in the scenario where they can influence the development of the EC towards the benefit of the wider world, and second, where they are unsuccessful in that task and have to aim towards a second rather than a first best outcome.

1.1 The nature of the external implications

Assessing the nature of the external implications of closer European integration is a multi-stage process. The obvious approach would be to begin by listing the changes in legislation and the regulatory environment which form part of the Single Market programme. To this should be added the legislative proposals which have emerged from the Maastricht Treaty on European Union, with suggestions on how it might be amended in order to achieve ratification by all the member states. Beyond this we can assess the further changes which seem likely to take place during the 1990s, extending full membership of the EC to some or all of the EFTA countries by 1995 and providing a closer association of various of the Central and Eastern European countries and the other applicants from Southern Europe: Cyprus, Malta and Turkey. We would then go on to assess how the various market players, both within the EC and outside it, react, and calculate the resultant impact.

For the case of the Single European Market, this is roughly how the analysis behind the *Cecchini Report* on *The Costs of Non-Europe* proceeds, although it tends to conflate the Single Market and EMU effects.[10] *One Market, One Money* has developed this further, by identifying the elements related to EMU as such – lower interest rates and transactions costs for intra-EC currency transaction – and by exploring some of the issues related to response, particularly on the subject of dynamics, rather more fully. The first step used there was to assess the implications of the Single Market measures in terms of potential cost reductions. Using models of how the economies have responded in the past, it then estimated the outcomes.

We could argue about the appropriate choice of models. The Commission employs a combination of limited sectoral assessments[11] and macroeconomic model simulation using models such as Interlink and Hermes. We have ourselves extended this sort of analysis, both at the detailed sectoral level (Mayes *et al.* 1991; Burridge and Mayes 1992) and at the broader macroeconomic level (Britton and Mayes 1992, based on the contributions to Barrell 1992). However, this is an artificial exercise as it assumes that all the Single Market measures will be implemented and that the market will respond to them fully. Thus the question of the most appropriate model is very much secondary to its use within the appropriate conceptual framework.

In practice we need to make a more complex assessment (see Figure 1.1). First, we cannot assume that any specific regulatory change achieves its objective. For example, it may not be the binding constraint. Permitting labour movement into an area achieves little if there is a shortage of housing or if the price differential is such that people cannot afford to move. Second, the market may react in order to frustrate the intention – a potential cost reduction may not be passed on in full in an oligopolistic market, for example. Third, it is

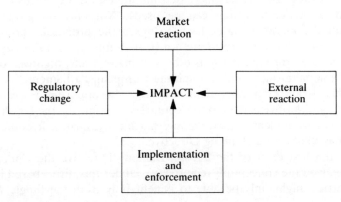

Figure 1.1

one thing to legislate, but another to enforce legislation. The UK government has struggled for years to control local authority spending, with singular lack of success, where the local authority did not share the same objectives. It is thus highly unlikely, where public purchasing is relatively small scale and highly decentralised, that any effective scheme can be devised to ensure that competition is fully open to all Community suppliers. Lastly, it cannot be assumed that third countries will sit idly by. They may themselves initiate legislation or behaviour which will offset the effects of changes in the SEM programme. This is thus not just a matter of replacing an increasingly sophisticated partial equilibrium approach by general equilibrium models (as in the case in Stoeckel *et al.* 1990), but by considering how the system of responses itself responds to such a major change of regime.

In part this is an application of the Lucas critique (Lucas 1976) of many standard econometric models, in which he argues that using models based on behaviour under a previous regime is inappropriate for assessing behaviour under a new regime. Given the dramatic nature of present changes under the Single Market, EMU, the EEA and, in particular, the transformation of the Central and Eastern European economies, that critique could scarcely be more appropriate. The point of the regime changes is to change behaviour, especially by unleashing stronger competition. However, the process of regime change is itself subject to competition, bargaining and uncertainty.

We therefore need to amend the simplistic views of impact by taking into account all three of these influences.[12] However, even this restriction does not grasp the full picture as the actual regulatory changes are themselves the result of internal and external pressures (Figure 1.2). The process of embodying the proposals set out in the 1985 White Paper in appropriate directives, regulations and other legislation is itself one of negotiation and compromise (although the Single European Act has increased the number of occasions on which qualified majority voting can be used). Not only do governments within the member states have to agree the proposals through the Council of Ministers, but there are strong lobbies, both directly to the Commission through Brussels offices of major firms, organisations and professional groups, and through the European Parliament.[13]

This period of development also gives the opportunity for governments and lobbyists from other countries to influence the legislation.[14] This has been clearly instrumental in achieving change in some areas, such as the Second Banking Directive.

In the first draft of the Second Banking Directive the Commission introduced the concept of 'reciprocity'. Under this, firms based in third countries might only be able to benefit fully from the Single Market

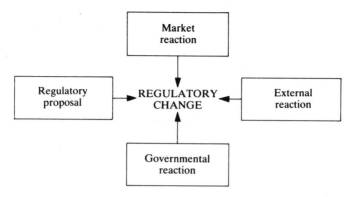

Figure 1.2

rules if their home country allowed access to EC companies on a comparable basis. It soon became clear that this was an unreasonable condition as US legislation, for example, excluded US banks from various operations across state boundaries. EC banks could not expect more favourable treatment in the United States than US banks, and the United States could not be expected to change rules designed to protect the US banking system from systemic collapse just because the EC had different views about how banking should be regulated. Subsequently, the Commission argued that the idea of reciprocity had been misinterpreted, but there was a clear change in approach between the first and second Commissions over which Jacques Delors presided (the second one coming into office at the beginning of 1989). No longer were there suggestions, for example, that only two Japanese cars should be admitted into the EC for every one European car sold in Japan.[15] External representations and threats were very successful in scotching the idea that there might be some form of 'Fortress Europe', whereby the openness of the Single Market was exploited behind more efficient external barriers for the Community.[16]

In some areas representatives from organisations in other countries are involved formally in the decision-making for the Single Market. Part of the process of technical harmonisation involves standard-setting through CEN and CENELEC to which the EFTA countries also belong. International rail standards in Europe involve the East European countries as well. The importance of being a party to negotiations such as these is emphasised by the United States' request for a seat at the table.

Influence by companies in third countries does not have to be external. It is possible to become a Community player by investing inside the EC. This can be by acquisition of an existing company, greenfield investment or indeed, by co-operation agreements and joint ventures.[17] Firms have a choice of routes of market entry, from the various stages of trading, linkages with other companies, to direct investment whether through acquisition or by setting up a new enterprise. This choice can be exercised in different ways across the various stages in the production chain, as past and potential decisions affect the impact on third countries and the way they and their companies choose to react.

It is no coincidence that Stephen Woolcock, writing on the United States (Chapter 5), distinguishes between policy reactions by the government and by firms, because they both have major market power. Trade with the United States is important to the EC, as the United States is the largest single external market. US support for the measures involved in European integration – or at least its acquiescence in them – is necessary for them to work properly. The mature US multinationals, whose European subsidiaries like to be thought of as European companies, are major players in the detailed lobbying and decision-making process in European integration. It is noticeable, as Woolcock points out, that the main US objectors are those who are not major players inside the Community, or who are concerned that they may not be able to continue to play such a role.

George Yannopoulos, writing on Japan, on the other hand (Chapter 6), focuses strongly on the response by Japanese companies, in the main because their maturity in tackling European markets is far less advanced than that of the United States. Companies rapidly building up a market share attract far more opposition from incumbents. This is revealed even more strongly in the case of ASEAN where concerns relate not so much to the Single Market *per se* but to Community commercial policy. Although efforts are made to separate these two issues by the authorities in Brussels, the two are related. While integration measures are aimed at improving the efficiency of the use of resources within the Community by removing unnecessary internal barriers, they are also aimed at improving the competitiveness of European industry with respect to the rest of the world.

Chapter 8 on Australia and New Zealand takes this emphasis on what is not involved in the current steps in European integration even further. In their case they do not have the strong growth in other areas to offset EC protection in their major export areas. Their concern is therefore far more with what the Single Market is not but could be, rather than what it is. Without the benefit of major bargaining power from their importance in trade with the EC, or a wide range of significant multinational companies, they are recipients of EC policy rather than effective participants in the process of policy determination. Like the ASEAN countries, trade with the EC, both as importers and exporters, is far more important to Australia and New Zealand than it is to the EC. Expansion of links with the East European countries may easily have further adverse effects on Australia and New Zealand, for example those relating to Polish agricultural products and the sale of East German butter to the Soviet Union in 1990, which meant that the Soviets did not buy on the open market in that year.

1.2   Closer European integration

Although the combined impact of the four elements of current European integration (the Single Market; European union; the EEA/ widening of membership; and the transformation and integration of the former Soviet bloc) should all be taken into account when discussing the impact on third countries (as indeed should the evolution of all the many other factors that will come to bear in the 1990s), it is probably helpful to separate them out, at least initially.

1.2.1   The Single Market

Table 1.1 summarises the changes being implemented in the Single Market programme; more detailed descriptions are readily available.[18] The structure of the influence of those measures on third countries is given in Table 1.2, and follows a similar framework to that of Yannopoulos (1990). The Single Market is an ambitious attempt to remove unnecessary regulatory divisions in the European Community, and involves both positive and negative measures. Negative measures in this sense involve removing existing discrimination, while the positive measures involve setting up new common regulatory frameworks which apply across the whole Community. (Ending discrimination may also involve new measures, so the positive/negative distinction should not be taken too literally.)

Taking the negative first, these measures are in effect a liberalising of the market, with the removal of barriers at the frontiers to the free flow of goods and services, the mutual recognition of others' qualifications, systems of accreditation, etc., the opening of public procurement to producers in other member states and a string of other measures set out in Cecchini (1988). Some of this liberalisation applies to all goods and services within the market irrespective of place of production, in that, with no internal frontiers, all can move freely.

Some opportunities within the EC to withhold these benefits of freedom of circulation of goods and services from third countries will

Table 1.1 The main features of the Single Market programme.

The '1992 Programme' calls for action in six main areas:

1. *Unified market in goods and services:* Removal of barriers to trade in financial and other services, and of remaining non-tariff barriers to visible trade. Simplification of customs procedures and elimination of vehicle checks. Harmonisation of technical standards and health/safety regulations, with mutual recognition of certification. Closer alignment of VAT and excise duties.
2. *Unified factor market:* Free movement of capital, with removal of exchange controls. Alignment of savings taxes. Free movement of labour, with mutual recognition of qualifications.
3. *Promotion of competition:* Common rules on regulation, takeovers, state assistance to industry, patents and copyrights, company accounting and disclosure of information. Opening of public procurement to competitive tender. Reduced intervention in agriculture.
4. *Monetary integration:* Exchange-rate alignment (via ERM). To be followed by adoption of a single currency and creation of a European Central Bank.
5. *Social protection:* Adoption of a Social Charter incorporating freedom of movement, fair wages and conditions of employment, vocational training, collective bargaining, consultation over technological change and company restructuring, protection of children, elderly and disabled people.
6. *United response to external challenges:* A common external tariff. Infrastructure projects, especially high-speed rail and road links and integrated telecommunications. Co-operative R&D, especially in microelectronics and information technology. A common energy policy.

Table 1.2 Application of major Single Market measures to third countries.

Measures	Applicability
Frontier restrictions	
single country quotas	Very difficult to enforce.
voluntary restriction agreements	Can continue but lack the sanction of the threat of an effective alternative.
removal of formalities	All benefit.
Technical barriers	
common standards	Could benefit some members more.
single certification and testing	All benefit.
Market entry	
public procurement	Members only, unless reciprocity.
right of establishment	Some benefit to member states.
takeover/merger	Unequal benefits in both directions.
Freedom of movement of persons	Members benefit more.
Other market regulations,	Some slight net benefit to members.
e.g. transport, financial services	
Fiscal (VAT, Corporation tax, etc.)	Largely neutral effect.
Financial (state aids, capital markets, etc.)	Net benefit to third countries.

continue to exist. In the case of motor cars, and other items like pharmaceuticals, which have to be registered before they can be used, it is possible to control foreign market penetration without internal border controls in the Community. But for goods such as clothing, which retail widely, any effective control would be difficult to envisage. Thus to a large extent the benefits are available to third country producers. Nevertheless, exporters still face the frontier barriers of getting into the Community at all. While the costs of the delays involved at the frontier may be relatively lower than the costs of shipping long distances to the EC, this still means that *relative* prices move in favour of EC producers as they have no frontiers to cross.

Services are a rather different matter, as most require local establishment, which again offers an opportunity for control of third country producers and, hence, discrimination against them even though third country banks, for example, can benefit from operating under home country control in their place of principal registration within the EC. But that is still a second administration to cope with in addition to that of their own country.

Public procurement continues as a discriminatory device against those in third countries, although there is the opportunity to participate if reciprocal benefits are offered. The preference of public purchasers for domestic products, despite price and quality disadvantages, is the norm round the world, so in many respects the EC is going further towards liberalisation than most other countries. Hence, seeking reciprocity is an understandable stance, even though it may deny EC purchasers the best value for money if they choose not to open their purchases unilaterally.

Where local capacity does not exist it is commonplace to ask for offsets when permitting foreign imports, i.e. requirements that part of the product is produced locally or that other activities are brought into the local area. Many of the reasons for preferring local supply (e.g. security and rapid response) are practised widely in the private sector too. The difference is that private firms are under no obligation to justify their purchasing decisions to the public. The appropriateness of their strategies will be reflected in their relative performance.

The application of mutual recognition is not as straightforward for third countries. In the first place it does not apply to qualifications and to the movement of people, unless they happen to have a qualification in a member state. Second, it would be normal for a third country to seek type approval or certification in its domestic market before going on to export. Companies in member states would be able to go on to export elsewhere in the EC provided their products meet the minimum requirements with respect to health, safety and the environment, but foreign companies need to obtain a second registration within the EC, thus slowing market entry and adding to costs.

In addition to *liberalising*, many of the Single Market measures involve *harmonising* existing rules and regulations to a common form (the positive measures referred to earlier). Although one of the main reasons why the 1992 programme has proved such a major step forward in the pace of European integration is that much detailed harmonisation no longer has to be agreed by Community institutions, harmonisation is still a major problem. First, in many cases an agreement is still required, but responsibility for it has merely been passed on to standards institutions, such as CEN and CENELEC. These organisations may very well be more adept at getting agreement and indeed may conclude 'better' agreements, but the initial consequence is that despite rapid progress a log-jam of cases has built up. As a result it will be a very long time before a Single Market is attained in technical requirements. Second, the way in which the harmonisation which is still required is taking place seems to have a penchant for combining the most restrictive aspects of each of the member states, rather than the lowest or a compromise.

Third countries are concerned that quarantine and health standards are being used as a covert means of protection. This results in both costs and benefits for third countries. They are excluded from discussions on the common standards – although, of course, if a third country company is a world leader and a major European producer to boot, as is IBM, it can still dominate the process. On the other hand, the third country does not have to adhere to safety or environmental requirements in production nor to the measures in the social dimension of the Single Market programme. While this may benefit some LDCs, this is of less help to developed countries which already impose strong social obligations on employers.

In general, a company will benefit if the common standards are closest to its own standards. This is least likely for companies outside the United States and Japan as their standards can differ from those in all other countries, thus giving some Community producers a competitive edge.[19] However, the need to adjust can occur even where there is little or no production in the EC. New Zealand, for example, is currently trying to attain EC standards certification for radiata pine (its main commercial timber), which is not normally grown commercially in Europe.

Two aspects of the Single Market which can offer a benefit to third countries are worth mentioning. The first comes from competition policy. EC companies are restrained both in the EC market share and in practices such as vertical restraint agreements within the Community. The EC authorities, whether Commission or national governments, have no such jurisdiction outside the EC.[20] Thus a third country company can benefit from a monopoly position in other parts of the world and from restrictive practices which boost its profitability. It can use this strong base to be a more aggressive competitor within the EC. However, the cross-subsidisation implied would only make sense if it were a temporary means of attaining a competitive position which would then be sustained without it. Of course, the converse may apply when local Trade Practices or Commerce Acts are harsher than those in the EC. In any case, a foreign company has two sets of legislation to worry about: its own domestic and that in the EC, which itself has both a Community and a member state component.

The second area of possible benefit comes in the form of state aids, which are heavily restricted in the Single Market to ensure equal treatment of companies from all member states. No such restrictions apply to third countries except those that might be caught under anti-dumping rules of the GATT. Again, therefore, the net effect depends on the relative circumstances that apply in the particular third country. In the case of New Zealand, the rapid rundown of state aids could mean that the balance is unfavourable.

All told, the net effect of the Internal Market on relative costs seems to be clearly negative for most third country companies, although some, like insurers and brewers, will have improved access and those in transport and distribution can benefit from market growth. In so far as reciprocal removal of restrictions cuts costs and removes distortions, there will be further gains. The crucial question, however, is the extent to which the European market expands as it is this that provides the possibility of a clear net gain to third countries.

The sensitivity of the external impact of the Single Market on the relative rate of growth and relative cost effects is demonstrated by Stoeckel *et al.* (1990), who provided one of the few attempts to quantify the effects of the 1992 programme on the world as a whole, using a general equilibrium model (both income and price effects are allowed for). They explore three scenarios ('simple', 'adjusted', 'restricted'; see Table 1.3) where in the simple case the reduction of costs in the EC plus the increase in demand leads to an improvement in the trade balance. Under these circumstances there are losses for both North America and Japan, but Australasia and ASEAN benefit.[21]

If, on the other hand, the EC countries were to expand their economies enough to eliminate this improvement in the balance of trade (the 'adjusted' case, referred to in Table 1.3), the picture is substantially changed. The North American loss is transformed into a small gain and the Japanese loss is largely eliminated, but this is in part at the expense of Australasia and ASEAN. However, these first two simulations assume that the new external restrictions placed on third

Table 1.3   Simulated effects of EC-1992, by region: changes in 1988 US$bn (Stoeckel *et al.* 1990).

Region	GDP	Exports	Imports
	Simple		
EC	230.8	88.3	−80.3
North America	−20.8	−36.2	25.3
Asia-Pacific	−12.3	−33.5	−31.7
Japan	−17.7	−21.6	7.6
Australasia	1.2	0.7	1.5
China	−0.2	−1.4	2.1
India	0.4	0.7	−1.3
Tigers	−0.8	−7.5	6.7
ASEAN*	3.9	−1.1	−11.6
Other Asia	−0.5	−0.4	−0.9
World	197.6	18.7	−137.2
	Adjusted		
EC	230.8	20.0	11.8
North America	5.4	2.1	2.7
Asia-Pacific	−0.3	−0.2	0.5
Japan	−2.0	−0.7	−0.4
Australasia	0.6	0.3	0.2
China	0.2	0.0	0.4
India	0.2	0.1	0.1
Tigers	0.0	0.0	0.0
ASEAN*	0.6	0.0	0.1
Other Asia	0.1	0.0	0.1
World	235.9	21.9	14.9
	Restricted		
EC	−52.2	−57.6	−33.9
North America	−39.5	−21.2	−27.4
Asia-Pacific	−16.4	−14.0	−15.7
Japan	−13.7	−7.6	−4.9
Australasia	−0.8	−1.0	−0.7
China	−0.6	−0.2	−2.2
India	−0.3	−0.3	−0.6
Tigers	−1.7	−3.7	−3.8
ASEAN*	0.8	−1.0	−2.9
Other Asia	−0.1	−0.2	−0.4
World	−108.1	−92.8	−76.9

Notes: The regions are defined in Table 1.4.
ASEAN* is all ASEAN members except Singapore.
World refers to all countries and regions in the table.
Figures are changes from base data in 1988 values.
See text for shock imposed on model.

Table 1.4   Regions used in Stoeckel *et al.*'s (1990) study.

ASEAN	Brunei, Indonesia, Malaysia, Philippines, Thailand
Tigers	Hong Kong, South Korea, Singapore, Taiwan
Other Asia	Bangladesh, Pakistan, Sri Lanka
EC	EC (12)
North America	Canada, United States
Australasia	Australia, New Zealand
ROW	Africa, Eastern Europe, South America, all other countries

countries at the Community level after 1992 are equal to the average of the restrictions imposed by the individual member states at the outset of the process in 1986. If a more pessimistic, 'restricted' view is taken and the agreed levels lie half way between the average and the most restrictive of the individual member states, the picture is transformed. Everybody, with the exception of ASEAN, loses, including the EC itself.

In many respects these results tell us rather more about the model than the economies involved as there is a very limited dynamic element in the model. As with all models calibrated on the past, policy and behavioural responses are not assumed to be affected by the shocks. In the case of the EC such changes are clearly hoped for as a deliberate consequence of the Single Market programme. Furthermore, in this form of simplified analysis only very general assumptions are made about the degree to which the Single Market proposals, as set out in the White Paper, are translated into legislation and about the direct impact of such legislation on costs. In general, the assumptions made in the background papers to the Cecchini Report are applied. Even with the low level of impulse from 1992 (simulated in Burridge and Mayes 1992), a third of the total impact comes from the feedback of the initial effect on the economy. If Stoeckel's simulations are to be believed, it is clear that the United States and Japan would have good reason to be unenthusiastic about the implications of 1992 under a range of plausible assumptions.

1.2.2   *Economic and monetary union*

Monetary union extends the scope of integration in a number of respects.[22] In the first place transaction costs are reduced since it is no longer necessary to change currencies between the member states. It also avoids the need for forward cover in those currencies. This is of disproportionate benefit to the member states themselves as they have a much larger proportion of their transactions with the other members.

Second, monetary union is expected to lead to considerable convergence among the member states in real terms, in policy and in structure, in itself contributing to what is described as economic union.[23] However, the emphasis in much of the discussions (see the various contributions to *European Economy*; No. 36, May 1988, for example) has been on convergence of inflation. As the rates of inflation in the member states fall towards that of the lowest (rather than the average) under the framework of the Delors Committee Report (1989), so real rates of interest can fall in the countries which currently experience more rapid inflation. It is argued, *inter alia* by Cecchini, that this fall in the cost of capital, aided by financial liberalisation under the Single Market, will tend to stimulate investment, and hence, productive potential and growth as the average age of the capital stock falls and its productivity rises (subject to diminishing returns of course). Foreign-owned producers within the EC will benefit to the same extent as domestic companies, but will still have a greater foreign exchange exposure than EC companies because of the greater need to deal in their own currencies.

However, a single currency in the EC is not without its problems, as it removes part of the adjustment mechanism to deal with external shocks. Regions within the EC may find that with nominal (but not, of course, real, as inflation can still vary) exchange rate adjustment no longer available to them they have to deflate in order to adjust, with consequent high unemployment. If demand for a third country's products is concentrated in parts of the Community experiencing adjustment problems (say, the United Kingdom), then the net impact will be less favourable than for countries focused on the fastest growing products and regions.

Again, therefore, as in the case of the Single Market, the balance of positive and negative factors will probably be close to call. Simulations with NIGEM (the National Institute's global econometric model) in *A Strategy for the ECU* suggest a net gain to third countries, but convergence may prove more difficult. (We have dealt with the issue of the achievability of EMU in considerable detail in Britton and Mayes (1992); and Barrell (1992) contains a range of views from many of the member states.) Under the Maastricht Treaty the EMU will be established in two further stages (the Community has already implemented stage 1). Stage 2 will be implemented on 1 January 1994, when the European Monetary Institute (EMI) will be set up, which has been charged with trying to bring the Community to stage 3 when exchange rates among the member states will become irrevocably fixed and the independent European Central Bank (ECB) will be set up. The EMI is effectively the embryo ECB.

The starting date for stage 3 depends on the success of the member states in converging according to five main criteria:

1. that they have not had to realign their exchange rates outside the permitted range within the last two years;
2. that their inflation rate has been within 1½ per cent of that of the three least inflationary member states over the period;
3. that their public sector deficit has been within 3 per cent of GDP;
4. that their public sector debt is less than 60 per cent of GDP;
5. that real interest rates have been within 1½ per cent of those of the lowest three member states.

In the first instance convergence according to these criteria has to be reviewed by mid-1996 and a decision taken as to whether to go ahead with stage 3 at the beginning of 1997. For that to occur a majority of the member states must have converged and the Council meeting in the form of heads of state/government must have agreed that it should go ahead. If convergence is insufficient, or it is decided not to proceed at that date, then stage 3 will come into operation on 1 January 1999 with whatever member states have converged by mid-1998.

The impact of EMU is thus contingent on its timing and how many members are in it. We attempted to forecast the outcome in Britton and Mayes (1992). In our opinion (1) it is unlikely that Greece will have converged by either date, unless there has been a dramatic political and economic change; (2) it will be difficult for Portugal and to a lesser extent Spain to converge by the earlier date; (3) there is no means of bringing Belgium's debt within the required range; and (4) for Italy to achieve the necessary budgetary reforms will require a major change of past behaviour – it is possible that the new government led by Mr Amato may be able to achieve that.[24] The remaining member states, including the United Kingdom, should be able to get close to convergence by either date.

There is therefore likely to be some pressure to go ahead in 1997, particularly because the interim stages of close alignment of exchange rates are difficult to sustain. Some shocks to the system are inevitable. With open capital markets, flows across the exchanges can readily reach unsustainable magnitudes despite central bank intervention if the interest rates required to prevent them become politically unacceptable. The temptation, therefore, will be to ease the criteria when it comes to making the decision. Otherwise the EC would be facing the prospect of stage 3 without Italy, Belgium and possibly Spain (and the United Kingdom if it chooses not to participate). That seems unlikely. The omission of Portugal and Greece might prove acceptable, but such a wide exclusion would fundamentally change the face of the Community and would entail that some of the member states would have to vote in favour of their own exclusion for the measure to be passed by qualified majority. Monetary union at an early stage by a smaller group of states is more likely only outside the Maastricht treaty.

Clearly, financial institutions and commercial companies in third countries will be affected by the introduction of stage 3, but the uncertainty which surrounds the progress to EMU must tend to limit the impact and the willingness to respond. However, although the stance of fiscal and monetary policy among the member states will be more predictable, EMU is likely to be a much less important feature of European integration for some time than the pervasive effects of the Single Market on the conduct of business.

There are very few forecasts of the impact of EMU, and the major source, the *One Market, One Money* issue of *European Economy*, is not very explicit. Although it identifies sixteen mechanisms by which EMU will have an impact, the chapter on 'the external dimension' is largely concerned with the impact on the world monetary system. Clearly, EC countries will gain from a reduction in transactions costs. They will need to keep smaller foreign exchange reserves as a result of pooling, and may reap gains from international seignorance as the external role of the ecu increases and supplants that of the US dollar.

Direct benefits to the member states from EMU are generally estimated to be small compared with GDP, perhaps as much as ½ per cent for the fall in transaction costs. The fall in interest rates for the higher inflation countries could, however, be much more striking, particularly since this is likely to have a dynamic effect. The report speculates on this effect, which is caused to quite a large extent because the average age of capital is likely to fall and the rate of product innovation increase with harsher competition. However, the report does not come to an explicit conclusion. Indeed, in this and the companion article by Baldwin (1992) in the second special issue of *European Economy*, these effects are bound up with those of the Single Market.

It is suggested that, taking into account the dynamic effects, the Single Market impact might lie between 3.6 per cent and 16.3 per cent of Community GDP, with a mean of 9.8 per cent, spread over a period of ten years, and continuing to increase thereafter. This works out at 0.4–1.0 per cent a year, with a mean of 0.7 per cent. The interest rate stimulus to growth can be added to this, contributing perhaps 5–10 per cent of GDP over ten years, and hence an average increase of some 1 per cent a year.

If this scenario comes close to reality, then the growth rate effect will dominate any diversion of trade or investment, and third countries will be clear beneficiaries, very much along the lines quoted above from Delors. However, these effects relate to the EMU once it is in operation, and this is not expected much before the end of the century, even on an optimistic assessment. Before that, convergence has to be achieved, and that is not without cost to those member states with high inflation rates. Inevitably, deflation will have to form part of the process of adjustment. It is possible then that, in the short run, any dynamic effects could initially be adverse. The net outcome is consequently much more debatable and dependent in part on the extent to which the increase of the structural funds helps offset the problems of adjustment, and the degree to which behaviour can change, thereby cutting the unemployment and output costs of meeting the conditions of nominal convergence required for stage 3 of EMU.

Our own view (Britton and Mayes 1992) is rather cautious, as is the Commission's: 'it seems justifiable . . . to consider a significant growth bonus from EMU, while unproven, to lie well within the bounds of plausibility' (*One Market, One Money*, p. 84). The debate about such dynamic effects seems destined to continue. Our own view is that a general attempt to try to squeeze deficits and reduce inflation, while simultaneously trying to avoid letting exchange rates fall, is bound to be deflationary for the European economy, with adverse spillovers for the rest of the world. Indeed, we expect that the pressures will be too great for some member states and they will have to devalue and adjust more slowly, as has already been demonstrated by Italy, Spain and the United Kingdom. Thus on balance, an adverse scenario for third countries seems a real possibility during the coming years.

1.2.3 The expansion of the Community

Although the response to Austria's application to join the EC in 1989 made it clear that the Single Market programme was to be complete before any expansion of the EC could be considered, this has been swiftly overtaken by events in Eastern Europe, and the Community was expanded by the entry of East Germany as part of a united Germany in October 1990. Negotiations over further expansion to include EFTA members are due to start in 1993 and some declaration to that effect is likely at the Edinburgh summit at the end of the British presidency in December 1992. The real question at present is not over whether there will be negotiations but over which countries will be included. Sweden and Finland have lodged formal applications, but it is not clear how far the other EFTA countries will join them.

One incentive to the countries to apply now is that the EC will not want to undertake overlapping negotiations, but will want to complete both the first set of negotiations and the assimilation of the new members before proceeding to a further round of negotiations. If the negotiations are with a relatively small number of EFTA countries, they could be completed quite quickly as the EC and EFTA countries have already been through the negotiations for the EEA agreement. But if the number of applicants were large, this would pose serious managerial problems for a Community already overburdened by a structure originally designed for six members, a smaller population and a more limited range of competences. Dealing with these problems would entail a reshaping of some of the EC institutions and proce- dures, and an agreement that not every member or every language be involved on every occasion, following the precedent laid down by the ECB.

A further inter-governmental conference is planned for 1995 which will discuss the wider issues of political integration and institutional change not covered by Maastricht, so a plausible timetable would be completion of the negotiations and accession before then. (The negotiations with East Germany show how rapidly work can be undertaken when the need arises.) A question remains over the three other states that have already applied for membership: Cyprus, Malta and Turkey. Turkey's application is likely to be postponed for political reasons, but even if they were not sufficient, the enormous differences in living standards and the sheer size and population of the country would make full membership very difficult to achieve in the light of the problems already encountered when including Spain, Greece and Portugal.

On the whole, this part of the expansion of the Community is very much a continuation and slight acceleration of existing trends. The EEA agreement has already extended the Single Market legislation to EFTA. Norway and Finland have been shadowing the ERM and are involved as observers in the discussions among the central banks, so movement to full membership is not likely to have a major impact on outsiders, except in so far as it affects agriculture, which to date has been excluded from EC–EFTA discussions. The EEA agreement already incorporates a contribution from EFTA countries to the structural policy of the EC, with a cohesion fund. Membership will extend this, but the main change for the new members will be an equal say in decision-making, rather than the present one-sided relationship (Brewin 1992).

For the other Eastern and Central European countries the time horizon is likely to be considerably extended, and any periods of accession long drawn out. At present it appears that the EC is prepared to consider the gradual accession of as many of these countries as wish to join through a series of steps, beginning with special agreements, progressing through association agreements and possibly some other interim stage to full membership. However, progress through the various stages requires measures of both political change and economic convergence.

On this basis, although there may be a number of more limited agreements during the coming years, moves towards either special status or full membership do not seem very likely before the end of the decade. However, the accession of EFTA countries with a long history of neutrality or previous closer economic ties with the region because of their proximity is likely to alter the orientation of the Community and may encourage a change of view. In any case, economic difficulties in those countries may become so acute that further action is required, advancing the pace of change. Third countries need to have regard to the sectors in which such rapid progress could occur, particularly agricultural and resource-based products, for example, and the impact any rapid increase in loans or investment funds might have. To some extent, any such increase will be a diversion and could increase the cost of capital. Rather greater uncertainty clouds the relationship with the components of the former Soviet Union (other than the Baltic states), both because of their much greater size and because of the debate over how far Europe actually extends.

In so far as this process of widening opens up new markets and accelerates their rate of growth, it will be of benefit to third countries. But if it closes agricultural markets, this will add to the problems of countries like Australia and New Zealand rather than reduce them. Furthermore, the East European countries are not just consumers but potential new producers, much closer to West European markets and, in the transition, likely to have lower unit costs than their Western counterparts and probably able to concentrate on the less highly processed products. This adds to the competitive threat to Australia and New Zealand not just in Europe but in wider export markets as others try to follow the same drive to efficiency. The United States and Japan are both regarding Eastern and Central Europe rather cautiously as an appropriate location for investment, but are unlikely to find that it affects them adversely. In the same way the ASEAN and other newly industrialised countries are unlikely to observe much in the way of a competitive threat in the more immediate future. Such threats would occur if Eastern and Central Europe were successful in emulating those countries' own experience.

On the whole there has been almost no quantification of either the impact of the EEA or integration with the countries of Eastern and Central Europe. The exception is Stoeckel *et al.* (1990), who have also simulated the impact of an expansion of the EC to include the East European countries, excluding the Soviet Union but including East

Germany. The pattern of impact suggested (Table 1.5) is very similar to that for the Single Market. The existing EC is a gainer, North America and Japan are losers, while any impact on Australasia and ASEAN is positive. These results run slightly at variance with our previous discussion, largely because of the relative weights of market growth and displacement, effectively assumed by the model.

1.3   Concluding remarks

European integration is not taking place in a vacuum. As the chapters in this book show, the reactions of Europe's major trading partners, particularly the United States, have influenced the 1992 programme. It is not clear how much the spectre of Fortress Europe was ever a reality rather than a negotiating position. Nevertheless, there have been significant reductions in the extent to which the benefits conferred by the Single Market would be exclusive to the member states, particularly through the rapid redefinition of the term 'reciprocity' in 1989 (as set out in CEPS 1989).

The road to integration is also strongly affected by the actions and reactions of foreign companies. Foreign-owned multinationals with a strong presence in Europe are full participants in the determination of the detailed characteristics of the internal market, not just in technical harmonisation but more widely with some of the US multinationals in

Table 1.5 Simulated effects of expanding the European trade bloc: changes in 1988 US$bn (Stoeckel *et al.* 1990).

Region	GDP	Eastern European growth plus preferential tariff Exports	Imports
EC	7.3	3.7	2.2
North America	−4.5	−4.2	−5.5
Asia-Pacific	−3.2	−4.0	−4.6
Japan	−3.4	−2.1	−1.3
Australasia	0.2	−0.3	−0.2
China	−0.1	0.0	−0.7
India	0.0	−0.1	−0.2
Tigers	−0.3	−1.0	−1.0
ASEAN*	0.5	−0.4	−1.0
Other Asia	0.0	−0.1	−0.1
World	−0.3	−4.5	−7.9

Notes: The regions are defined in Table 1.4.
ASEAN* is all ASEAN members except Singapore.
World refers to all countries and regions in the table.
Figures are changes from base in 1988 values.
See text for shock imposed on model.

particular the best organised and informed lobbyists in the system. Because of the ability of such multinationals to alter the effects of the 1992 programme by major direct investment, whether 'offensive', 'defensive' or 'rationalising', as explained by Yannopoulos and illustrated for the case of Japan, simple calculations of the impact of the process of European integration are likely to be erroneous.

Such estimates as there are suggest that the nature of the overall impact will be affected by two important features. First, in a purely static context, it will depend upon the policy response to the improvements in the trading balance for Europe which are forecast. In particular, it depends upon how much integration leads to an increase in the rate of economic growth. It is this dynamic response, which has on the whole been poorly modelled, that is the second major contributory factor to whether, on balance, European integration will have a favourable external effect. In so far as it is weak, it appears from an analysis of the individual measures in the 1992 programme that even though many advantages may be open to companies from outside the EC, the net static effect could well be adverse for the major trading partners, such as the United States and Japan, before an assessment is made of the consequences of direct investment.[25] ASEAN countries, on the other hand, seem set to benefit in any event, while the impact on Australasia seems likely to be relatively small.

To some extent the assessment of the impact of integration is conflated with the evolution of the EC's trade policy in general. However, the advent of the Single Market does necessitate some changes in external trade barriers on sensitive products such as textiles and clothing and motor cars, all of which will have a positive effect on some external suppliers. It is also clear that the particular scope of the changes does not answer the major trade policy complaints of some third countries heavily involved in agriculture, as represented by the Cairns Group. Here the impact of integration and the progress of the Uruguay Round are clearly intertwined. If, as widely forecast, the results of the Uruguay Round are rather limited, continuing pressure for the extraction of gains by the formation of trade groupings round the Pacific Rim can be expected, where such groupings would hope not just to emulate the EC by reaping efficiency gains from removal of barriers between the members but to reap gains from increased bargaining strength with the Community.

The process of further integration with Economic and Monetary Union and closer links with EFTA and especially East European countries will modify the position in two important respects. On the one hand, it will result in a redistribution within the Community as part of the process of nominal and real convergence entailed by EMU. But on the other, there will be a major revision of investment and trading patterns with the East. In so far as initial measures involve more favourable treatment of agricultural products in the form of exports or imports, this will exacerbate rather than help those already discriminated against by the CAP. However, the nature of the internal redistribution will itself cause the process of integration to change as those countries and companies which find themselves adversely affected are not likely to sit idly by. As in the case of the Single Market, the proposals will evolve as the participants perceive their potential impact and internal and external pressure will affect the final agreement. Alterations in behaviour by companies and third country governments will affect the impact of the measures stemming from these agreements.

The evolution of the path forward is more complex than some of those describing an inexorable and irreversible process would like to think. The external impact of European integration plays an important role in that evolution.

Notes

1. I am grateful to Albert Meyer for research assistance and to Alan Bollard, Andrew Britton, Arthur Knight, Hans Liesner, Geoff Mason, Nick Oulton, Jon Stanford and Bob Webb for comments and advice.
2. These negotiations, which were begun in the late 1980s, were originally under the heading of a European Economic *Space* but it was suggested that a space has nothing in it so the title was changed to *Area*.
3. Calculations of loss and benefit are usually carried out in welfare terms, thus it is not the changes in trade shares as such which matter, but the resource gains which stem from them. Thus, trade-creation, the gain among members from substituting trade for domestic production, and trade-diversion, the gain for members from switching trade from non-members (and concomitant loss for the non-members), are readily overshadowed by an increase in the rate of growth of the market. First, because the whole of that increase is a welfare gain, and second, because the gain is dynamic not static. It is not a constant once and for all shift, but increases every year.
4. As is pointed out in Mayes *et al.* (1991), none of these publications claims to estimate what will happen. They discuss the benefits which Europe is missing out on. It may appear implicit that the programme of measures designed to implement the market will result in the realisation of those gains but this is not actually said. The studies show various micro- and macroeconomic mechanisms by which gains could be achieved.
5. We can construct an elementary calculation on the basis of the Commission's macroeconomic simulations for the Cecchini Report (Catinat *et al.* 1988). After six years EC imports from third countries rise by 7.2 per cent while exports to them rise by 10.5 per cent if the Internal Market is completed (Catinat *et al.* 1988, Table A.3.1). Since the EC starts from a position of deficit this represents a net improvement in the trade balance

of 31bn ecu in 1985 prices, or 1 per cent of GDP. However, as imports from outside the EC were 406bn ecu in 1985 prices, it requires only a small annual increase in EC demand to reverse the sign of the trade balance effect.

6. Many definitions of this core would include the south-eastern part of England, extending perhaps as far as Manchester (see Hingel 1991, for example). However, for the purposes of the argument set out here, it is not necessary to draw any arbitrary dividing lines between a core and a periphery, merely to establish that some parts of the EC are considerably more integrated than others and hence are likely to respond differently to increasing integration. Such lack of integration applies not just to mutual trade but to differences in legal, social and other structures as well.

7. There is a major debate about the definition of the extent of Europe and where the boundaries might be drawn and for what purposes (see the discussion in Wallace 1991, for example). However, the detail of that is not relevant to the current argument as all we are suggesting is that central and eastern European countries have aspirations about becoming full members of the EC or at least more closely linked to it and that over the coming years such links will develop both in practice, through the course of economic activity, and through explicit agreements at a variable pace, dependent on political imperatives and the rate of convergence of the particular countries to the EC's market-based system.

8. The problem of lack of representation by major forces was one of the prime motives for the formation of the Cairns Group of countries, which was influential in getting the Uruguay Round to start and focus on issues of 'minority' interest.

9. We have already mentioned that Latin America is not included in our range of Pacific countries.

10. The calculated cost reductions are combinations of the reductions theoretically available and those which will actually be realised.

11. With the honourable exception of the report by Smith and Venables (1988), which seeks to take into account the number of major players in the various sectors of the European economy and then by use of simple game theory assess how the market might respond. However, even there, there are limits as to how far the assessment of firms' responses from third countries, through inward investment and other product market strategies, might proceed.

12. Yannopoulos (1990) argues further that reduction in non-tariff barriers has a weaker effect than their tariff equivalent. What is certainly clear is that it is not possible to apply the same methods that would be required for a tariff reduction of the same size to the cost reductions suggested by Cecchini.

13. This is outlined clearly by Mazey and Richardson (1992).

14. Brewin (1992) has developed these ideas in a further project, which forms part of the ESRC's Single European Market research initiative, mainly looking at the influence of EFTA countries on the bargaining process.

15. This issue is dealt with more comprehensively in CEPS (1989), the report of a working party on '1992: the Environment for European Industry', chaired by Edmund Dell, for which the author was the rapporteur.

16. It was suggested that this combination of harsh internal competition and effective external protection had been a major ingredient in the Japanese success and that that should be emulated within the EC.

17. The ability to participate through direct investment has its limitations as there is an attempt to discourage 'screwdriver' assembly operations where the European share of the value added of the final product is rather limited. (The limitation is not specific, although there was pressure from some member states to make it 60 per cent.) There is only a formal limitation when the firm concerned is also subject to anti-dumping measures.

18. The Commission provides descriptions of the legislative changes themselves, but assessments of their impact are rather harder to find. The latest edition of El Agraa, *The Economics of the European Community* by Philip Allan is a good example of what is available.

19. With some explicit counterexamples, like HDTV, where the EC appears tempted to use standards as a weapon in the struggle for greater competitiveness, the general tendency has been to try to align EC standards with international (ISO) standards so that Community firms do not have the disadvantage of idiosyncratic local standards when trying to compete in international markets.

20. Although, as in the case of the de Haviland takeover, there can be effective extra-territoriality.

21. The result in the 'simple' case poses a problem when we look at the implications for the rest of the world. The total for the countries included in the table, rather misleadingly labelled 'World' by Stoeckel *et al.*, implies a net improvement in the balance of trade of $156bn. This presumably is netted out in the rest of the world, i.e. LDCs, non-EC Europe and the Soviet Union. This seems rather unlikely. (I am grateful to Nick Oulton for this point.) The other two simulations have plausible implications for the rest of the world.

22. This is set out in more detail in *A Strategy for the ECU* (Ernst & Young 1990, ch. 7).

23. This is rather more limited than what most people might expect from the words 'economic union'.

24. However, the run on the lira in September 1992 suggests that the market is not very confident about this outcome.

25. This source of 'gain' is much more debatable from the point of view of the investing country. It is a switch of resources away from the investing country to the recipient country. Thus while the rate of return to the investing firm may be maintained a different view may be taken of the net impact on employment. It is this inflow of resources to the EC which is one factor contributing to the expected increase in the growth rate.

References

Barrell, R. (ed.) (1992) *Economic Convergence and Monetary Union in Europe* (London: Sage).

Begg, I. and Mayes, D. G. (1991) 'Social and economic cohesion among the regions of Europe in the 1990s', *National Institute Economic Review*, no. 138, November, pp. 63–74.

Bollard, A. and Mayes, D. G. (1992) 'Regionalism and the Pacific Rim', *Journal of Common Market Studies*, vol. 30, no. 2, June, pp. 195–209.

Brewin, C. (1992) 'External influences on the 1992 programme', paper presented at ESRC Single European Market meeting, March, NIESR.

Britton, A. and Mayes, D. G. (1992) *Achieving Monetary Union* (London: Sage).

Burridge, M. *et al.* (1991) 'Oxford Economics Forecasting's System of Models', *Economic Modelling*, July.

Burridge, M. and Mayes, D. (1992) 'Industrial change for 1992', in *Structural Change and the UK Economy*, ed. C. Driver and P. Dunne (Cambridge: Cambridge University Press).

Catinat, M., Donnie, E. and Italianer, A. (1988) 'Macroeconomic consequences of the completion of the internal market: the modelling evidence', in *Studies on the Economics of Integration*, vol. 2. Research on the Cost of Non-Europe (Brussels/Luxembourg: EC Commission).

Cecchini, P. (1988) *The European Challenge 1992: The Benefits of a Single Market* (Aldershot: Wildwood House).

CEPS (1989) *1992: The Environment for European Industry*, Report of a Working Party (Brussels).

Delors, J. (1989) *Report on Economic and Monetary Union in the European Community* (Brussels: EC).

Ernst & Young, NIESR and AUME (1990) *A Strategy for the ECU* (London: Kogan Page).

European Commission (1990) 'Economic and monetary union', Sec. (90) 1659 final, October, Brussels.

Hager, W., Knight, Sir A., Mayes, D. G. and Streeck, W. (1992) *Public Interest and Market Pressures: problems posed by Europe 1992* (London: Macmillan).

Hingel, A. (1991) 'Archipelago Europe – Islands of Innovation', Monitor/ FAST Programme dossier, April.

Journal of Common Market Studies (1990) 'Europe 1992 and the Developing Countries', Special Issue, vol. 29, no. 2.

Lucas, R. E. (1976) 'Econometric policy evaluation: a critique', in *The Phillips Curve and Labour Markets*, Carnegie–Rochester Conference Series on Public Policy.

Mayes, D. G. *et al.* (1991) *The European Challenge: industry's response to the 1992 programme* (Hemel Hempstead: Harvester Wheatsheaf).

Mazey, S. and Richardson, J. R. (1992) 'Interest groups and European integration', paper presented at ESRC Single European Market meeting, March, NIESR.

Smith, M. A. M. and Venables, A. J. (1988) 'The costs of non-Europe: an assessment based on a formal model of imperfect competition and economies of scale', in *Studies on the Economics of Integration*, vol. 2. Research on the Cost of Non-Europe (Brussels/Luxembourg: EC Commission).

Stoeckel, A., Pearce, D. and Banks, G. (1990) *Western Trade Blocs* (Canberra: Centre for International Economics).

Trela, I. and Whalley, J. (1990) 'Global effects of developed country trade restrictions on textiles and apparel', *Economic Journal*, December.

UNCTAD (1989) *Trade and Development Report 1989* (Washington: UN).

Wallace, W. (1991) 'From twelve to twenty-four? Challenges to the EC posed by the revolutions in Eastern Europe' (Andrew Schonfield Association, Trinity College, Oxford).

Yannopoulos, G. N. (1990) *The External Implications of the Completion of the Internal Market of the Community*, Report of a Working Party (Brussels: CEPS).

2

The Community's external trade policy

Dermot McAleese

The European Community's external trade regime is in the process of rapid transformation. The 1992 programme has been followed by the prospect of Economic and Monetary Union (EMU) later in the 1990s. In addition, the European Economic Area (EEA) is scheduled to come into operation in 1993. The absorption of East Germany into the Community and the opening of trade with Eastern Europe will have direct and indirect implications for the pattern of EC trade. While, at the time of writing (1992), the fate of the Uruguay Round hangs in the balance, the negotiating process itself has changed the trade policy perspective. All this makes writing about the Community's trade policy an unusually difficult task.

As the world's major trade bloc, the EC exercises an important influence on the outside world's economic prospects. In many cases the influence is asymmetric: the Community's market matters more to individual countries than their markets matter to the Community. Australia illustrates the point: trade with the EC accounts for 15 per cent of Australia's exports and 24 per cent of its imports (Mayes 1990), but for only 2 per cent of EC exports and imports. For many non-EC countries, the uncertain evolution of the Community's trade policy is a matter for considerable concern. The United States does not suffer from asymmetrical dependence, but is still uneasy. A front-page report in *IMF Survey* (1 April 1991) quotes Professor Weidenbaum, a former chairman of President Reagan's Council of Economic Advisers, as predicting that 'the trade wall around the European Community (EC) has risen and will rise even higher in the years ahead.' The image of a vigorous, expanding and protectionist EC does not accord with my view of the future, nor with the record of the Community to date, but many believe otherwise. Hence the need for regular reviews of the

Common Commercial Policy (CCP) and its impact on the EC's trading partners.

The plan of this chapter is as follows. First, the main features of the CCP are described. Second, the characteristics and pattern of EC trade are outlined, thus explaining the context within which the CCP has been and continues to be formulated. The third section provides a review of the effects of three major changes in the trade environment on EC trade policy: closer EC integration, EC enlargement and the Uruguay Round. The final section contains conclusions. These suggest that the general thrust of change is likely to be in a 'liberal' direction: an expanding EC market will offer enhanced opportunities to extra-EC exporters and any changes in EC trade policy, while continuing to be selective as regards countries and sectors, are unlikely to prevent third countries from exploiting these opportunities.

2.1   Elements of the Common Commercial Policy (CCP)

A common trade policy is an essential characteristic of a customs union. The creation of such a policy has not, however, been an easy task for the Community; indeed, it has yet to be fully accomplished. To take a somewhat inglorious example, the external trade regime of the Common Agricultural Policy (CAP) took ten years (1957–67) to be decided, with tough arguments among member states at every stage concerning the choice of trade instrument (the variable levy), the level of support prices and the method of financing (Pinder 1991).

The basic features of the CCP are well known. The June 1991 GATT Trade Policy Review (GATT 1991), however, provides a particularly useful insight into how the Commission sees the CCP and how it is perceived by GATT officials and GATT delegations. In addition, there is a growing descriptive and analytical literature on the subject (recent examples include Yannopoulos 1988; McAleese 1990; Molle 1990; Fielding 1991; Pelkmans 1991; Tsoukalis 1991).

The essential features of the policy are incorporated in Articles 110–16 of the Treaty of Rome. These much-cited articles propose two major principles. First, member states aim to contribute to the 'harmonious development of world trade', the 'progressive abolition of restrictions' and the 'lowering of trade barriers' (Article 110). The Community was not designed to be an exclusive rich-man's club, no more than a 'Fortress Europe'. Second, the CCP was to be based on uniform principles with respect to tariffs, the conclusion of trade agreements, liberalisatior of export policy, anti-dumping measures and subsidies (Article 113). The same article provides for exclusive Community competence in the realm of trade policy, for decision by majority voting and for a substantive executive and negotiating role of the Commission. The CCP has been further strengthened by the Court of Justice's determination that, wherever a common policy is developed internally, the external aspects of that policy are automatically a matter of Community competence.

The Community's record in trade matters has its critics. Like other OECD countries, it has presided over a rapid growth of NTBs during the past two decades, particularly in farm products. The MFA and VERs in automobiles, electronic goods and steel are obvious examples. There are also 'grey area' measures, such as subsidies, anti-dumping procedures and rules of origin. Whether the Community's record in this respect has been any worse than Japan's or the United States' is unclear. Summary measures of NTBs are bedevilled by definitional problems, coverage and time-frames. For example, Laird and Yeats (1990a) conclude that the share of EC imports affected by NTBs is greater and has increased faster than the OECD average. Yet the same authors show elsewhere (1990b) that the average EC trade coverage is lower than Japan and the United States (see Table 2A.1). In the EC's favour, Laird and Yeats (1990a) report that the EC share of imports covered by (non-MFA) VERs was 4.4 per cent compared with 11.3 per cent in the United States. Moreover, if an effort is made to calculate the trade-distorting effects of trade barriers instead of the stock of barriers, a relatively favourable picture of the EC emerges. A study by Hufbauer, for example, cited in *The Economist* (22 September 1990), shows that elimination of hard-core non-tariff measures would lead to a 12 per cent expansion of EC imports compared with a much higher 20 per cent expansion of Japanese imports and 13 per cent of US imports.[1] All this is not to deny that there are wide gaps between principle and practice with regard to progressive liberalisation and uniformity.

The key development in recent years has been the effect of the 1992 programme in enforcing greater uniformity in the Community's trade policy. Abolition of frontier controls within the Community will undermine the system of national MFA quotas, Article 115 derogations, national VERs and ceiling quotas under the GSP. This is so, particularly when such abolition is accompanied by a strengthened competition policy. Competition policy and free internal circulation together reinforce the tendency to uniformity.

Uniformity means a trade policy which is common to all member states. It does not imply that this common trade policy will be the same for all extra-EC countries. In fact, the CCP has become highly differentiated through a series of associations, free trade agreements and special preferential areas concluded under Article 228 of the Treaty. The intention has been to create positive discrimination in favour of certain areas (Lomé countries, GSP, EFTA, etc.). Although industrialised countries at the bottom of the hierarchy of preferences (Australia, New Zealand, United States, Canada and Japan) object to such discrimination, this much-criticised feature of the CCP is unlikely to disappear – witness the continuing pressure for special preferential arrangements with Eastern Europe and the close integration between EFTA and the EC within the European Economic Area.

2.2 Characteristics and patterns of EC trade

EC trade patterns set the context within which EC trade policy is formulated. The central issue for the EC is how to remain competitive against the formidable challenges posed by new technology and new commercial competitors. The CCP is perceived as playing an important role in achieving this objective.

EC trade has a strong regional concentration (Table 2.1). No less than 60 per cent of trade is intra-EC trade. If EFTA is added, the figure rises to about 70%. Intra-European trade has been the fastest growing element of EC trade in recent years. With the exception of agricultural trade, the rise in intra-EC trade has not been at the expense of non-EC countries; external trade-creation has also taken place. Indeed, over a long period of thirty years, Lloyd (1992) finds only weak evidence that regional trade groups such as the EC give rise to an increased share of intra-group trade in the total import trade of the group. Like other industrial countries, EC trade is mostly intra-industry in character. The search for more intensified exploitation of potential gains from trade has driven the Community towards measures to achieve greater integration of EC trade and closer trade ties with its neighbours. In this sense, the EC could be described as more inward-focused than other countries.

A second characteristic is the absence of any major imbalance on current balance of payments account since the early 1980s. The trade imbalances experienced by the United States and Japan, which continued through the 1980s and which have impacted strongly on their respective commercial policies, have not been replicated in the Community. The broad EC-wide balance, however, coexists with troublesome bilateral trade imbalances, notably the persistent deficit with Japan (totalling $32m in 1990) and the rapid erosion of the US surplus (Table 2.2). Individual member states also have balance of payments problems (Greece, Spain and the United Kingdom had deficit/GNP ratios of 6 per cent, 3 per cent and 3 per cent, respectively, in 1990) and until German unification West Germany's

Table 2.1   Structure of EC12 merchandise trade by region, 1985 and 1990 (% shares).

	Exports		Imports	
Europe				
Intra-EC	61.0		58.8	
EFTA	10.5		9.5	
Other OECD-Europe	1.5		1.4	
		73.00		69.7
America				
United States	7.1		7.6	
Canada	0.9		0.8	
Latin America	1.6		2.5	
		9.6		10.9
Asia				
Japan	2.1		4.1	
Four Asian NICs*	2.3		2.5	
		4.4		6.6
Eastern Bloc (including China)		3.1		3.7
Australia		0.6		0.4
Other		9.9		9.9
Total (Value)		100.0 ($1,360bn)		100.0 ($1,415bn)

*Hong Kong, Singapore, South Korea and Taiwan.

Source: *European Economy*, December 1991.

huge surplus was able to shelter behind the EC aggregate, thus saving itself from mercantilist opprobrium. But these individual member state imbalances have rarely been translated into particular stances at Community trade policy level. Whatever problems are encountered by third countries with the Community do not originate from an intrinsic structural problem in the EC's balance of payments.

A third feature is what the Commission describes as the 'unfavourable' product composition of Community exports (*European Economy*, December 1991, p. 142). Trade performance in high-tech products has been a source of concern for many years (see *European Economy*, November 1989, for an analysis). High-tech exports to extra-EC have grown by only 2 per cent per annum during the period 1982–90, a low growth rate in absolute terms and one which reflects a rapidly declining world market-share (Table 2.3). Most of the growth in high-tech exports has occurred within the confines of the Community. Moreover, imports from extra-EC have grown faster (7.7 per cent per annum) than intra-EC imports (7.3 per cent per annum). This

Table 2.2 Exports, imports and trade balances of the EC, 1980 and 1990 (US$bn).

	United States			Japan			EFTA			Developing economies			Total extra-EC		
	1980	1989	1990	1980	1989	1990	1980	1989	1990	1980	1989	1990	1980	1989	1990
Exports	38.6	85.0	95.9	6.7	23.1	28.5	76.3	117.2	139.1	122.9	134.5	157.4	305.0	456.0	530.6
Imports	66.0	91.2	105.8	19.7	52.6	60.7	67.9	113.1	130.1	180.2	151.5	159.2	393.9	499.3	593.6
Merchandise trade balance	−27.4	−6.2	−9.9	−13.0	−29.5	−32.2	+8.4	+4.1	+9.0	−57.3	−17.0	−1.8	−88.9	−43.3	−63.0

(−) = deficit
(+) = surplus

Source: GATT, *International Trade 90–91*, vol. 2 (Geneva, 1992).

Table 2.3 EC's high-technology trade growth rates, 1982–90.

			Exports			Imports	
		Intra	Extra	Total	Intra	Extra	Total
SITC 54	Pharmaceutical	5.3	0.8	3.0	5.6	5.6	5.4
58	Plastics	8.1	2.1	6.0	7.9	9.4	8.2
71	Power equipment	2.4	−1.1	0.3	1.3	5.4	2.8
72	Specialised equipment	2.6	−3.0	−1.0	3.4	2.4	3.0
75	Computers, etc.	12.1	10.2	11.6	12.7	10.6	11.6
76	Telecoms and comm. electronics	10.0	0.7	5.0	9.9	7.3	8.1
77	Electrical machinery	7.8	4.6	5.9	7.2	9.6	7.9
79	Ships, aircraft	10.4	2.2	3.4	10.1	9.9	5.7
87	Professional and scientific equipment	6.7	5.8	6.1	6.6	5.7	6.2
88	Photo and optical equipment	5.5	5.6	5.8	5.7	5.8	5.6
Total High Technology		7.5	2.0	4.6	7.3	7.7	7.1

Note: Growth rates for trade with world may lie outside interval determined by intra- and extra-EC growth rates because of the particular methodology used in compiling the data.

Source: *European Economy*, December 1991.

trade pattern suggests an erosion of comparative advantage in these products. The EC's trade balance in high-tech products shows a marked deterioration during the 1980s (Table 2.4). In the case of office and telecom equipment, the Community ran a $36 billion deficit in 1990, six times higher than 1980, while its large surplus in machinery and transport equipment was reduced by $17 billion during the same period. The EC's position in high-tech industries has attracted much academic comment; a recent study reaches the rather chilling conclusion that:

> European firms in ICT (information and computer technology) are significantly weaker than their Japanese and American competitors and we cannot simply assume that the enlargement of the European market and the removal of remaining barriers in trade and competition will in themselves be sufficient to ensure improvements in the electronics, telecommunications, automobile and every other industry. (Freeman and Oldham 1991, p. 9)

The Commission has not chosen to regard this loss of market share in 'strong-demand' sectors as the inevitable result of changing trends in comparative advantage, to be accepted passively. A key sentence in the Cecchini Report bears repetition: 'Comparative advantage is no longer seen as divine inheritance, nor are market structures and rivals' behaviour set in tablets of stone' (Cecchini 1988, p. 85).

Table 2.4   Extra-EC trade in selected products 1980 and 1990 (US$bn).

		Exports	Imports	Trade balance	Change in trade balance, 1980–90
Chemicals	1980	35.7	17.2	+18.5	
	1990	65.2	38.6	+26.6	+8.1
Machinery and transport equipment	1980	115.9	58.0	+57.9	
	1990	217.7	176.9	+40.8	−17.1
Other non-electrical machinery	1980	43.1	13.6	+29.5	
	1990	75.6	34.0	+41.6	+12.1
Electrical machinery	1980	11.9	5.7	+6.2	
	1990	23.7	18.4	+5.3	−0.9
Office and telecommunications equipment	1980	11.3	17.2	−5.9	
	1990	27.7	63.9	36.2	−30.3
Automotive products	1980	27.5	8.2	+19.3	
	1990	49.0	26.7	+22.3	+3.0

Source: computed from Table A12; GATT; *International Trade 90–91*, vol. 2 (Geneva, 1992).

The 1992 programme drew much of its inspiration from the need to establish conditions for the successful relaunching of high-tech industries. Commercial policy is also being deployed with vigour for this purpose, in particular, anti-dumping measures and VERs, to combat what is perceived as, and in many cases undoubtedly is, predatory competition by the Japanese.

Despite these interventions, the operation of the law of comparative advantage has brought about major changes in EC's pattern of specialisation. Considerable adjustments in the EC economy have taken place and deserve better documentation than normally received. The share of agricultural employment in EC12 total employment has fallen from 13.8 per cent in 1970 to 7.4 per cent in 1988. Employment in the steel industry has declined since 1974 by 72 per cent in the United Kingdom, 43 per cent in Germany and 64 per cent in France. Coal production levels have fallen by 17.5 per cent in Germany and 13.1 per cent in the United Kingdom over the period 1979–88. EC12 shipbuilding production (tonnage of merchant ships) has fallen to half its level of the early 1980s. Textile and clothing employment has declined precipitously throughout the Community: in the decade to 1983, by 46.9 per cent in Germany, 52.8 per cent in France, 54.6 per cent in the United Kingdom and 63.9 per cent in the Netherlands. A significant part of this decline in employment can be attributed to the direct or indirect (via induced productivity increases) impact of import penetration. Moreover, the percentage job loss in the EC textile and clothing industry contrasts with much lower corresponding figures for

Japan and the United States of 18.6 per cent and 29.7 per cent, respectively (Trela and Whalley 1990). The downward trend in employment has continued through the 1980s. Numbers employed in the combined textile clothing and footwear sectors, during the period 1981–9, fell by 24.2 per cent in Germany, 32.3 per cent in France, 34.1 per cent in the United Kingdom and 36.7 per cent in the Netherlands.

Measures of import penetration likewise indicate a continuing process of change. Extra-EC imports/consumption ratios have risen steeply in clothing, transport equipment and machinery and a range of other goods (Table 2.5). Food and agriculture are the predictable exceptions to this generalisation and, as mentioned earlier, the penetration of markets via intra-EC trade has proceeded at a more rapid pace than extra-EC trade. Nevertheless, where 'sensitive' manufactured goods are concerned, the CCP may have slowed down the pace of change, but has certainly not brought it to a halt.

2.3 Changing trade environment

Three changes in the trade environment will forcefully impact on the Community's external trade in the 1990s: (1) closer European integration (1992 and EMU); (2) the enlargement of the Community (EEA, association agreements with Eastern Europe and expanded full membership of the Community); and (3) the Uruguay Round.

Table 2.5 Import penetration of the European Communities (EC12), 1982–7 (imports as a percentage of apparent consumption).

	Intra-EC trade			External trade		
	1982–3	1984–5	1986–7	1982–3	1984–5	1986–7
Food, beverages, tobacco	9.91	10.23	10.79	4.28	4.10	3.63
Textiles	21.05	22.79	22.82	10.00	10.68	10.82
Clothing	26.60	29.03	30.37	20.68	22.86	25.14
Chemicals	21.35	23.19	23.28	8.93	9.75	8.92
Ferrous and non-ferrous metals	11.38	12.67	11.68	6.80	7.23	6.13
Transport equipment	24.43	24.89	26.09	8.05	9.28	9.20
Machinery and other manufactured goods	26.87	28.73	31.35	20.71	23.33	23.29
Total manufactures	17.03	18.31	19.29	10.51	11.67	11.15

Note: Apparent consumption is defined as gross output plus external imports minus external exports.

Source: UNCTAD (1990), *Handbook of International Trade and Development Statistics.* Table 1.3 of GATT (1991), vol. 1.

2.3.1 *Closer European integration*

Although not explicitly treated in the early 1992 documents, the external trade effects of 1992 have by now been extensively studied (*JCMS* special issue 1990; Pelkmans 1991; Mayes 1990; McAleese 1991; Winters 1991; Yannopoulos 1990). 'A confusing debate downplaying the benefits' is how Pelkmans (1991) summarises the discussion of the 1992 impact on non-EC countries. The main findings of these studies can be surveyed under a select number of headings.

First, the effects of the integration process on EC growth is likely to be strongly positive. This expected income effect will increase the demand for imports and will, for most third countries, overcompensate for any adverse repercussions via loss of preference or competitive position in the EC market. The income effect will benefit third countries through (1) increased demand for their exports, (2) higher prices for primary products as a result of higher EC activity, (3) lower prices for EC and competing manufactured exports to rest of world as EC efficiency improves, and (4) foreign investment effects. On the last, some stress the effects of outward EC investment as Community markets tighten; others focus on the benefits to countries such as Australia (Mayes 1990) and Japan (Yannopoulos 1990) from investment by their nationals in the more prosperous post-1992 EC market. All these 1992 effects are, of course, subject to the *ceteris paribus* clause: the position relative to what would otherwise be the case.

Income effects of 1992 have to be analysed in conjunction with sectoral trade implications as national trade barriers are replaced with uniform EC-wide trade rules. The textiles and automobile sectors are obvious examples. High-tech industries will also be affected as public procurement is opened up and technical barriers removed. The key issue concerns whether the new trade regime will be more liberal or less liberal than the old, recognising that we are discussing the matter at a high level of generalisation.

Those anticipating a more liberal trend draw sustenance from considerations such as: (1) the importance of extra-EC trade in imposing competitive behaviour on EC industry (Jacquemin and Sapir 1991); (2) the stronger competitive position of EC industry in the context of a unified market;[2] and (3) the effect of mutual recognition and common standards in opening the EC market to third countries (much stressed by Pelkmans, who sees the third country benefits of 1992 downplayed because of misunderstanding of the new technical standards regime). The EC's decision not to press for equal treatment in its definition of reciprocity but to be satisfied with national treatment and 'effective market access' is also seen as evidence of a more open approach and a model for liberalisation by other countries.

Thus Tsoukalis concludes that the Single European Act is 'likely to have a liberalising effect both directly through the elimination of intra-EC barriers and indirectly by acting as a catalyst for further international liberalisation' (Tsoukalis 1991, p. 277).

The counter-argument revolves around the proposition that the 1992 programme will involve strong redistributive effects within the Community. Losers will become defensive ('countries and companies which find themselves adversely affected will not stand idly by' in Mayes' phrase (1990, p. 83)). Rather than allow the internal 1992 programme to fail, the Commission will have to give way on external trade policy by enforcing tighter restrictions than it would wish. This argument obviously carries weight and there is evidence of such extreme defensiveness in, for example, the restricted access given to East European food products. But there are strong countervailing considerations in addition to those mentioned above.

The brunt of further liberalisation of extra-EC trade in Heckscher–Ohlin-type goods is likely to impose the heaviest adjustment costs in the less developed regions and states of the Community. However, these member states have, so far, concentrated on enlarging the amount of Structural Funds available in the Community budget rather than stiffening the CCP. Pressures will, however, be exerted by states and affected firms on securing adequate safeguard measures. These must not necessarily be equated with protectionism. In another context, Margaret Sharp (1991) has argued persuasively that EC anti-dumping procedures and competition policies have combined to give the optimal policy mix for the cultivation of competitive high-tech industries. Given the increasing elusiveness of the concept of a national company in a world dominated by multinationals, she foresees the 1990s as being a decade of continued ambiguity and schizophrenia in trade diplomacy and the conduct of international economic policy. Nationality of a firm's ownership is likely to matter less; and the types of function and degree of responsibility attached to the 'European' operation to matter much more. Simplistic protectionist policies will not work and could be disastrously counter-productive in this situation. Sharp and Walker, however, call for policies to ensure that Europe captures the beneficial spin-offs of foreign investment:

> both American and Japanese multinationals establishing manufacturing facilities [in the EC] should be required to make commitments to establish research, development and design laboratories, to source components locally and to train Europeans in both management and technical grades. (Sharp and Walker 1991, p. 390)

How to achieve this within GATT rules is, of course, another matter. Following the Maastricht Summit in 1992, the 1992 programme has been supplemented by the prospect of EMU. This will further deepen the integration process. From a trade policy point of view, it raises an additional consideration. The regional effects of dollar fluctuations in the EC economies will need to be carefully evaluated in determining ecu/$ exchange rate policy. Recent work by Michalopoulos (1991) shows that dollar fluctuations have radically different effects on different EC economies. In the case of the United Kingdom and Italy, a devaluation *vis-à-vis* the dollar leads primarily to higher prices (via 'imported' commodity prices effects, etc.), whereas, in the case of Germany and France, a fall in the dollar exchange rate leads primarily to changes in trade volumes. Given the disruptive effects of sustained misalignments of the dollar exchange rate, this issue merits a place in the research agenda in the 1990s.

2.3.2 Enlargement

Enlargement of the Community will involve the creation of a wider *European Economic Area (EEA)*, and also the possibility of accession to full membership of some EFTA countries (e.g. Austria, Sweden and Switzerland). The EFTA countries are ideal additions to the Community in the economic sense. They are affluent, have few major social or regional problems, are able and willing to contribute to the Community budget, face few industrial adjustment costs (apart from pharmaceuticals) and, starting off from a high level of agricultural protection but no net food export surpluses, will impose no further burden on the CAP. EFTA rates of protection in 'sensitive' manufacturing sectors tend to be lower than EC levels. Prompted by the prohibitive cost of agricultural protection, Sweden is turning towards more market-oriented approaches and others may follow. Hence the net effect of EFTA involvement in the CCP should be to strengthen the tendency towards openness and liberalisation. New issues will surface, notably in transport (Austria, Switzerland), fisheries (Iceland) and also in services, competition policy and direct foreign investment but these are unlikely to impact much on third countries.

The effects on trade policy of closer economic relations with *Eastern Europe* are more difficult to predict. The starting point is one of exceptionally low trade volumes. In 1989 EC exports of industrial goods to Eastern Europe amounted to $22.7 billion and imports to $25.2 billion (Table 2.6). This was equivalent to some 6 per cent of total EC trade in industrial products with third countries. The former Soviet Union accounted for more than half this trade, with Poland and Hungary next. Their lack of hard currency made them poor markets for EC exports, while their own goods carried little attraction in Western markets. At the bottom of the EC's preferential ranking until

Table 2.6 Imports of industrial products of the EC from Eastern Europe by groups of products and by EC countries, 1989 (%).

Products (CN)/EC countries	East European countries						Total
	Soviet Union	Poland	Romania	CSFR	Hungary	Bulgaria	
25–27 Mineral products	58.6	19.9	35.4	10.7	5.1	11.2	41.4
28–38 Chemical products	4.9	6.6	4.1	8.9	10.4	14.7	6.0
39–40 Plastics, rubber	0.4	2.7	1.4	5.8	6.2	4.7	1.9
41–43 Hides, travelling goods	1.1	1.3	0.5	1.2	2.8	1.3	1.2
44–46 Wood, cork, articles thereof	6.2	5.2	3.1	7.6	3.9	2.3	5.6
47–49 Paper, paperboard	1.6	1.3	1.0	6.2	1.4	4.1	2.0
50–63 Textiles	2.6	13.5	18.2	11.0	21.0	15.3	8.1
64–67 Footwear, headgear, etc.	0.0	2.0	1.5	1.8	4.2	1.0	1.0
68–70 Stone, ceramic prod., glass	0.1	1.7	2.1	6.5	2.4	1.6	1.3
71 Pearls, precious metals	5.0	1.2	0.0	0.6	0.4	0.6	3.1
72–83 Base metals, articles thereof	13.0	22.0	13.0	17.0	16.5	18.9	14.9
84–85 Machinery, electr. equipment	1.2	9.4	4.2	8.9	16.6	15.9	4.8
86–89 Vehicles/transport equipment	2.6	6.2	1.8	6.9	1.6	1.0	3.3
90–92 Optical/measuring instruments	0.3	0.6	0.2	1.2	0.8	0.9	0.4
93 Arms, ammunition	0.0	0.0	0.0	0.3	0.1	0.1	0.1
94–96 Furniture, toys, etc.	0.2	4.7	13.2	3.6	3.8	3.0	2.8
97–99 Works of art, etc.	2.2	1.4	0.1	1.8	2.7	3.7	1.9
25–99 All industrial products	100.0	100.0	100.0	100.0	100.0	100.0	100.0
US$bn	14.4	3.2	2.7	2.5	2.0	0.4	25.2
Germany, Federal Republic	21.9	45.6	27.9	46.2	54.6	28.7	30.7
Italy	19.6	9.4	32.8	12.7	14.4	19.3	18.8
United Kingdom	8.9	14.1	6.9	10.6	7.8	9.3	9.4
France	17.5	8.8	16.1	9.7	9.7	11.2	14.7
Spain	8.3	2.0	3.8	2.8	1.8	5.6	5.9
Netherlands	11.7	6.8	6.8	6.5	4.5	7.5	9.4
Portugal	0.4	0.3	0.2	0.5	0.2	0.7	0.3
Belgium/Luxembourg	8.2	3.3	2.2	3.5	3.1	3.8	6.0
Greece	1.7	2.0	2.8	3.9	2.2	13.0	2.3
Denmark	1.5	5.4	0.4	3.0	1.4	0.6	2.0
Ireland	0.4	2.3	0.2	0.7	0.2	0.1	0.7

Source: Schumacher and Mobius (1991, Table 1b).

recent years, and with even the small amount of trade riddled with interventions on both sides, past trade trends are an unreliable guide to the future. (Eastern Europe attracted between 12 per cent and 18 per cent of the Commission's anti-dumping investigations during the period 1985–8 and 34 per cent during the period 1980–8; by contrast, only one case was initiated against Australia/Oceania 1980–8 (Schumacher and Mobius 1991).)

The fear of 'catastrophic' immigration will push the Community to favouring trade (movement of goods) as a substitute for factor mobility (movement of people). Association agreements between the EC and the Czech and Slovak Republic, Hungary and Poland came into force on 1 March 1992 which provide free access for these countries' industrial exports, with special deals for textiles, steel and processed food products and the usual safeguard provisions. There is a political commitment to full membership of Poland, Hungary and the Czech and Slovak Federal Republic as soon as circumstances permit.

The trade patterns to emerge from closer association are likely to vary by country and over time. Initially, one might expect the adjustment problems of the Community to be exacerbated. Pressure will be placed on EC's protected agriculture, steel, textiles, clothing and footwear industries and other semi-skilled activities. But Eastern Europe supply constraints will be an important limiting factor on this pressure in the short to medium term. Schumacher and Mobius conclude that third countries 'do not have to expect trade diversion effects on a large scale because of the changes in the EC's trade policy *vis-à-vis* Eastern Europe' (1991, p. 23). Nevertheless, there will be some trade diversion and some increased competition for EC Structural Funds. The direct beneficiary of Eastern Europe's increased demand for imports is likely to be the contiguous and better-off areas of Europe (Germany, Austria, North Italy). Association and/or accession of such countries will lead to adjustment problems though, as in the case of 1992, the income effects of a successful integration could more than compensate for adjustment costs.

The same considerations apply to *Turkey*, from which approximately 60 per cent of the total population increase in OECD-Europe is expected during the period 1985–2000, and to the *Mediterranean countries*. These countries, especially Turkey, have already made quantum inroads on the EC textile and clothing markets and need to extend their exports further. Although full membership is not a serious possibility for some considerable time, the Community will be under an obligation at least to maintain, if not enhance, access to its market. Pressure to reform CAP will intensify because of sheer cost considerations. The necessity to encourage trade in order to avoid pressures on immigration is likely to lead to further liberalisation with these countries, or at least to no further restrictiveness.

2.3.3   *Uruguay Round*

The EC has been consistent in its support for a stronger and extended
multilateral system. Attention of politicians may have been diverted by
1992 but the programme, in so far as it anticipated many of the
Uruguay Round problems and has acclimatised member states to
resolving them, has had a positive effect on the negotiations. Irrespective of the specific outcome of the Round, the process of reform of the
CAP will continue under the dictates of 1992, the financial and
environmental costs of CAP and the enlargement pressures referred to
above. The Uruguay Round is just one further reason for undertaking
a reform which was always necessary. Commissioner MacSharry's
reference to 80 per cent of CAP expenditure going to 20 per cent of
EC farmers did more to command popular support for reform than any
pressure from outside the Community. In other respects, the EC's
experience may serve as a model for the Uruguay Round: on services,
technical standards, rules of origin, local content and public procurement, the problem is the capacity of the United States and others to
match the EC. On procurement, the EC has chosen a 50 per cent EC
content and a 3 per cent EC price preference rule, but the United
States is not in a position to reciprocate. A phased tariffication in place
of bilateral MFA quotas is also likely. Further market-led adjustment
and globalisation will reduce protectionist pressures to a vigilant
anti-dumping policy combined with appropriate origin rules.[3] Successful conclusion of the Round would be helpful in reinforcing the
openness of the Community market. If the Round does not succeed,
the EC is better placed than the two other groups to proceed on the
basis of regionalised agreements. It would be a pity if the prospect of
agreement were to be jeopardised by an unreasonable insistence by the
United States on more progress in lowering CAP supports than is
politically acceptable within Europe.

2.4   Conclusions

'The single market will be open, but it will not be given away' (Jacques
Delors, address to the European Parliament, January 1989).
    An 'open' market is an elusive concept. We all want open markets –
in sectors in which we enjoy a comparative advantage! Even under an
optimistically liberal scenario, it will be a considerable time before
Australia and New Zealand will be able to sell agricultural produce, or
China textile and clothing products, into the EC market without let or
hindrance. This paper has argued that the direction of change is likely
to be towards easier rather than more restricted access. Within this

general framework we can expect continuing strong differential treatment across sectors. As the overall level of protection falls, the value of special preferences, which have been such a distinctive characteristic of the CCP, will diminish. In this sense, the single market will be 'open'.

The 'not given away' clause in President Delors's statement has been clarified to mean not equal treatment but the less exacting national treatment, with provision for change in cases where national treatment provides a level of market access inferior to that provided to third country suppliers in the EC market. Access to the Community market will not, however, be left open to third countries without qualification. The Community has a long history of interventionism. But the way in which 1992 is being handled suggests that significant areas of the EC market are being opened up to third country competition, notably in services and government procurement and also in other sectors as a result of mutual recognition and common technical standards.

The Community is trade-dependent and continues to rely on extra-EC countries as a source of trade gains. Its policy will be dictated by a number of factors in the years ahead.

First, the maintenance of a strong growth performance remains crucial. Enthusiasm for integration within and without the EC gathers momentum when the economy is doing well. To some extent European integration is a fair weather phenomenon. But it is also true that the process of integration itself tends to improve the weather! The spin-off from EC growth to imports has been emphasised: between 1973 and 1985 each percentage point of additional EC GDP led to an accompanying increase of 1.5 per cent in imports from non-member countries (Wagner 1991).

Second, within the context of a strong EC economy, the maintenance of regional balance is important in order to prevent the emergence of protectionist lobbies. The effects of the 1992 programme on the EC's less developed regions is a matter of controversy. Neven argues that the main beneficiaries are likely to be the southern European countries – 'both in terms of exploiting comparative advantage and in terms of exhausting scale economies' (1990, p. 46), but others take a less sanguine view. Jacquemin (1990), for instance, foresees the possibility of 'lower economic growth, higher unemployment and increased emigration' as the outcome of liberalised capital flows. A pessimistic scenario (for the less developed regions) is also sketched by Doyle (1989) and by the Padoa-Schioppa Report (1987). The cohesion issue is far from resolved given our present state of knowledge of the production and trade effects of integration.

Protectionist lobbies may be kept away by increased flows of Structural Funds but will be permanently put out of action only if these funds succeed in making the less developed regions competitive. According to Pelkmans, 'the cohesion programme as well as the temporary derogations prevent a non-conciliatory stance of EC-South on Fortress Europe in the product markets . . .. Cohesion is a necessary condition for a Community open to the world economy in these sensitive sectors' (1991, p. 39).

Third, awareness of the cost of protection has increased, not only in relation to agriculture, which is of crucial interest to Australia, but also in the case of manufacturing industries. At the same time, economists and business strategists have developed new perspectives on the potential gains from trade. The new trade theories stress the importance of economies of scale and competition, both of which require large, open markets for their full realisation. Extensive though the EC12 market already is, these gains require global competition if the dangers of oligopoly are to be avoided. Hence, a go-it-alone Fortress Europe would run the risk of inducing stagnation in many leading edge industries of the future.

Fourth, there is a new culture of free markets, deregulation and lower taxes as sources of higher prosperity which gives intellectual backing to the adherents of freer trade.

Nevertheless, what Max Corden has termed 'conservative resistance' will continue as a force within the Community. Its influence will be greater in Europe because of the lower degree of labour mobility (and widely divergent views as to the desirability of such mobility within the EC). The legitimate expression of this resistance can be met by means of comprehensive codes of safeguards and anti-dumping and anti-subsidy actions. Recourse to the hitherto largely unused New Community Instrument cannot be ruled out either, especially in the event of failure of the Uruguay Round. There have been many legitimate criticisms of such measures but strong assurances are needed if the case for a more liberal Common Commercial Policy is to be fully effective.

From a third country perspective therefore there is reason for optimism. But an element of regionalism in trade measures for specific sectors cannot be ruled out. Much will depend on the outcome of the Uruguay Round and on how the European economy performs in the present uncertain economic climate. The Community's trade policy, no more than the Community itself, cannot stand still. Old issues may be exacerbated, such as the Japanese trade surplus with the Community, and new issues will appear on the trade agenda. The relation between environmental issues and trade is an example – very relevant in the case of Eastern Europe and the Community. The linkage between trade (and aid) policy and security policy is another issue which will occupy a higher place on the agenda as the Community becomes more closely integrated.

Notes

1. Because of the EC's high trade ratios, the absolute import expansion is different to the percentage: EC +$115m, Japan $113m, US +$55m.
2. EC industry does not necessarily mean EC-owned industry (see below). Moreover, as Michael Porter (1990) points out, a larger home market can be a danger in so far as it acts as a disincentive to globalise – another argument for keeping the EC market open. To compete successfully, even within Europe, erstwhile national champions will need to set their sights on global markets and global competitiveness.
3. There has been much discussion over the protectiveness or otherwise of the EC anti-dumping procedures. Messerlin (1989) and Weidemann (1990) present conflicting arguments, from a large country–large economy perspective. Industrialists from small EC countries generally criticise the EC procedures as far too demanding and slow-acting. During the period 1980–8, the EC concluded 264 investigations with positive findings (duties, price undertakings or other measures). By comparison, during the same period there were 109 cases with positive findings by Australia and 134 by Canada (Nicolaides 1990).

Table 2A.1 Frequency ratios and non-tariff measure trade coverage ratios for individual OECD countries, 1981 and 1986.

Importer	Frequency ratio[1]			Trade coverage ratio[1]		
	1981	1986	1981–6 change (points)	1981	1986	1981–6 change (points)
Belgium–Luxembourg	8.4	8.6	0.2	12.6	14.3	1.7
Denmark	9.0	9.2	0.2	6.7	7.9	1.2
Germany (Fed. Rep.)	11.1	12.5	1.4	11.8	15.4	3.6
France	13.5	14.1	0.6	15.7	18.6	2.9
Greece	10.4	10.6	0.2	16.2	20.1	3.9
Great Britain	10.1	8.1	−0.2	11.2	12.8	2.4
Ireland	6.3	6.5	0.2	8.2	9.7	1.5
Italy	18.1	18.3	0.2	17.2	18.2	1.0
Netherlands	11.0	11.1	0.1	19.9	21.4	1.5
EC(10)[2]	11.4	11.5	0.1	13.4	15.8	2.4
Switzerland	9.7	9.7	0.0	19.5	19.6	0.1
Finland	3.4	3.4	0.0	7.9	8.0	0.1
Japan	12.7	12.5	−0.2	24.4	24.3	−0.1
Norway	19.8	17.4	−2.4	15.2	14.2	−1.0
New Zealand	45.0	38.8	−6.2	46.4	32.4	−14.0
United States	4.8	6.5	1.7	11.4	17.3	5.9
All above	12.2	12.0	−0.2	15.1	17.7	2.6

Notes:
1. Refers to hard-core non-tariff measures such as variable import levies, quotas, VERs, MFA trade restraints, prohibitions including seasonal prohibitions.
2. Excludes EC intra-trade.

Source: Laird and Yeats (1990b).

References

Cecchini, P. (1988) *The European Challenge 1992: The Benefits of a Single Market* (Aldershot: Wildwood House).

Doyle, M. F. (1989) 'Regional policy and European economic integration', in Committee for the Study of Economic and Monetary Union, *Report on Economic and Monetary Union in the European Community* (Delors Report) (Luxembourg).

Fielding, Sir L. (1991) *Europe as a Global Partner*, UACES Occasional Paper 7 (University Association for Contemporary European Studies).

Freeman, C. and Oldham, C. (1991) 'Introduction: beyond the Common Market', in C. Freeman, M. Sharp and W. Walker (eds) *Technology and the Future of Europe* (London: Pinter).

GATT (1991) *Trade Policy Review: The European Communities*, vols 1 and 2 (Geneva).

Hufbauer, G. C. (1990) *Europe 1992: An American Perspective* (Washington, DC: The Brookings Institution).

IMF Survey (1991) 'The coming emergence of three giant trading blocs', 1 April (Washington, DC: International Monetary Fund).

Jacquemin, A. (1990) Discussion of Neven's chapter in *Economic Policy*, April.

Jacquemin, A. and Sapir, A. (1991) 'Competition and imports in the European Market', in L. A. Winters and A. J. Venables (eds), *European Integration: Trade and Industry* (Cambridge: Cambridge University Press).

Journal of Common Market Studies (1990) 'Europe 1992 and the Developing Countries', Special Issue, vol. 29, no. 2.

Laird, S. and Yeats, A. (1990a) 'Trends in nontariff barriers of developed countries 1966–1986', *Weltwirtschaftliches Archiv*, vol. 126.

Laird, S. and Yeats, A. (1990b) *Quantitative Methods for Trade-Barrier Analysis* (London: Macmillan).

Lloyd, P. L. (1992) 'Regionalisation and world trade', *OECD Economic Studies*, Spring.

Matthews, A. (1990) *The European Community's Trade Policy and the Third World: an Irish Perspective* (Dublin: Gill and Macmillan).

Mayes, D. G. (1990) 'The external implications of closer European integration', *National Institute Economic Review*, November.

McAleese, D. (1990) 'External trade policy', in A. El-Agraa (ed.), *The Economics of the European Community* (3rd edition, London: Philip Allan).

McAleese, D. (1991) 'The EC internal market programme: implications for external trade', in N. Wagner (ed.), *ASEAN and the EC: the Impact of 1992* (Singapore: Institute of Southeast Asian Studies).

Messerlin, P. (1989) 'The EC antidumping regulations: a first appraisal', *Weltwirtschaftliches Archiv*, vol. 125, no. 3.

Michalopoulos, G. T. (1991) 'Macroeconomic consequences of the US dollar exchange rate movements for the EC economy: an empirical analysis', PhD Thesis, University of Reading.

Molle, W. (1990) *The Economics of European Integration* (Aldershot: Dartmouth).

Neven, D. (1990) 'Gains and losses from 1992', *Economic Policy*, April.

Nicolaides, P. (1990) 'Anti-dumping measures as safeguards: the case of the EC', *Intereconomics*, November/December.

Padoa-Schioppa, T. (1987) 'Efficiency, stability and equity: a strategy for the evolution of the economic system of the European Community', Report of a Study Group to President Delors (Commission of the European Communities, April).

Pelkmans, J. (1991). 'Completing the EC internal market: an update and problems ahead', in N. Wagner (ed.), *ASEAN and the EC: The Impact of 1992* (Singapore: Institute of Southeast Asian Studies).

Pinder, J. (1991) *European Community: the building of a union* (Oxford: Oxford University Press).

Porter, M. (1990) *The Competitive Advantage of Nations* (London: Macmillan).

Schumacher, D. and Mobius, U. (1991) 'Eastern Europe and the EC: trade relations and trade policy with regard to industrial products', paper to Joint Canada Germany Symposium, November 1990, revised January 1991 (Berlin Deutsches Institut für Wirtschaftforschung (DIW)).

Sharp, M. L. (1991) 'The Single Market and European technology policies', in C. Freeman, M. Sharp and W. Walker (eds), *Technology and the Future of Europe* (London: Pinter).

Sharp, M. L. and Walker, W. B. (1991) 'The policy agenda – challenges for the new Europe', in C. Freeman, M. Sharp and W. Walker (eds), *Technology and the Future of Europe* (London: Pinter).

Trela, I. and Whalley, J. (1990) 'Unravelling the threads of the MFA', in C. B. Hamilton (ed.), *Textiles Trade and the Developing Countries: Eliminating the Multi-Fibre Arrangement in the 1990s* (Washington, DC: The World Bank).

Tsoukalis, L. (1991) *The New European Economy: The Politics and Economics of Integration* (Oxford: Oxford University Press).

Wagner, N. (1991) 'The EC internal market and ASEAN: an overview', in N. Wagner (ed.), *ASEAN and the EC: The Impact of 1992* (Singapore: Institute of Southeast Asian Studies).

Weidemann, R. (1990) 'The anti-dumping policy of the European Communities', *Intereconomics*, January/February.

Winters, L.A. (1991) 'International trade and 1992', *European Economic Review*, April.

Yannopoulos, G. (1988) *Customs Unions and Trade Conflicts* (London: Routledge).

Yannopoulos, G. (1990) 'The effects of the Single Market on the pattern of Japanese investment', *National Institute Economic Review*, November.

3

European multinationals' competitiveness: implications for trade policy[1]

John M. Stopford

The progressive deepening of the internal integration of EC markets, together with the EC/EFTA treaty, which will create in 1993 a new European Economic Area embracing 380 million consumers and accounting for 40 per cent of world trade, has renewed and heightened fears in many quarters that the EC will adopt a protectionist stance towards the rest of the world. Such fears have undoubtedly provided one strong reason for the rapid rise of inward foreign direct investment (FDI) to the EC in recent years. Not only would an invested position within the market mitigate many of the costs of tariff protection, but it would also provide the possibilities of establishing an 'insider' position, sometimes supported by local purchasing preferences.

This chapter argues that, although such fears are largely unfounded, they may indeed be real in some of Europe's most threatened sectors. In very general terms, multinational corporations most typically oppose the protectionism. None the less, there are three conditions that may lead to the emergence of a Fortress Europe in which some non-European firms may be at a disadvantage. First is where multinationals rely much more on trade than on FDI to serve foreign markets, as in textiles. Second is in those sectors, such as automobiles, where FDI is important but where European multinationals are weak relative to world competitors. Third is where there are particular European fears about Japanese competition and where arguments have been advanced to regulate Japanese multinationals, irrespective of whether or not they have invested within the borders of the EC.

The central proposition is that public policy is critically affected by the 'bargains' that governments strike with firms, especially the leading players in any politically salient industry (Stopford and Strange 1991). In the European case, though there is a high degree of penetration by non-EC firms in many industries, it is to the European firms that EC governments listen most carefully. How leading European firms calculate and express their interests thus becomes an input to policy choice in Brussels.

To provide some clues as to how firms behave in these matters, this chapter reviews the evidence of how trends in FDI have affected both the configuration of world industries and the accompanying policy shifts. The strength of European multinationals relative to their global rivals is then assessed to indicate the special considerations that act to modify the impact of general trends. More detailed evidence on automobiles and electronics is used to illustrate the force of protectionist arguments in those sectors where Europe is relatively weak and to suggest some implications for non-EC firms.

3.1 FDI blunts protectionism

Milner (1987) argues that both France and the United States resisted the protectionist temptation most strongly in those industries where multinationals' interests were pervasive and that firms' trade preferences were relatively independent of state influence. Milner shows that firms determined their trade policies in broadly similar ways, regardless of the country of origin. Moreover her data show convincingly that the supposedly 'strong' state of France has been much more open to pressure from the corporate sector than is generally asserted. To the extent these arguments remain true, firms make obsolete the view that 'the democratic state [is] an autonomous entity capable of shaping societal preferences in accord with its own' (Nordlinger 1981, p. 100).

More generally, it can be argued that there are many reasons why multinationals should find protectionism unduly costly. First, they are concerned about retaliation. Second, they wish to avoid the additional costs of seeking to develop new markets to compensate for the loss of those closed by protectionism and of import costs for operations established behind tariff walls. Third, intra-industry rivalry can place multinationals at a disadvantage relative to protected, domestically oriented rivals. Firms dependent on a web of global trade and production will view protection as a cost that may undermine the status quo.

Some examples serve to make the point. The failure of US tyre producers to develop a radial tyre led to a surge of imports in the early 1970s. The smaller US producers launched a trade complaint against Michelin from France, who had established a plant in Canada to export to the United States. Despite opposition from Goodyear, the largest and most international US producer, the US government ruled against Michelin in a countervailing duty action, but imposed only a 'nuisance' tariff. The suit was later halted at the combined urging of Goodyear and Michelin, who had acted quickly to invest in US production. Later protectionist pressures were quashed by Goodyear in its controlling role over the Tire Producers' Association. Thereafter, the largest US producers met import competition by internal consolidation and specialisation. For its part, Michelin faced enormous problems of adjustment to new competition after the mid-1970s. Like the Americans, Michelin eschewed offers of government aid and relied on its own resources for further internationalisation, by both greenfield expansion and acquisition.

Much the same happened in the television industry. The smaller domestic US producers started trade actions against Asian imports, but were opposed by RCA, the largest and most internationally integrated producer. RCA tried to respond unilaterally to the threat, but ultimately failed and was sold, first to GE and later to Thomson of France. French producers had, during the 1960s and 1970s, relied on protection and government aid. But growing Europeanisation sparked interest in freer intra-European trade and harmonisation of technical standards. Thomson's wider world interests, however, combined policies of Europeanisation with the maintenance of selective protection against the Japanese (Milner 1987, chapter 6). The story was repeated in the US semi-conductor industry (Milner and Yoffie 1989).

Such examples suggest how firms' policy perspectives shift as their international strategies evolve. The question then arises as to how much those perspectives are also shaped by national policy. For many European firms, it is quite likely that the creation of the Common Market and the development of 'national champions' were influential in promoting a liberalisation of policy. But it is also evident that many of the largest European multinationals were strong supporters of the Common Market *before* its inception (Hanreider and Auton 1980, p. 123). Further, as Panić (1991) observed, multinationals were acting to integrate Europe faster than could adequately be accommodated by matching changes in national attitudes and economic institutions. The calculations of institutions' and firms' interests were interdependent.

The creation of national champions has, however, provided only equivocal support for freer trade. Some have remained domestically oriented and have opposed moves to challenge their *chasses gardées*. Yet, others have expanded abroad, often despite government opposition, and like St Gobain, the French glass producer, have added to the anti-protectionist interests.

There are several extra considerations which also affect European responses to emerging regional trade policy. These have to do with competitive forces at work to change the nature of global competition.

Whereas in the past, nationality seems to have affected managers' perceptions of the available options strongly and to make, say, the British response quite distinct from the French, common competitive threats are increasingly eliciting common European responses.[2] Some lingering nationalistic differences still, to be sure, exist, but they seem exceptions now rather than the rule.

Perhaps paradoxically, while national differences have lessened, sectoral and firm-level differences have increased. Strong firms in industries where FDI is important, as in many chemicals and consumer goods, have typically reacted to calls for protectionism with either indifference – the 'big yawn' described by Wells (1992) for the Americans – or overt opposition. By contrast, many weaker firms in trade-sensitive industries have reacted more defensively and called for political help.

3.2 Trends in FDI, competition and trade policy

These seemingly contradictory responses have been shaped by the uneven impact of the trends in the form of global competition. During the latter half of the 1980s, there have been marked changes in the preferences between exports and FDI, changes in the direction and form of the investment flows and changes in the position of individual firms. Taken together, these shifts strongly suggest that the determinants of international economic activity have been transformed into a configuration significantly different from what it was.

Between 1983 and 1989, FDI outflows grew at an annual rate of 28.9 per cent, much faster than world exports (9.4 per cent) and world GDP (7.8 per cent) during the same period.[3] Much of the growth has been among 'Triad' countries, as Table 3.1 shows. The long-standing concentration of FDI outflow from a few, richer countries has recently been accompanied by a growing share of the investment in the same countries, and a relative reduction of investment flows to developing countries.

Such aggregate indicators obscure considerable divergence in preference and practice for the balance between foreign trade and investment.[4] Here the analysis is complex, for useful generalisations based on some notion of industry are elusive. To explain why this is so, a short digression from the main argument is needed. Conventional, economic explanations emphasise sectoral differences in the importance of scale, costs and transaction costs as prime determinants of the configuration of a firm's foreign assets.[5] That sense of industry determinism has, in recent years, been modified to show that firms have wide degrees of latitude in the specific choices they make within

Table 3.1 Growing concentration of FDI within the 'Triad'.

	1980	1988
	% Share of stock of inward FDI	
EC	37	33
(excluding intra-EC)	(31)	(23)
USA	16	27
Japan	1	1
Share of 'Triad'	54	61
World total (US$bn)	509	1,219
	% Share of stock of outward FDI	
EC	39	43
(excluding intra-EC)	(33)	(34)
USA	42	30
Japan	4	10
Share of 'Triad'	85	83

Note: The data for Japan and several European countries exclude reinvested profits. The data for EC exclude Ireland, Greece and Luxembourg.

Source: adapted from UNCTC, *World Investment Report* (1991, Table 10).

an industry. Porter (1986), Prahalad and Doz (1987), Bartlett and Ghoshal (1989) and others have shown the importance of modifying the drive for scale by integrating activities across national boundaries to allow greater responsiveness to differences in national conditions of demand. Rather than regarding the balance to be struck as a matter solely of industry economics, these more recent analyses have indicated that the balance is equally affected by *firm-specific* resources.

History affects how a firm exercises choice in building its asset base. As a first approximation, one can depict US and British multinationals as having initially expanded abroad by emphasising responsiveness to differences in local demand structures in their preference for FDI over exports. Later on, the Japanese expanded in the same industries by emphasising integration and exporting, thereby changing many of the 'rules' of competition and forcing earlier investors to respond. National differences are indicated in Table 3.2, which shows the export/foreign production ratio for a large sample of industrial firms. Furthermore, these national differences were also apparent within industries, albeit to a lesser extent (Stopford and Dunning 1983). More recent events, however, have served to create a degree of convergence towards the earlier US position. Japanese and German exporters have radically stepped up their FDI, while maintaining their exports.

That convergence has, however, been uneven, as Table 3.3 indicates. The US/European balance has remained dominated by FDI,

Table 3.2 Changing balance between overseas production and exports from home country, 1977–90.

	Exports/overseas production ratio		
	1990	1981	1977
United States	0.15	0.16	0.17
Europe*	0.44	0.44	0.50
United Kingdom	0.17	0.24	0.32
France	0.57	0.63	0.58
Germany	1.09	1.38	1.76
Japan	1.64	3.76	4.30

*'Europe' includes Austria, Belgium, Finland, France, Germany, Italy, Netherlands, Sweden, Switzerland, and the United Kingdom.

Sources: for 1977 and 1981, Stopford and Dunning (1983, Table 4.4), based on data for 500 industrial multinationals. For 1990, Wells (1992) for United States using 1988 data; Stopford (1992b) for a sample of 105 leading European industrial multinationals; the figure for Japan was calculated by Professor Urata from MITI data (Wagakuni Kigyo no Kaigai Jigyo Katsudo, No. 19) for all Japanese manufacturing firms.

Table 3.3 Regional balance of trade and FDI, 1989.

Region	Export/ FDI ratio
North America	
to Western Europe	0.6
to Japan	2.6
to rest of Asia	1.6
intra-regional	1.8
Western Europe	
to North America	0.4
to Japan	5.6
to rest of Asia	1.5
intra-regional	4.8
Japan	
to North America	1.4
to Western Europe	2.1
to rest of Asia	2.8

Source: author's calculations based on OECD export data (fob values for intra-OECD trade, otherwise cif values) and estimates of stocks of FDI drawn from national sources.

whereas in other regional relationships, exports are of roughly similar or greater importance in the balance. The ratios shown in Table 3.3 are, to be sure, artificial in that they compare a book-value stock figure for FDI with an annual flow figure for exports: they merely suggest the relative importance of the balances.[6]

Table 3.3 also shows the continuing importance of trade within Europe. Intra-EC integration has, so far, been driven much more by trade expansion than cross-border investment. For example, British FDI in the region has remained almost static (expansion by some firms being offset by disinvestment by others), while the share of British exports going to the EC has risen from 32 per cent in 1972, the year of accession, to over 50 per cent by 1990. Data from other EC members show the same trends. In other words, there are divergent trade and investment trends within and between trade blocs.

3.2.1   The 'new' global competition

Major industries have 'gone global' at different times and for different reasons. Table 3.4 is a gross simplification of reality, but it indicates that the process has been going on for many decades, involving progressively more sectors. Indeed, it is becoming difficult to identify a major industry where a purely national position is defensible any longer. Moreover, those affected earliest have been changed again as technologies have developed.

The factors identified in Table 3.4 can act together to alter the relative importance of trade and FDI in any one sector. In electronics, for example, much of the early US and European internationalisation emphasised FDI. Later on, the then new Japanese entrants changed the 'rules' to emphasise trade for as long as possible. Today, the threat of protectionism, combined with further technical advance, has begun to swing the pendulum back towards FDI. In other words, a snapshot of the trade/investment balance for an industry can mislead: the balance is shifting continuously.

Four developments were needed to spur these innovations and make them profitable. One was the impact of information and transport technologies on lowering the real costs – and risks – of managing at a distance. A second has been the effect of deregulation, especially in financial markets, to permit cross-border transactions. A third has been the creation of new technologies that have altered, and often lowered, the scale needed for efficient operation. Yet another has been the fragmentation of demand as customers and consumers in industrial and consumer markets have demanded ever greater variety of products and services. Though it is possible that demand for variety was always

Table 3.4   The changing nature of global competition.

Decade	Factor •	Threatened national industries
Pre-1960	Natural resources	Oil, aluminium
1960s	Labour-intensity	Textiles, shoes, simple assembly
1970s	Capital-intensity	Automobiles, machinery, chemicals
1980s	Technology	Consumer electronics, telecoms
1990s	Information, Service	Financial services, media

present, such demand can now be supplied profitably by those firms that have invested in flexible supply 'systems' and managerial processes that reduce the cost of supplying variety. Failure to invest in the new systems has often caused erstwhile leaders to lose competitive position.

Where new technology has reduced factory scale, it has usually increased the need for greater scale elsewhere in the firm. Smaller plants can be geographically dispersed, but they need to be linked together by costly systems of information and control. For example, Ford of Europe spent over $1.5 billion during the early 1980s to improve its European network. Such system developments act to heighten the barriers to entry and are critical in shaping the emerging form of supply networks described below.

3.2.2   Emerging regional networks

Changing economics of supply affect how firms choose where to source their goods. Despite much rhetoric about global integration, very few multinationals appear to have succeeded in achieving more than regional integration of their supply systems (Morrison *et al.* 1990). Within regional blocs, where there are already the advantages of both proximity and unrestricted, cheap transfer, they are creating networks of trade in physical goods to increase the gains from specialisation. The greater the importance of FDI, the greater is the extent of intra- rather than inter-regional trade.

One consequence of the development of intra-regional supply is shown by the growth of intra-industry trade among northern European countries, where the greatest historical weight of assets is located and where the multinationals' moves to specialise their operations are most pronounced. Simultaneously, trade from Spain, Portugal and, to a lesser extent, Greece, is becoming more specialised, helped in part by multinationals' supply-oriented investments in these countries after they joined the EC. The same is beginning to happen in Eastern Europe. But there are limits to the extent of the expansion of the 'catchment area'; most developing countries have not been affected, as Langhammer (1990) shows, though there are some signs that supply networks around the Mediterranean basin are being enhanced.

Simultaneously, as Figure 3.1 shows, leading multinationals have been building parallel networks of inter-regional trade in the 'intangibles' of knowledge, engineering, design, brand management, and the like. Given the demands of scale for the underlying systems, the investments are primarily global in scope. These systems can be transferred across national borders to change the basis on which competitiveness is established in each country. The configuration of the networks indicated in Figure 3.1 is merely notional; in practice the distinctions are not so clear. Where demand is homogeneous at the global level, as for many components, corporate resources and supply facilities are managed on an integrated basis, thus permitting some inter-regional trade in goods. Because neither trade statistics nor FDI measures take account of the growing trade in FDI-related 'intangibles', the generality of the argument must necessarily be speculative. Yet case evidence, shown later, suggests that some firms have constructed parallel networks to such an extent that their costs are increasingly divorced from national factor costs.

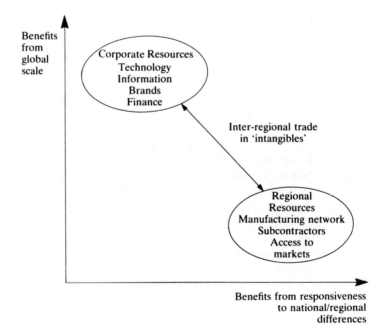

Figure 3.1   The differentiated global network.

3.2.3 Trade policy responses

The emergence of parallel supply networks calls into question the basis of national accounts as a measure of national competitiveness (Julius 1990) and suggests that trade policy is of decreasing regulatory power. Much of the trade in manufactured goods has long been internal to the multinationals in the form of inter-affiliate trade.[7] These internal transfers are relatively insensitive to exchange-rate shifts, though they are exposed to the risks and costs of tariff and non-tariff obstacles. The adjustments of the 1980s, though not fully understood in their generality, indicate that the volume of such 'captive' trade has been increasing to add fuel to an old debate.[8]

The managerial response to protection has often been such that trade policy has alleviated, but not cured, the problem of declining European competitiveness in trade-sensitive industries. There is evidence that many European firms, especially the British, respond to tariff protection by increasing dividends, not by making the needed long-term adjustments in investment (see, for example, Sharp 1986). European prices for computers and workstations are 40–50 per cent above world prices and the price for Lotus 1-2-3 software is almost double that charged in the United States. Trade protection may keep European firms in business, but may also reduce their ability to export outside the region. This concern is indicated by the decline in the European index of trade specialisation, in a period when the United States and Japan are becoming more specialised. For Europe, one possible explanation is that previously strong exporters are becoming weaker and insufficient numbers of newcomers are emerging to offset the decline.

Under these circumstances, the appropriateness of Brussels' concentration on developing EC-wide policy as its main instrument of control is questionable. There are two issues. First is whether the EC Commission can use its exclusive powers, under Article 113 of the Treaty of Rome, to implement a coherent policy at all: second is whether a continental policy can be effective in building competitiveness. Member states maintain over 1,000 national, quantitative import restrictions, including specific restrictions on the Japanese in sixty-one product categories. Changing many of these arrangements will be difficult: some preceded accession to the Community and are subject to grandfather clauses; others are part of more general agreements such as the Multifibre Arrangement (MFA); yet others affect issues of national political salience that make accession to Brussels' demands difficult.

Most experts agree that a trade regime by itself will not be sufficient to promote a greater European presence in the most globally competitive industries. Lawrence (1991) makes the point that external, GATT-type negotiations are no more than efforts to solve problems at the border; 1992 concerns issues of 'deep integration', which go beyond border problems. Furthermore, the extent of both external and internal adjustment varies greatly among sectors. Figure 3.2 illustrates the extent of the differences for some industries. The diagram is notional, even though it is based in part on careful and systematic attempts to measure the differences, and on the EC Commission's identification of particularly threatened sectors. Some industries, like chemicals and ball-bearings, had adjusted to both regional economics and global competition well before the 1992 programme was launched in 1985. Others, like pharmaceuticals and retail banking, shaped by strong and quite different national regulations, have substantial internal adjustments to make.

The effectiveness of an external trade policy will be determined in part on progress made to eliminate continent-wide barriers to trade. Continuing state intervention on such matters as pricing (as for

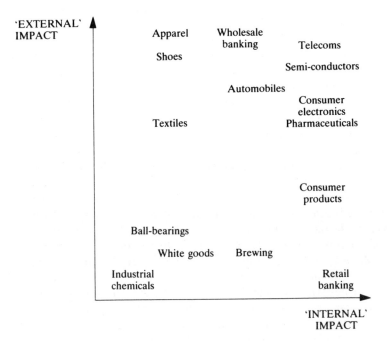

Note: The axes are notional. The positioning of each industry indicates the author's assessment of relative impact, based on numerous industry studies.

Source: adapted from Calori and Lawrence (1991, Table 7.1).

Figure 3.2 1992 affects industries unevenly (selected industries).

semi-conductor memories), state subsidies for loss-making enterprises (as the French support for its computer firm, Bull) and the interpretation of the 'local content' and anti-dumping rules all impede price competition and can unduly cushion inefficiency. In part also, the outcomes will be determined by the impact of the firms' relative competitive strengths on managers' perspectives on feasible adjustments to regulatory change.

3.3   Assessing European competitive strength

It might be inferred from these general arguments that moves towards globalisation heighten the advantages of the leaders. By raising the resource costs, global competition typically means that only a few players can hope to remain profitable and thus able to finance the needed offensive, resource-building investments. Yet many of yesterday's leaders have fallen by the wayside. That so many Japanese firms have succeeded in coming from behind to assume leadership by changing the 'rules' shows that it is possible to overcome initial resource disadvantages. So too for Europeans, though fewer have so far succeeded. Michelin (in tyres), Bekaert (in steel cord for radial tyres) and smaller firms like Edwards High Vacuum (vacuum pumps) are notable examples; all have emphasised internationalisation and global networks of intelligence.

Under these *dynamic* conditions, measures of market share – one measure of relative strength – need to be taken over a considerable period of time. Moreover, they should be made at the global level, for strength within one country or even within Europe may not be sufficient to create strength elsewhere. Lacking reliable data for world market shares, a rough proxy is the relative shares held by the leading players. Franko (1991) has provided some long-run trends up to 1990 for the twelve leaders in many sectors, some of which are shown in Table 3.5. Continuing and growing European leadership in chemicals and consumer goods contrasts starkly with losses elsewhere. In automobiles, the gains achieved during the 1960s and 1970s were not extended during the 1980s. Indeed, the figures shown overstate the European position, because much of the volume recorded lies within Europe, and the share of markets outside has been declining. In textiles and apparel, the erosion of the European position has been much more severe (due in part to the challenge from new entrants from Turkey and South Korea) and has led to a pervasive sense of threat (Cline 1987).

The data in Table 3.5 indicate no more than the fluctuating fortunes of the leading firms; they do not indicate the totality of the industry,

Table 3.5   Shares of world industries, 1960–89 (per cent of sales of top twelve firms).

	1960	1970	1980	1990
Chemicals				
Europe	32	60	69	73
United States[1]	68	40	31	23
Japan	0	0	0	4
Consumer goods (food and beverages)				
Europe	34	33	50	52
United States	62	67	50	48
Pharmaceuticals[2]				
Europe	13	30	45	51
United States	87	70	55	49
Petroleum products				
United States	77	78	66	47
Europe	23	22	34	45
Other	0	0	0	8
Automobiles and trucks				
United States	83	66	42	38[3]
Europe	17	22	40	39
Japan	0	12	17	23
Electrical equipment and electronics				
Japan	8	17	21	47
Europe	11	24	32	31
United States	71	59	47	11[3]
South Korea	0	0	0	11
Computers and office equipment				
United States	95	90	86	70
Japan	0	3	7	23
Europe	5	7	7	7
Textiles				
Japan	7	32	21	42
Europe	35	23	30	26
United States	58	44	41	21
Other	0	0	8	11

Notes
1. Excludes the petroleum and coal interests of DuPont.
2. Includes pharmaceuticals divisions only of Hoechst and Bayer.
3. Excludes revenues of financial subsidiaries: equivalent adjustments for non-US firms were not possible, thus understating the US share.

Source: Franko (1991).

nor the competitiveness of firms in individual segments. Additional measures are needed. Two are shown in Table 3.6 for seven manufacturing industries. One measures the configuration of the industry in terms of the export/foreign production ratio. This ratio indicates the relative ordering of priorities; the absolute numbers are of little importance for the argument here.[9] The other indicates world strength in terms of sales outside Europe, where the benefits of any European protectionism do not apply.

Table 3.6 The 'global' position of European firms, selected industries, 1988.

	Number of firms	% sales outside Europe	Export/ foreign production ratio	% sales in top twelve[1]
Emphasis on FDI				
Pharmaceuticals	6	50	0.27	51
Consumer goods	10	40	0.07	52
Petroleum	6	37	n/a	45
Chemicals	10	27	0.67	73
Emphasis on trade				
Electronics and computers	10	24	0.92	19
Textiles	5	15	n/a	26
Volume autos	5	14	2.84	39

1. The share of European firms' sales in the world's twelve largest firms. For details, see Table 3.5.

The data show that Europe is well endowed with leading firms in industries where FDI is of predominant importance: chemicals, consumer products, petroleum and pharmaceuticals. By contrast, leading European firms are weaker where trade is more important. These weaker firms – in electronics, textiles and volume automobiles – are also much more concentrated within Europe. Given the trends that the non-EC proportion has fallen for many of these weaker firms during the 1980s, but grown for the stronger ones, the differences are being magnified over time.

The divergence of the responses now audible in Brussels owe much to these increasingly stark differences. Weaker firms that become defensive and inward-looking are more prone to lobby Brussels for protection of all kinds (Hamel and Prahalad 1985; Prahalad and Doz 1987). For some of these threatened firms, the new opportunities in Eastern Europe look relatively attractive where they can be captured within integrated continent-wide systems of supply, thus intensifying the sense of a continental perspective. At the same time, stronger competitors can maintain a global perspective, in which Europe is but one region of strategic importance.

The differences should not, however, be exaggerated. The data provide no more than an indication of relative balance. Moreover, within a 'weak' industry, there is a wide range of position. Peugeot has more to lose than VW, because of its far greater reliance on a high share of a protected home market. To illustrate the range of further consideration that needs to be taken into account when measuring competitive strength, attention is now turned to two of the threatened industries. The discussion that follows includes some of the public policy debate to highlight the interlocking nature of the bargains struck between the firms and government.

3.3.1 Automobiles

The mass-market automobile industry has been transformed as the development of global systems has altered the rules of competition. Not only has demand for variety of model increased sharply around the world, but also advances in production technology have created new production possibilities profitably to supply variety and to accelerate the pace of new model introduction. The Japanese leaders in the new systems have gained market share at the expense of the earlier leaders from the United States and Europe.

Table 3.7 provides some measures of how costs have been reduced and time-scales collapsed in the Japanese 'lean' system of production (Womack *et al.* 1990). The effect of these advantages in terms of productivity and quality is shown in Figure 3.3. Most revealing, for the purposes of indicating the possibilities of divorcing the costs of operation from national factor costs, is the advantage of the Japanese 'transplants' in the United States over Ford and GM in their own backyard, and, to a lesser degree, of the transplants operating in Europe. The European differences are today rather greater than as shown for 1988, as the recent Japanese investments have subsequently started up.

While the Japanese have been building global position, most of the European mass-market producers (Mercedes-Benz, for example, is excluded) appear to have been concentrating on a Europe-first strategy. Table 3.8 shows the extent of the concentration of their sales within Europe. In terms of the locus of production, the concentration is even greater. For example, Peugeot had only about 1 per cent of its production outside Europe and like many others (excepting VW) has been reducing capacity outside Europe.

Table 3.7 The challenge of variety plus time (automobile industry).

	Japan	United States	Europe
Model development time (months)	46	60	54
No. in project team	485	903	904
Ratio of delayed projects	1:6	1:2	1:3
Return to normal quality after model change (months)	1.4	11	12
Return to productivity (months)	4	5	12

Source: Womack *et al.* (1990).

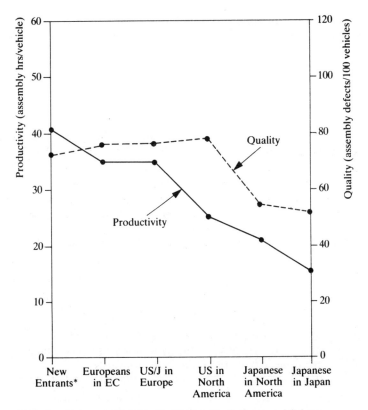

*Includes thirteen plants in Brazil, Mexico, South Korea and Taiwan.

Source: Womack *et al.* (1990).

Figure 3.3 Regional productivity and quality differences (automobile assembly, volume producers, 1989) (weighted average).

Table 3.8 Leading European automobile producers' concentrate on the regional market, 1988.

	% of Sales in:		
Producer	Home market	Rest of Europe	Rest of world
VW (Germany)	38	38	24
Rover (UK)	59	24	17
Renault (France)	51	37	12
Fiat (Italy)	54	35	11
Peugeot (France)	75	20	5

Source: Lynch (1990).

The European supply systems of both the local producers and the US transplants have been extended across national borders. They are predominantly intra-regional, though as suggested earlier in Figure 3.1, there is some inter-regional supply. For example, GM's UK-assembled Vauxhall Cavalier had only 56.5 per cent of its manufacturing cost in the United Kingdom in 1986: the rest came from Germany (28.5 per cent), Australia (10 per cent, engine) and Japan (5 per cent, gear box) (Page 1986). VW imports parts and assemblies from its affiliates in Brazil, Mexico and South Africa. The success of these systems is critically dependent on local collaboration, for no one in the industry is wholly vertically integrated. Thus, the relative inefficiency of European parts suppliers constrains the emergence of greater export competitiveness of the finished product (Boston Consulting Group 1991).

GM, VW and Fiat have also been expanding their reach into Eastern Europe with large acquisitions, licence deals and modernising investment programmes. They and Ford have also made large investments in Spanish assembly plants to supply the rest of Europe. These investments were made either in anticipation of Spain's accession to the EC or shortly thereafter. Low labour costs and adequate levels of skill, combined with ready access to the wider market, have made Spain (and more recently Portugal) a newly important magnet pulling the centre of gravity of the industry southwards.

Whether the European response to the new global challenge will prove sufficient has become, in part, a question of whether the scale of group resources is sufficient to develop the 'system architecture' of control and production as fast and as extensively as the Japanese. It is also a matter of the speed of transformation from a long history of cushioned protection that has affected both managerial attitudes and work practices. High degrees of national protection inhibited the development of even continental-scale efficiencies (Pearce and Sutton 1985). The 1992 developments are, to be sure, designed to remove such protection, but they are likely to decrease trading margins at the very time that greater capital spending is needed (Waverman 1991). These problems of internal adjustment exacerbate the sense of external threat and appear to be making the European industry more inward-looking and prone to divert resources away from other territories.

The urgency of the need for transformation is not reflected in current trade policy. Under Article 115 of the Treaty of Rome, EC countries have been permitted to limit imports from Japan. In 1988, Japan's informal voluntary export restraint of automobiles into the EC was 1.21 million cars. Italy's quota, approved by the GATT, limits imports to 3,300 units. France and the United Kingdom have specific market share limitations, and there are also bilateral controls in Portugal and Spain. Elsewhere in Europe, where there are no such restraints, the Japanese now command market shares as high as 40 per cent. Protectionism, it would seem, has served merely to preserve some national shares but failed to provide the spur for the protected firms to hold on to share in neighbouring EC countries.

National policies have also varied with respect to local-content regulations and transitional arrangements.[10] At the heart of the local-content debate is a dispute about the application of the previously informal 60 per cent guideline for the Japanese 'transplants', mainly located in the United Kingdom. Even though Article 5 of the 802/68 EC regulation applies to automobiles,[11] the French have argued for at least an 80 per cent content before free EC-wide circulation can be permitted. The United Kingdom has also favoured an 80 per cent level, but has argued for a transitional period.

Though all European producers – whether indigenous or long-established US transplants – feel threatened, there has been much debate on the most appropriate response to the Japanese threat. The Committee of European Community Automobile Makers (CCMC) was disbanded in November 1990, when M. Calvet, the chairman of Peugeot, remained implacably opposed to any reduction of the trade barriers and to a proposal that the CCMC move from unanimity to majority voting for proposals submitted to the Commission. A new body, the Association des Constructeurs Européens d'Automobiles (ACEA), was created in 1991 and excluded the Japanese. By July 1991, the ACEA and the Commission agreed on a plan that would allow Japan's share of cars and light vans to rise from 11 per cent to 16 per cent by 1999. Direct imports from Japan would be frozen; any expansion was to be supplied by the transplants. But Peugeot and the Japanese have remained opposed to the plan and final agreement has yet to be reached.

These are circumstances where the lack of consensus within the European industry permits the Fortress mentality among the most threatened producers to delay moves to liberalise the regulations. Even though ACEA members now seemed prepared to take the gamble that they can catch up sufficiently within the next eight years to take on the Japanese without further protection, they still rely on anti-Japan policies to provide time to adjust.

3.3.2 *Electronics*

The globalisation of the electronics industry happened rapidly, fuelled by advances in technology, the adoption of open systems and the proliferation of alliances.[12] For instance, when the 256K chip was introduced in 1986, many thought this would be the lasting standard. Yet, Fujitsu and Toshiba introduced a 1MB chip in 1988. As so often, Europe was left behind: the JESSI project for technical co-operation is still working on trial production of its own 1MB chip. Of perhaps greater concern is the domestic orientation of most of Europe's leading players, as Table 3.9 shows.[13] Even Philips, the largest firm and one of the most territorially spread, suffers from persistent unprofitability and is currently undergoing deep surgery to cut costs.

One measure of the threat facing the European industry is the large trade deficit: about $17 billion in consumer electronics and $10 billion in computers. Another is the fact that most of Europe's declining share of world semi-conductor production, down from 22 per cent in 1978 to about 10 per cent in 1990, has been unprofitable.

As in automobiles, the long history of protection has provided a cushion muffling any drive for world-scale competitiveness (Porter 1990). One measure is the evidence of prices. As noted earlier, European prices are well above the differences that might be expected from tariffs. Yet they have not led to superior profits for European producers. On the contrary, most are in financial difficulty and France has provided Bull with a massive subsidy to keep it in business. Only the non-European suppliers seem to be able to benefit from the price umbrella. IBM, for example, earned two-thirds of its total 1989 net income in Europe, benefiting considerably from its world 'system', which has lowered its European costs below that of the locals.[14]

Government purchases from favoured local suppliers are one cause for the blunted response to world competition. Another is the extensive government support for collaborative research in a proliferation of programmes like ESPRIT (information technology), RACE (broadband communications) and JESSI (micro-chips). Even with a budget of ecu 5.7 billion for the period 1990–4, little was achieved to help catch up with the leaders. The issue is not one of throwing money at the problem, but of getting proven technologies into operation more quickly and with fewer resource costs.

These are circumstances that have bred great dissent among producers, among governments and between industry and government. There are no solutions that satisfy everyone. Consider, for example, the issue of setting a continental standard for the telecommunications system. To enhance efficiencies from 1993 onwards, the Brussels Commissioner for Research has called for a 'European nervous system' based on the inter-operability of the national communications systems. But free-traders, such as the Commissioner for Competition Policy, objected to the protectionist overtones of the proposals. Moreover, opponents of central control have pointed to the effect of high prices in

Table 3.9 Ten major European electronics firms, sales by region, 1988.

Firm	% of sales in:		
	Home country	Rest of Europe	Rest of world
Thomson (France)	29	22	49
Racal (UK)	40	15	45
Philips (Netherlands) (est.)	22	46	32
GEC (UK)	60	12	28
CGE (France)	42	35	23
Olivetti (Italy)	37	42	21
Siemens (Germany)	64	22	14
STC (UK)[1]	73	14	13
Nixdorf (Germany)[2]	52	41	7
STET (Italy) (est.)[3]	90	5	<5

Notes:
1. Includes ICL, now acquired by Fujitsu; the remainder of STC was bought by Northern Telecom in 1990.
2. 1987 data: now acquired by Siemens.
3. Subsidiary of IRI.

Source: Lynch (1990).

slowing down the rate at which demand can grow to fuel further innovation. UNICE, the industry lobby, is opposed to a single system, arguing the need for flexibility to allow everyone to benefit.

Dissent is further confused by arguments about the extent to which ownership of Europe-based assets now matters. In the wake of Fujitsu's purchase of ICL, there are Japanophobe voices raised to warn against the possibilities of further purchases that reinforce already dominant positions. ICL has been ejected from the European IT Roundtable and from JESSI, even though many consider it to be just as 'European' as the remaining members both in strategic terms and in terms of where it adds value.

The waters of the debate have been muddied by competitive shifts that have made it increasingly difficult to define what constitutes a European firm. Almost all of the largest European electronic firms are dependent in one way or another on alliances with US or Japanese competitors. Siemens buys its mainframes from Fujitsu and is developing its D-ram chips with IBM. Olivetti has had numerous alliances with AT&T and Hitachi. Thomson relies on JVC for many of the critical technologies in consumer electronics. As one senior official in Olivetti, itself a threatened player in the industry, put it:

> In the 1990s, competition will no longer be between individual companies but between new, complex corporate groupings. A company's

competitive position no longer (solely) depends on its internal
capabilities; it also depends on the type of relationships it has been able
to establish with other firms and the scope of those relationships.[15]

The implication is that the electronics industry in Europe is not the
same as the European electronics industry and that the focus of the
debate should be on creating conditions that enhance Europe's
value-adding capability, regardless of ownership. Proponents of such
an argument point to the fact that, for example, IBM's added value
within Europe (both absolutely and proportionately) has long been
greater than that of national champions. Yet many in both industry
and government would disagree. Ownership matters, they maintain,
because it conditions future prospects in any one region: firms give
preference to the home territory, making the burden of adjustment to
adverse trading condition fall at the periphery of the system. And
where there is weakness, the effect of inter-regional trading networks
in the alliances adds to Europe's trade deficit.

The weakness of the industry as a whole creates a dilemma that
seems incapable of solution by rationality alone. None of the obvious
options is wholly satisfactory. Further protection shows no sign of
arresting the decline and would merely maintain higher prices. Forced
inward investment by importers threatens the incumbents more
directly and heightens the debate about the consequences of a collapse
of a European player. The dilemma is illustrated by Regulation No.
288/89 [OJL 33, of 4.2.89], which requires the diffusion process for
semi-conductor manufacture to be located in a member state to
guarantee free EC circulation. Many regard this restriction as likely to
lead to inefficiency. Selective encouragement for some segments does
not appear to have helped in the past, because of technical changes
that have eroded the protectability of the segment 'boundaries'.
Moreover, mergers to gain greater scale do not provide a clear
solution. For example, Thomson's proposal to merge much of the
chip-making capacity was opposed by Siemens and Philips on the
grounds that it would merely serve to reduce the impetus for further
development. Besides, Siemens announced in July 1991 that it was
merging its interests in next-generation chip development with those of
IBM. This move underscores the fact that attempts to create a
centrally planned future will be overtaken by events: it is a case of
sauve qui peut.

The sense of dilemma can cause leading industrialists to make
inconsistent statements. For example, one top official in Philips, the
troubled leader at the centre of the storm, reaffirmed his support for
free trade, but then went on to argue for policies that would 'oblige
governments to buy European' (van der Klugt 1986). Moreover,

Philips successfully argued for European price protection for video tape recorders to keep inefficient local production going. The extra margins awarded to the Japanese had the perverse effect of adding to their cash-flow capability to fund the development of next-generation products faster than the protected Europeans could achieve.

The threat to European electronics is so great that the industry is rife with speculation about future defensive mergers, even though the gains appear illusory. Yet the position is not unremittingly bleak. Some, like Thomson in France and Racal in Britain, are clearly determined to persist in maintaining an aggressive stance outside Europe. Yet, as argued earlier, even Thomson relies on selective protection at home. None the less, Thomson's position is so different from, say, Philips', that it can negotiate from greater strength. Where European fortunes are so divergent, the industry's lobby pressure in Brussels is perhaps understandably inconsistent.

3.4 Conclusions

The evidence from a variety of industries points clearly to a growing divergence in positions taken by leading EC multinationals in responding to shifts in global competition and regionalisation. Where competitive strength is measured at the world level, the strong are able to adjust aggressively to changes within Europe without disturbing their global strategies. The weaker are prone to become more inward-looking and to call for protectionist help from Brussels. Though multinationals (and indeed the official position of Brussels) may in general resist protectionism, there are so many special cases of weakness, especially in trade-oriented industries, that the fears of a Fortress Europe developing selectively may prove to be justified.

One reason why this may be so is that the impact of these two sides of industry's 'voice' is likely to be one-sided. The weak, and particularly weak French firms, are much more vociferous in lobbying both their national governments and Brussels than are most of the strong players. Strong leaders in investment-intensive industries have been relatively silent, reflecting perhaps their confidence and sense of indifference to changes in trade policy. Few have gone as far as British Petroleum, which stated in 1990 that 'as an international company, BP's commercial success is crucially dependent on . . . the maintenance and enhancement of the GATT-based multilateral trading system.' The problem of such asymmetry is exacerbated by the fact that weakness in even the most threatened sectors is a relative term; most have some strong firms that do not necessarily agree on a unified lobby position.

There are other factors at work to complicate the position and to suggest that the actions taken in Brussels will most likely be those of compromise. One is the continuing difference of approach taken by national governments. The British have emphasised the need to attract value-added investments, leading one observer in Britain to predict 'that by the year 2000, one in six people in the UK manufacturing sector will work for Japanese firms, while one in four will be employed by EEC firms based outside of the UK'.[16] By contrast, the French and Italians have emphasised the continuing importance of national ownership. A second is the position of smaller firms and unions that may feel particularly threatened both by the global changes and by integration within Europe. Where the drift to the South has been important, Northern labour interests have raised fears about loss of employment; established employers in the South have raised fears about the loss of competitiveness. The issues of 'Social Europe' are an inescapable part of the political response to the changing fortunes of the major firms.

The implications for non-EC firms of the cross-currents of these developments are unclear: much depends on specific circumstance. None the less, two broad lines of enquiry can be drawn out of the foregoing analysis. One concerns the need to develop 'insider' positions within the EC. The other concerns the need to examine the durability of the competitive strength of prospective partners in a co-operative drive to establish position.

The rapid rise of US and Japanese FDI into Europe in recent years suggests that there is a race to develop 'insider' positions in all sectors. Japanese FDI grew by 32 per cent in Fiscal 1990 alone. In sectors dominated by FDI, the development of multinationals' dual networks of supply needs careful consideration. It may not be sufficient to build an intra-regional network for the supply of physical goods: the inter-regional networks of knowledge and control are of growing salience. Not only must non-EC firms consider their investments in continental rather than national terms, but also they need to pay attention to the increasing scale requirements for 'system' investments that harness new information technologies and permit even greater levels of service to local customers. Thus, the barriers to entry are rising, not because of regulation but because of the changing economics of competition.

For trade-intensive sectors, the likelihood that the weakness of indigenous producers will continue to be offset by protection also raises the barriers. Purely 'arm's length' trading will suffer from perhaps rising discrimination in purchasing preferences. Moreover, customer demands for enhanced levels of service need to be satisfied, often by means of adding FDI selectively in such activities as warehousing and after sales service. In addition, the tendency to link trade and investment in the 'ownership matters' debate adds further pressure to develop insider positions in partnership with a local player.

Where partnership is important, non-EC firms need to examine the underlying strengths of the prospective partner firm, not the strength of the industry. Here the metric is not the European, but the firm's global position. The ideal is to collaborate actively with firms that are sufficiently strong and durable to continue delivering the desired additions to local resources over long periods. Strength and durability do not necessarily mean today's leading firms; many erstwhile leaders have disappeared as competition has changed. Deals with weak and inflexible firms, even if they seem to meet short-term goals, are likely to lead to disappointment. When threatened by global competition, weaker firms tend to divert resources to cope with the most pressing competitive agendas where they have unambiguous control. Thus, there are occasions when collaboration with smaller firms may be preferred, even if their political clout is small. Above all, the analysis above suggests that non-EC firms should address these issues of entry with some urgency; the current turbulence is likely to settle down into a new structure of competition that may make future entry even harder to achieve profitably.

Notes

1. This chapter draws on data contained in Stopford (1992a), a study commissioned by the OECD Development Centre.
2. For some data on the earlier European preferences, see Franko (1976), Savary (1984), Stopford and Turner (1985), and Onida and Viesti (1988).
3. These figures are drawn from UNCTC (1991), Table 1.
4. Given the limitations of space, the other alternatives of licensing, franchising and contractual arrangements are ignored.
5. For good summaries of the economic literature, see Buckley and Casson (1985), Caves (1982), Dunning (1988), Rugman (1986) and Teece (1985).
6. The extent to which this is possible and how changes occur over time has been the subject of much controversy. For reviews of the alternative interpretations of the data, see, for exampe, Dunning (1988), Kojima (1990) and Vernon (1979).
7. For early evidence, see Helleiner (1981). More recent data are available from national statistics collected in the United Kingdom and United States.
8. For example, Urata (1991, Table 11) shows that the inter-affiliate exports of Japanese electronics firms doubled between 1983 and 1988, but that the share of 'captive' imports to Japan declined slightly as more third-party supply deals were made.
9. The export/foreign production ratios are estimates based on data from annual reports. The export data refer to exports from the home country.

The ratio is thus only a proxy for the balance of effect for serving non-EC markets. Where partial data on the non-EC markets are available, they show a similar ordering of relative importance.

10. Cesare Romiti, paper presented at a European Parliament Conference, *A Strong Europe – A Competitive Industry*, 7 March 1989. Similar views were expressed earlier in EC Commission, *The Future of the European Automobile Industry*, Brussels, November 1987.

11. This Article states that a product is considered to have originated in the country where the last substantial transformation of the product occurred. The argument is about the definition of 'substantial'.

12. For general background see, for example, Soete (1985) and Booz, Allen and Hamilton (1985a, b). For a summary of European business–government responses, see Cawson *et al.* (1986). For an analysis of world trends and British weakness, see Electronics Industry Sector Group (1988).

13. The domestic orientation in electronics is understated in Table 3.9, because much of the non-European volume for some firms, such as GEC, is in electrical equipment.

14. Even IBM, however, was threatened by the Asian invasion and was forced to announce large-scale cost-cutting moves in 1991.

15. Cited in the *Financial Times*, 29 May 1990. This statement may prove to be directly apposite to Olivetti's own fluctuating fortunes, for the firm announced at the end of June 1992 that Digital Equipment of the United States might purchase up to 10 per cent of the voting stock in the new cross-holding arrangement.

16. Douglas McWilliam, of the Confederation of British Industry, cited in *Siemens Review*, June 1991.

References

Bartlett, C. A. and Ghoshal, S. (1989) *Managing across Borders: The Transnational Solution* (Boston, MA: Harvard Business School Press).

Booz, Allen and Hamilton (1985a) *Outlook, Special Report: The Information Industry* (New York).

Booz, Allen and Hamilton (1985b) *Consumer Electronics Industrial Policy*, Report to the Commission of the European Communities (New York).

Boston Consulting Group (for the EC Commission) (1991) 'The competitive challenge facing the European automotive components industry' (London).

Buckley, P. J. and Casson, M. (1985) *The Economic Theory of the Multinational Enterprise* (London: Macmillan).

Calori, R. and Lawrence, P. (eds) (1991) *The Business of Europe* (London: Sage).

Caves, R. (1982) *Multinational Enterprises and Economic Analysis* (Cambridge: Cambridge University Press).

Cawson, A., Shepherd, G. and Webber, D. (1986) 'Government–industry relations in the European consumer electronics industry: contrasting responses to competitive pressure in Britain, France and West Germany', University of Sussex, working paper series on government–industry relations, July.

Cline, W. R. (1987) *The Future of World Trade in Textiles and Apparel* (Washington, DC: Institute of International Economics).

Dunning, J. H. (1988) *Explaining International Production* (London: Unwin Hyman).

Electronics Industry Sector Group (1988) 'Performance and competitive success: strengthening competitiveness in UK electronics', report prepared for National Economic Development Council by McKinsey & Company.

Franko, L. G. (1976) *The European Multinationals* (New York: Harper & Row).

Franko, L. G. (1991) 'Global corporate competition II: Is the large American firm an endangered species?', *Business Horizons*, vol. 34, no. 6, November–December, pp. 14–22.

Hamel, G. and Prahalad, C. K. (1985) 'Do you really have a global strategy?', *Harvard Business Review*, July–August.

Hanreider, W. and Auton, G. (1980) *The Foreign Policies of West Germany, France and Britain* (Englewood Cliffs, NJ: Prentice Hall).

Helleiner, G. K. (1981) *Intra-firm Trade and the Developing Countries* (New York: St Martin's Press).

Julius, D. (1990) *Global Companies and Public Policy* (London: Pinter/The Royal Institute of International Affairs).

Kojima, K. (1990) *Japanese Direct Investment Abroad* (Tokyo: International Christian University, Monograph Series 1).

Langhammer, R. J. (1990) 'Europe 1992 and the developing countries: fuelling a new engine of growth or separating Europe from non-Europe', *Journal of Common Market Studies*, vol. XXIX, no. 2, December.

Lawrence, R. Z. (1991) *Scenarios for the World Trading System and their Implications for Developing Countries* (Paris: OECD Development Centre Technical Paper no. 47, November).

Lynch, R. (1990) *European Business Strategies* (London: Kogan Page).

Milner, H. V. (1987) *Resisting Protectionism: Global Industries and the Politics of International Trade* (Princeton, NJ: Princeton University Press).

Milner, H. V. and Yoffie, D. (1989) 'Between free trade and protectionism: strategic trade policy and a theory of corporate demands', *International Organization*, vol. 43, no. 2, Spring, pp. 239–72.

Morrison, A. J., Ricks, D. A. and Roth, K. (1990) 'Globalisation and regionalisation: which way for the multinational?', *Organizational Dynamics*, Winter, pp. 17–29.

Nordlinger, E. (1981) *On the Autonomy of the Democratic State* (Cambridge, MA: Harvard University Press).

Onida, F. and Viesti, G. (eds) (1988) *The Italian Multinationals* (London: Croom Helm).

Page, F. (1986) 'What is a "British" car?', *Atlantic*, July, pp. 13–15.

Panić, M. (1991) 'The impact of multinationals on national economic policy', in Bürgenmeier, B. and Mucchielli, J. L. (eds), *Multinationals and Europe 1992* (London: Routledge).

Pearce, J. and Sutton, J. (1985) *Protection and Industrial Policy in Europe* (London: Routledge & Kegan Paul).

Porter, M. E. (ed.) (1986) *Competition in Global Industries* (Boston, MA: Harvard Business School Press).

Porter, M. E. (1990) *The Competitive Advantage of Nations* (New York: The Free Press).

Prahalad, C. K. and Doz, Y. (1987) *The Multinational Mission* (New York: The Free Press).

Rugman, A. M. (1986) 'New theories of the multinational enterprise: an assessment of internationalisation theory', *Bulletin of Economic Research*, vol. 38, pp. 101–18.

Savary, J. (1984) *French Multinationals* (London: Pinter/IRM).

Sharp, M. (1986) *Inward Investment and National Industrial Competitiveness: a comparative study of Western Europe* (SPRU, University of Sussex, September).

Soete, L. (1985) *Technological Trends and Employment: 3 Electronics and Communications* (Aldershot: Gower).

Stopford, J. M. (1992a) *Offensive and Defensive Responses by European Multinationals to a World of Trade Blocs* (Paris: OECD Development Centre Technical Paper no. 64, May).

Stopford, J. M. (1992b) *The Directory of Multinational Enterprises* (4th edition, London: Macmillan).

Stopford, J. M. and Dunning, J. H. (1983) *Multinationals: Company Performance and Global Trends* (London: Macmillan).

Stopford, J. M. and Strange, S. (1991) *Rival States, Rival Firms* (Cambridge: Cambridge University Press).

Stopford, J. M. and Turner, L. (1985) *Britain and the Multinationals* (Chichester: Wiley).

Teece, D. J. (1985) 'Transaction cost economics and the multinational enterprise: an assessment', *Journal of Economic Behaviour and Organization*, vol. 7, pp. 21–45.

United Nations Centre on Transnational Corporations (UNCTC) (1991) *World Investment Report 1991* (New York: United Nations).

Urata, S. (1991) 'Globalisation of the Japanese electronics industry', draft chapter in Urata, S. *Japanese Corporations in Globalisation and Regionalisation* (Paris: OECD Development Centre Study).

Van der Klugt, C. J. (1986) 'Japan's global challenge in electronics – the Philips' response', *European Management Journal*, vol. 4, no. 1, pp. 4–9.

Vernon, R. (1979) 'The product cycle hypotheses in the new international environment', *Oxford Bulletin of Economics and Statistics*, vol. 41, pp. 255–67.

Waverman, L. (1991) 'Strategic trade policy and 1992', in Bürgenmeier, B. and Mucchielli, J. L. (eds), *Multinationals and Europe 1992* (London: Routledge).

Wells, L. T. Jr (1992) *Conflict or Indifference: US multinationals in a world of regional trading blocs* (Paris: OECD Development Centre Technical Paper).

Womack, J. P., Jones, D. T. and Roos, D. (1990) *The Machine that Changed the World* (New York: Rawson Associates).

4

European integration in the 1990s: implications for Australia

Kym Anderson

At the close of the 1980s, people outside Europe concerned with developments there were focusing on the EC92 programme of removing remaining trade barriers among the twelve members of the European Community. Since then, however, the focus has had to broaden very substantially: East and West Germany have united; most EFTA member countries plan to sign the European Economic Area (EEA) accord with the EC and some are applying for full EC membership; both the EC and EFTA countries are arranging association pacts with the Baltic states and East European countries; and Mediterranean countries and former Soviet republics are seeking closer relations with the rest of Europe. The European market of interest has thus expanded beyond the 340 million people in the EC or 370 million in the EEA to 500 million when East Europe is added, or more than 800 million if the former Soviet republics and Turkey are included.

This chapter assesses the likely impact of this increasing economic integration in Europe on the rest of the world and especially on Australia.[1] The first section provides a brief summary of the relative importance of Europe in global production and trade and in the trade of Australia. Section 4.2 examines the possible impact of pertinent developments in Europe, including integration initiatives, on its output and trade growth during the 1990s, and their effects on Australia. The latter involves examining not only the direct effects but also the indirect effects via East Asia, because that is where the majority of Australia's exports are now destined. The final section discusses possible responses Australia might make to these developments.

4.1   Europe's importance in world production and trade

Europe, defined here to include the former Soviet republics, has 15 per cent of the world's population, slightly less than half of which is in Western Europe. Its shares of world output and trade are much larger, at 35 and 51 per cent, respectively. Western Europe dominates both those shares, with Eastern Europe and the former Soviet republics (hereafter EEFSR) contributing only 4 and 6 of those percentage points in 1989, according to Table 4.1.[2] Europe's 51 per cent share of world trade compares with just under 20 per cent each for North America and East Asia. True, three-quarters of Europe's trade is with other European countries, but a third of North America's trade also is intra-regional (Table 4.2). When both sources of intra-trade are excluded, Europe and the Americas account for 27 per cent of world trade each as of 1989 (down from more than 30 per cent each in the early 1960s), while East Asia contributes about one third (double its share of the early 1960s; see Figure 4.1).

Traditionally, Australia's trade was very much focused on Europe. In the 1950s, for example, more than one third of the country's exports were destined for the United Kingdom and another 30 per cent for other European countries. In recent years, however, only 20 per cent of those exports have found their way to Europe. That is, Europe switched from being nearly twice as important to being less than half as important to Australian export trade as one might expect given Europe's share of world imports.

The majority of Australia's exports now go to East Asia, which has also become the source of more than a third of Australia's imports (Figure 4.2). This redirection was partly a consequence of the negative effects of the United Kingdom entering the EC and the EC becoming ever-more protectionist towards its farmers, and partly due to the

Table 4.1   Importance of Europe, North America and Japan in the world economy, 1989 (%).

	Share of world:		
	Population	GDP	Trade
Western Europe	7	31	45
Eastern Europe and the former Soviet Union	8	4	6
	15	35	51
United States and Canada	5	29	19
Japan	2	14	8

Source: World Bank (1991).

Table 4.2   Network of inter- and intra-regional trade in merchandise, 1963 and 1989 (%).

Reporter	Partner:	Europe 1963	Europe 1989	Western Pacific 1963	Western Pacific 1989	North America 1963	North America 1989	Rest of World 1963	Rest of World 1989	Total
Europe[1]	exports	71	75	8	8	8	8	13	9	100
	imports	68	75	6	10	12	8	14	7	100
Western Pacific[2]	exports	31	20	44	43	19	29	6	8	100
	imports	31	20	36	50	25	20	8	10	100
North America[3]	exports	34	24	22	26	26	34	18	16	100
	imports	25	20	16	37	35	28	24	15	100
Rest of World[4]	exports	52	33	4	19	24	26	20	22	100
	imports	48	41	5	16	25	22	22	21	100
World	exports	57	50	10	20	15	19	18	11	100
	imports	54	50	9	23	19	16	18	11	100

Notes:
1. Europe includes all West, Central and East European economies plus the USSR.
2. Western Pacific includes the market economies of Northeast and Southeast Asia plus China, Australia and New Zealand.
3. North America includes Canada and the United States.
4. Rest of World includes Latin America, Africa, the Middle East and South Asia.

Source: GATT (1987, 1990).

positive effects of rapid industrialisation in East Asia, the related development of Australia's mining sector, and the reduction in protectionist barriers to imports from East Asia (Anderson and Garnaut 1989).

This redirection of Australia's trade does not mean, however, that developments in Europe are no longer of significance to Australia. On the contrary, in addition to still being of considerable direct significance, they are also very important indirectly in so far as they affect East Asia's economies and thereby the derived demand for Australian exports to East Asia. And East Asia is becoming increasingly dependent on trade with Europe. Japan, for example, increased the share of its exports going to Europe from 16 per cent to 24 per cent between 1984 and 1990, during which time Europe's share of Japan's imports rose from 11 per cent to 20 per cent.

Nor is Australia's interest restricted to just farm products. It is true that prior to the 1960s agriculture contributed more than four-fifths of Australia's exports. But by the end of the 1960s that share had fallen to below two-thirds of merchandise exports because of the expansion of the mining sector and associated metal manufacturing, and by the end of the 1980s it was less than one third (Figure 4.3). Moreover, services exports have grown and farm exports fallen even further of

(a) *Including intra-bloc trade*[1]

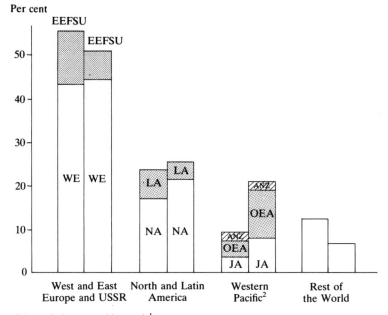

(b) *Excluding intra-bloc trade*[1]

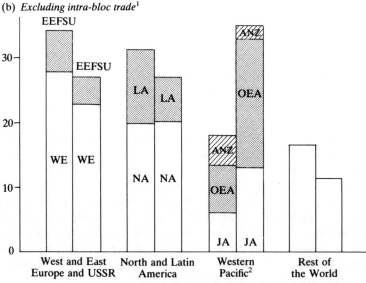

Notes:
1. Figure 4.1(b) is distinguished from Figure 4.1(a) in that it excludes from regional and global trade totals the value of trade between countries in Western Europe; between East Europe's former Comecon members; between the United States and Canada; and between Australia and New Zealand.
2. Japan; the market economies of Northeast and Southeast Asia plus China (collectively Other East Asia); and Australia and New Zealand (ANZ).

Source: GATT (1987, 1990).

Figure 4.1 Regional shares of world merchandise trade, 1963 and 1989 (exports plus imports as a percentage of global exports plus imports).

a) *Exports*

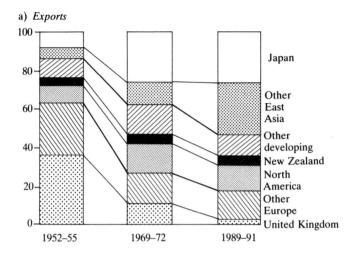

b) *Imports*

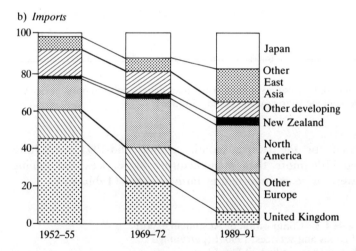

Source: Australian Bureau of Statistics, *Overseas Trade* (Canberra, various issues).

Figure 4.2 Direction of Australian trade, 1952–91 (percentage shares, years ending 30 June).

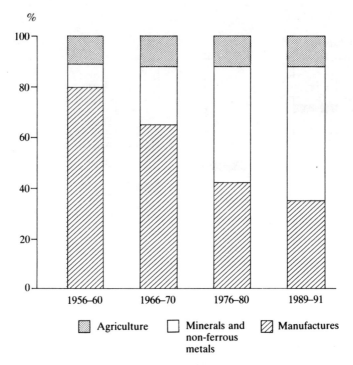

Source: Australian Bureau of Statistics, *Overseas Trade* (Canberra, various issues).

Figure 4.3 Composition of Australian merchandise exports, 1956–91 (percentage shares, years ending 30 June).

late, so that for the twelve months ending mid-1991 agriculture contributed little more than manufacturing or services and mining products were twice as important as farm products (Table 4.3).

Table 4.3 Composition of Australian exports of goods and services, 1990–1 (percentage shares, years ending 30 June).

Agriculture, forestry and fishing	22
Fuels, minerals and metals	43
Other manufactures	15
Services	20
	100

Source: Australian Bureau of Agricultural and Resource Economics, *Agriculture and Resources Quarterly* (Canberra, December 1992).

4.2 Effects of integration on Europe's growth and trade

To assess the external effects of European integration it is helpful to think first about its effects in boosting European economic growth, then to ask how faster growth will change its comparative advantages, and finally to speculate about the extent to which these developments will be accompanied by changes in the policy distortions to Europe's external trade.

4.2.1 *Faster European economic growth*

One of the key motivations for the EC92 Single Market programme was the belief that it would boost the rate of economic growth in member states. The basis for this belief is that with the abolition of remaining border controls on intra-EC trade as well as the harmonisation or mutual recognition of standards and other regulations, the efficiency of resource use and investments would increase through greater intra-EC competition and better exploitation of economies of scale.

Provided external trade barriers are not increased (see below), the likelihood is that faster economic growth will indeed eventuate. Cecchini *et al.* (1988) suggest the programme will generate a one-off increase in GNP of between 4.3 and 6.4 per cent, while Baldwin (1989) estimates that when the dynamic effects of the reform on investment are also taken into account, the programme could provide an ongoing increase in the EC's GNP growth rate of at least 0.6 percentage points per year.[3] Moreover, while these studies take into account gains from economies of scale and increased competition between firms, they do not include the possibility of faster growth from two other sources. One is competition between national governments which, in an environment of freer factor mobility, would compete more vigorously to retain/attract productive factors by taxing them less and increasing the efficiency of public sector enterprises.[4] The other is greater macroeconomic policy discipline. As EC countries move closer towards monetary union, their governments are coming under greater pressure to reduce inflation, exchange rate fluctuations, public debt, current account imbalances and the like. Indeed that has already been happening, as Figure 4.4 illustrates with respect to inflation.

The greater growth prospects in the EC led investors in recent years to divert funds from the other West European countries (the EFTA members) to the EC. The consequent slowdown in EFTA's growth in the early 1990s was a major factor in swinging public opinion in those countries towards supporting closer economic integration with the EC.

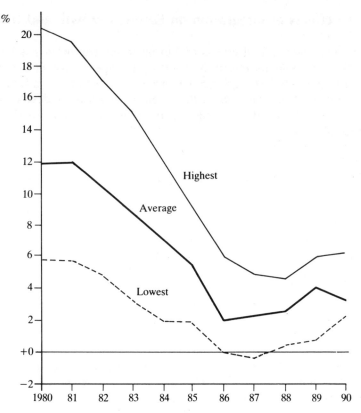

Note:
1. Private consumption deflator for Belgium, Denmark, France, West Germany, Ireland, Italy, Luxembourg and the Netherlands.

Source: Eurostat, as reported in *The Economist*, 30 November 1991.

Figure 4.4 Convergence of West European inflation rates, 1980–90 (annual average percentage).

Initially, this has taken the form of the European Economic Area (EEA) agreement, whereby EFTA countries in most respects effectively become part of the EC's Single Market. But because EFTA countries have only limited scope to influence EC policies under the EEA, they are increasingly looking on the EEA as an interim arrangement. Austria, Finland and Sweden have already applied for full EC membership from 1995 and Norway and Switzerland may well do likewise in a year or so. As a lead-up to membership, those countries are beginning to reform the more wasteful of their economic policies so that their producers are better able to face the rigours of stronger competition. In the case of Sweden this has included phasing down its high agricultural support levels and welfare programmes to EC levels. An effect of these changes is already showing up in the reversal of capital flight from Sweden, and it will soon show up more generally in the form of faster economic growth in EFTA countries.

The immediate effect of the dramatic reforms in Eastern Europe and the former Soviet republics during the past two years has been to lower output and incomes. But their medium- and longer-term prospects are very bright if their polities can be stabilised and the reform process maintained – and it is in the clear strategic as well as economic interests of Western Europe to ensure that that happens, which is why it is busy signing association accords with these former socialist economies.

Thus it seems highly likely that output and income growth in Europe will be somewhat higher in the 1990s than it was in the 1980s as a consequence of these various integration initiatives, and higher than it would be without those initiatives. If the share of Europe's GNP that is traded with the rest of the world were to be at least maintained, as has happened for the EC during the past three decades (see the white bars in Figure 4.5), this would be good news for Europe's trading partners as a group. But growth in Europe will be accompanied by changes in comparative advantage, and in policy distortions to external trade, that will affect trading partners unequally through altering the direction and composition as well as the total value of Europe's external trade. It is to these developments that we now turn.

4.2.2 Changes in comparative advantage

As integration in Western Europe leads to the more efficient location and use of its productive factors and induces investment which enlarges its stocks of various forms of capital, that part of Europe is likely to enjoy a net increase in the effective availability of capital relative to labour time and natural resources.

The effect of this change in factor endowment ratios on Western Europe's comparative advantage can be best seen with the help of the Leamer (1987) triangle depicted in Figure 4.6. That triangle represents graphically various countries' relative endowments of three factors, denoted N for natural resources, L for labour time and C for capital (human, physical, knowledge, etc.). Proxies used here to represent the natural resources to labour ratio and the capital to labour ratio are land area per capita and national product per capita. (Crude though these proxies are, more sophisticated indexes are unlikely to change the relative positions of the country groups shown in Figure 4.6.)

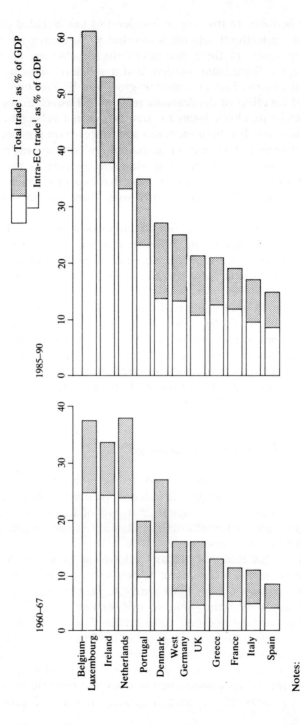

Notes:

1. Average of merchandise imports and exports.

Source: Eurostat, as reported in *The Economist*, 30 November 1991.

Figure 4.5   Intra-EC and total trade as a percentage of GDP, various EC countries, 1960–90.

These ratios are measured in log terms along the *NL* and *LC* sides of the triangle, respectively, the mid-point of each being the world average which is taken as the numeraire. Thus point *W* represents the global average endowment of all three factors. Countries located in space *WCB* – which includes Western Europe as a group – have above (below) average per worker endowments of capital (natural resources), and so would have a comparative disadvantage in primary products and unskilled labour-intensive manufactures and a comparative advantage in skill- and knowledge-intensive products.

Economic growth involving an increase in Western Europe's availability of capital relative to the other two factors, compared with the rest of the world, would shift its endowment point towards point *C* and away from line *NL*. Other things equal, this suggests that a consequence of Western Europe's integration programmes is its comparative advantage in capital- (especially skill-) intensive industrial and service activities would strengthen at the expense of primary production and labour-intensive manufacturing.

Such a change would appear to be good news for resource-rich Australia as well as East Asia's developing countries which export either primary products or labour-intensive manufactures in exchange for capital-intensive goods and services: both their volume and terms of trade would improve. In terms of Figure 4.6, Western Europe's endowment point would move further away from those of Australia/New Zealand, the Asian NIEs and Other Southeast Asia, increasing the scope for mutually beneficial trade between the Western Pacific region and Western Europe.

There are almost no quantitative studies of the likely external effects of European integration. One exception is by Stoeckel *et al.* (1990), using a straightforward (non-dynamic) computable general equilibrium model of the world economy to estimate the effects of the EC92 Single Market programme. That study suggests the gains to the EC12 would be about 5 per cent of GDP (within the range suggested by Cecchini *et al.* 1988), that Australia/New Zealand would enjoy a gain of 0.2 per cent of GDP, that East Asia's developing countries would benefit by 0.1 per cent of GDP, but that Japan would lose slightly, by 0.07 per cent of its GDP. A more recent and more detailed simulation study of West European integration by Haaland and Norman (1992) provides almost the same result for Japan (a 0.08 per cent loss).[5] These results are consistent with the expectation that the West European endowment point in Figure 4.6 would move closer to Japan's. But these studies ignore an important change since the mid-1980s, namely the emergence of Japan as a major net exporter of capital. In so far as some of its capital is attracted to the new investment opportunities in Western Europe (where, according to the Haaland/Norman study, the

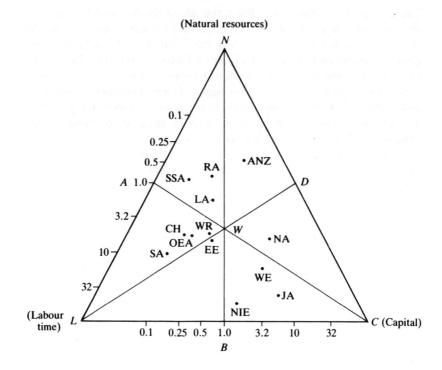

Notes:
The distance along *NL* from *N* measures the population density as a ratio of the world average (0.39 people per hectare of land). The distance along *LC* from *L* measures national product per capita as a ratio of the world average (US$3,980). Both scales are in logs. Along any ray from *C* to the *NL* line the population density is constant, and similarly for rays from the other two corners of the triangle. *W* is the world's endowment point. Countries are represented as follows: ANZ Australia and New Zealand, CH China, EE the East European economies, JA Japan, LA Latin America, NA the United States and Canada, NIE East Asian's four newly industrialised economies, OEA other East Asian market economies, RA Russia and the five former Soviet central Asian republics, SA South Asia, SSA Sub-Saharan Africa, WE the West European economies, WR the nine western republics of the former Soviet Union. The estimates used for per capita income for Eastern Europe and the former Soviet Union are US$2,350 and US$1,780 respectively, based on World Bank (1991) and other estimates reported in CEPR (1990, p. 33). The relative incomes and population densities within the former Soviet Union are derived from data in the report by the IMF *et al.* (1991). Purchasing power parity measures of income, if they were available for all countries, would show less differences across countries but this would alter little the relative position of country groups in the above triangle.

Source: adapted from Leamer (1987) using data from the IMF *et al.* (1991) and the World Bank (1991).

Figure 4.6 Relative endowments of natural resources, labour and capital, various economies, 1989.

returns to capital would increase by 0.6 per cent), this would more or less offset the loss to Japan resulting from greater competition from Western Europe in capital-intensive goods and services.

Table 4.4 gives some idea of the orders of magnitude of the effects on various manufacturing industries that might be expected from the EC92 Single Market programme and the EEA initiative. As expected from the above discussion, the EC92 programme boosts the EC's labour-intensive industries least and its skill-intensive industries most. Also as expected, this bias is modified somewhat as a consequence of the higher-wage EFTA countries becoming more integrated into the EC's single market under the EEA (cf. columns 1 and 2 of Table 4.4): Southern Europe's textiles, etc., industries expand at the expense of those labour-intensive firms previously supplying EFTA markets, both from within EFTA (see column 3) and from elsewhere (most notably East Asia). The combined impact of the two integration programmes on Japan is manifest in a reduction in output of some skill-intensive industries but an almost offsetting expansion of other capital-intensive industries.

In which directions will the comparative advantages of Eastern Europe and the former Soviet Union move, as a consequence of their

Table 4.4 Projected effects on manufacturing of West European integration (percentage changes).

	Effects on EC production of:		Effects of EC92 plus EEA programmes on production in:		
	EC92 Single Market programme alone	EC92 plus EEA programmes	EFTA	Japan	United States
Labour-intensive industries					
Textiles and clothing	0.1	1.1	−6.6	0.01	0.10
Timber products	0.4	1.2	−1.0	−0.03	0.10
Metal products	0.3	0.6	0.4	−0.01	0.01
Plastic products	0.7	1.1	−0.4	−0.01	0.03
Physical capital-intensive industries					
Paper products	0.3	0.3	1.8	0.00	0.00
Metals	−0.5	0.0	−1.8	0.44	0.15
Chemicals	1.4	1.6	1.5	0.00	−0.03
Skill-intensive industries					
Production machinery	1.3	−0.1	12.7	−0.10	−0.07
Office machinery	4.7	5.0	4.1	0.08	−0.20
Electrical goods	2.1	1.7	11.6	−0.10	0.00
Transport goods	4.5	3.4	18.8	−0.60	−0.04

Source: Haaland and Norman (1992).

transition from socialism and greater integration with Western Europe? In the short run it is arguable that, until foreign investors feel confident about the stability of the new regimes, output growth will come mainly from the primary sectors, particularly agriculture (so long as land is promptly privatised) since even the mining sector in the former Soviet Union is in desperate need of foreign capital (Anderson 1992b). But what about in the medium to longer term, which is the focus of this chapter?

Consider first where these former socialist economies are currently located within the Leamer triangle of Figure 4.6. The East European economies (EE) are all two or three times as densely populated as the rest of the world. And the western republics of the former Soviet Union (WR) also have about twice the global population density. It is only Russia and the central Asian republics (RA) that are relatively well endowed with natural resources per worker, with four times the global average land area per capita. These economies' capital stocks per worker (their position along the ray from C to the NL line in Figure 4.6) are of course much more difficult to determine. The indices shown in Figure 4.6 may seem low for these relatively well-educated communities, but on the other hand many of their stocks of physical capital appear to have little commercial value at international prices.

If the locations shown for EE, WR and RA in Figure 4.6 fairly represent these economies' relative resource endowments once they have adjusted to privatisation and to price, trade and exchange rate liberalisations, then accumulations of capital or inflows via aid and direct foreign investment will have clear effects on the comparative advantages of these groups of economies. Eastern Europe and the western republics of the former Soviet Union will strengthen their competitiveness in manufactures relative to primary products and, within manufacturing, will gradually move from strength in labour-intensive goods to strength in more sophisticated products. That is, their exporters will be competing in similar product lines with the more advanced of East Asia's developing countries, while their dependence on imports for primary products will increase. If these changes in their competitiveness reduce income growth in East Asia, Australia's exports to that region will slow down, offsetting any growth in Australian primary exports to the East European region.

Russia and the central Asian republics, by contrast, would get the highest return from employing additional capital in primary production. Whether Russia becomes a stronger competitor in farm or mineral and energy products will depend heavily on (1) the relative degree of security offered to property rights in the two sectors, and (2) the extent to which the underpricing of the output of these two sectors is reduced absolutely as well as relative to each other. Whatever those changes, Russia is likely to become a stronger competitor in similar product markets to those of Australia, potentially putting downward pressure on international prices for various primary products and thereby more or less neutralising the positive direct effect on Australia of likely developments in Eastern Europe. Should Russia take longer than the new nations to its west to take off, however, that neutralising tendency may not have much impact before the next century.

The above is premised on the assumption that labour does not migrate from east to west now that the East's borders are more open. This is something West European countries seem very keen to avoid. One way to reduce the probability of westward migration is to boost prosperity in the East, and by far the most effective means of doing that quickly – in addition to sending aid and investable funds – would be to allow these transforming socialist economies preferential access to West European markets. Already association accords have been signed by the EC and some EFTA countries with several of these former planned economies, and more are expected. We turn now to examine the effect of such preferences in the context of other possible changes to Western Europe's external trade policies as a consequence of the various integration initiatives.

4.2.3   *Changes in distortions to external trade*

The EEA agreement with EFTA countries and the association accords with East Europe build on the EC's already elaborate multi-tiered structure of trade preferences. Other components include agreements with the Mediterranean countries of Turkey, Malta and Cyprus, and with the African, Caribbean and Pacific island (ACP) developing country signatories to the Lomé Convention. In the wake of closer integration initiatives on the European continent, these other two country groups are likely to seek greater preferential access to West European markets. (Turkey, Malta and Cyprus have applied to become full members of the EC.) So assuming the United States continues to use its economic might to ensure its export products are affected relatively lightly by West European import restrictions, that leaves the economies of the Western Pacific among the most discriminated against by this hierarchy of preferences.

Moreover, there is the possibility that barriers to West European imports from the Western Pacific will be increased further as a consequence of (1) new preferences being given to East European, Mediterranean and ACP countries, and (2) strengthened competition among firms within the EEA. The former arises because East European, Soviet and Turkish export growth initially is likely to be in farm products, fossil fuels and labour-intensive manufactures – and among the most powerful protectionists in the EEA are farmers, coal miners and producers of textiles and clothing. If such exports are given preferential access to West European markets, the interest groups from these declining industries are sure to demand reduced imports from third countries to ease the additional structural adjustment pressures they will face. A protectionist response to those demands would have direct adverse effects on both Australia and East Asia's developing economies.

The other potential trigger to the raising of external barriers to West European markets is the greater internal competition that EC92 and EEA market integration generates. The earlier integration within the EC in the 1960s and 1970s involved relatively little economic dislocation because much of the intra-EC trade growth was of an intra-industry nature. Greenaway and Hine (1991) argue that further integration in the 1990s, by contrast, is likely to involve more inter-industry adjustments. The least competitive manufacturers may well be successful in seeking protection from the full force of those adjustment pressures, the most likely form being policies which inhibit competition from non-Europeans. More stringent use of provisions to impose anti-dumping duties is already occurring and is likely to continue (Hindley 1988), as well as a strengthening of local content and rules of origin provisions – and all the more so if increased direct assistance to selected industries is ruled out. It is likely that Japan and the East Asian NIEs will be the countries most adversely affected. Moreover, in order to reduce European consumer and East Asian producer opposition to such increased protection, market- (and hence rent-) sharing policy instruments such as 'voluntary' export restraints rather than more transparent import tariffs are likely to be used (Hillman and Ursprung 1988).

East Asian export manufacturers could respond in several ways to these developments. One possible response is simply to continue to search imaginatively for ways to circumvent West European import barriers. Non-tariff barriers have been found to be porous in the past (Yoffie 1983; Bhagwati 1988), and they are likely to continue to be so in the future.

A second possibility for East Asian manufacturers is to invest in Europe behind the external trade barriers. Indeed Japanese firms have been doing precisely that for at least two decades, and are likely to do so even more in the 1990s unless higher barriers to foreign direct investment are erected.[6] While this strategy reduces the cost of trade barriers to East Asia, the relocation of manufacturing to Europe lowers the demand for Australian raw materials since Australia would be less competitive in Europe than in Asia.

4.3   Possible Australian responses

How might Australia respond to these likely developments in both Europe and East Asia? Four suggestions are offered by way of conclusion. First and most obviously, Australia will adjust more appropriately the stronger and more stable its own economy, which underscores the need for it to continue its own unilateral process of microeconomic reform.

Second, it should continue to put pressure on the West Europeans to reduce their external trade barriers, and not only to preferred neighbours. Cairns Group pressure via the Uruguay Round of GATT negotiations has been very effective in keeping agriculture high on the Round's agenda, and similar pressure could be brought to bear against West Europe's coal protection. In addition to the usual economic arguments as to why those distortionary trade policies should be reformed, one might add plausible environmental reasons (Anderson 1992a).

Third, Australia needs to continue the process of integrating its economy with those of New Zealand, East Asia and North America. It seems unlikely – for political economy reasons – that a Free Trade Area will encompass the Asian–Pacific region in the near future (Anderson 1991b). But at least some regionally negotiated lowering of barriers to integration on a non-discriminatory, most-favoured-nation basis may be politically feasible. Most of the benefits from such reform would remain in the region because its trade barriers are highest for goods in which other countries of the region are the most competitive. Such a reform also would have the effect of strengthening APEC, the Asian–Pacific Economic Co-operation grouping. A key role that grouping has begun to play, and may be able to play even more effectively in the future, is to champion the cause of the rules-based multilateral trading system.

And finally, Australia must follow more closely the Japanese example of investing in Europe. The prospects for doing so are much wider than is commonly assumed, especially now that Eastern Europe and the former Soviet republics are opening up. The most obvious possibilities there are in agricultural and mineral technology and management consulting services, but many others are emerging as well. Former emigrants from that region to Australia could no doubt play an important role in overcoming language and other cultural barriers to such activities.

In short, the closer economic integration of Europe is not necessarily bad news for Australia provided the fears of a more protectionist Fortress Europe turn out to be excessive. Moreover, if the reforms there have the effect of raising substantially the importance of Europe in the world economy, this may have the additional beneficial effect of causing Australia to adopt a more global perspective in its international economic relations.

Notes

1. The present chapter builds on an earlier one that focused mainly on the EC92 programme (Anderson 1991a).
2. It is true that from now on inter-republican trade between the former Soviet republics (FSRs) will be measured as international trade. For 1989 that adjustment raises EEFSR's share of world trade from 6 to about 12 per cent, and hence Europe's total to 57 per cent. But since 1989 intra-EEFSR trade has collapsed, so in 1992 Europe's share may still be around 50 per cent even after making this adjustment.
3. For an elegant theoretical treatment of the endogenous effects of trade on growth, see Grossman and Helpman (1991). A specific application of the growth effects of integration is provided by Rivera-Batiz and Romer (1991). While some of that growth would come from greater competition and improved X-efficiency (Haaland and Wooten 1992; Horn, Lang and Lundgren 1991), some would require increased investment funds, a portion of which would be attracted from abroad (see, for example, Balasubramanyam and Greenaway 1991).
4. Indeed it has been argued that this type of competition (between governments of proximate nations with mobile factors) is a key part of the explanation for why it was Europe, rather than East or South Asia, where modern economic growth began (Jones 1981). There is also the possibility, however, that such a growth stimulus will be offset by the dampening influence of the EC's supra-national bureaucracy and parliament, which are becoming responsible for an increasing proportion of policy decisions.
5. Unfortunately, the latter study does not disaggregate the rest of the world apart from separating out Japan and the United States.
6. See, for example, Thomsen and Nicolaides (1991), Yamazawa (1991) and Balasubramanyam and Greenaway (1991). The latter note that the share of Japan's foreign direct investment going to the EC rose from 10 to 20 per cent over the 1980s – a period when the real value of total Japanese FDI grew at 31 per cent per year!

References

Anderson, K. (1991a) 'Europe 1992 and the Western Pacific economies', *Economic Journal*, vol. 101(409), November, pp. 1538–52.

Anderson, K. (1991b) 'Is an Asian–Pacific trade bloc next?', *Journal of World Trade*, vol. 25(4), August, pp. 27–40.

Anderson, K. (1992a) 'Effects on the environment and welfare of liberalizing world trade: the cases of coal and food, in *The Greening of World Trade Issues*, ed. K. Anderson and R. Blackhurst (Hemel Hempstead: Harvester Wheatsheaf).

Anderson, K. (1992b) 'Will Eastern Europe and the former Soviet republics become major agricultural exporters?', in *Improving Agricultural Trade Performance Under the GATT*, ed. T. Becker, R. Gray and A. Schmitz (Kiel: Vauk-Verlag).

Anderson, K. and Garnaut, R. (1989) *Australian Protectionism: Extent, Causes and Effects* (London and Sydney: Allen and Unwin).

Balasubramanyam, V. N. and Greenaway, D. (1991) 'Economic integration and foreign direct investment: Japanese investment in the EC', CREDIT Research Paper no. 91/12, University of Nottingham, December.

Baldwin, R. (1989) 'On the growth effects of 1992', *Economic Policy*, vol. 9, Fall, pp. 247–81.

Bhagwati, J. N. (1988) *Protectionism* (Cambridge, MA: MIT Press).

Cecchini, P. *et al.* (1988) *The European Challenge 1992: The Benefits of a Single Market* (Aldershot: Wildwood House).

CEPR (1990) *Monitoring European Integration: The Impact of Eastern Europe* (London: Centre for Economic Policy Research).

GATT (1987) *International Trade 1986–87* (Geneva: General Agreement on Tariffs and Trade).

GATT (1990) *International Trade 1989–90*, vol. II (Geneva: General Agreement on Tariffs and Trade).

Greenaway, D. and Hine, R. C. (1991) 'Intra-industry specialization, trade expansion and adjustment in the European economic space', *Journal of Common Market Studies*, vol. 29(6), December, pp. 603–22.

Grossman, G. M. and Helpman, E. (1991) *Innovation and Growth in the Global Economy* (Cambridge, MA: MIT Press).

Haaland, J. I. and Norman, V. D. (1992) 'Global production effects of European integration', Paper presented to the CEPR Conference on Trade Flows and Trade Policy after 1992, Paris, 16–18 January.

Haaland, J. I. and Wooten, I. (1992) 'Market integration, competition and welfare', Paper presented to the CEPR Conference on Trade Flows and Trade Policy after 1992, Paris, 16–18 January.

Hillman, A. L. and Ursprung, H. W. (1988) 'Domestic politics, foreign interests, and international trade policy', *American Economic Review*, vol. 78(4), September, pp. 729–45.

Hindley, B. (1988) 'Dumping and the Far East trade of the European Community', *The World Economy*, vol. 11(4), December, pp. 445–64.

Horn, H., Lang, H. and Lundgren, S. (1991) 'Managerial effort incentives, X-inefficiency and international trade', Seminar Paper no. 507, Institute for International Economic Studies, University of Stockholm, December.

IMF, IBRD, EBRD and OECD (1991) *A Study of the Soviet Economy* (Paris: OECD).

Jones, E. L. (1981) *The European Miracle* (Cambridge: Cambridge University Press).

Leamer, E. E. (1987) 'Paths of development in the three-factor, n-good general equilibrium model', *Journal of Political Economy*, vol. 95(5), October, pp. 961–99.

Rivera-Batiz, L. A. and Romer, P. M. (1991) 'Economic integration and endogenous growth', *Quarterly Journal of Economics*, vol. 106(2), May, pp. 531–55.

Stoeckel, A., Pearce, D. and Banks, G. (1990) *Western Trading Blocs* (Canberra: Centre for International Economics).

Thomsen, S. and Nicolaides, P. (1991) *The Evolution of Japanese Direct Investment in Europe* (Hemel Hempstead: Harvester Wheatsheaf).

World Bank (1991) *World Development Report 1991* (New York: Oxford University Press).

Yamazawa, I. (1991) 'The new Europe and the Japanese strategy', Paper presented at a conference on Building the New European Single Market, Rome, 7–9 January.

Yoffie, B. D. (1983) *Power and Protectionism: Strategies of the Newly Industrializing Countries* (New York: Columbia University Press).

5

US views on 1992[1]

Stephen Woolcock

5.1   A history of support for European integration

North American, and in particular US, views of 1992 must be seen in
the broad political context of transatlantic relations. The United States
has shown consistent support for the idea of European integration.
Initially, this took the form of linking Marshall Aid to greater
European economic co-operation, then organised by the Organisation
for European Economic Co-operation (OEEC). There was also strong
political support for Monnet's supranational approach to European
integration as a means of helping to bring about Franco-German
reconciliation and to stabilise Europe. In the early days of European
integration there were strategic and political reasons for American
concerns to see a stronger (Western) Europe. The possible adverse
effects of economic integration for the United States were seen as
more than manageable, given the strength of the US economy in
relation to those of the European countries. With the promise of
enhanced markets for US exports and US production, the creation of
the EC was seen as being trade creating rather than trade diverting.

   In any case, in order to ensure that the EC did not become
inward-looking the United States sought to influence the shape and
level of the Common External Tariff, as it did, for example, during the
Kennedy Round of GATT multilateral trade negotiations. Even as
President Kennedy asked for negotiating authority from Congress in
order to launch the Round in 1962 he stressed the positive nature of
European economic integration:

> For the first time, as the world's greatest trading nation, we (the United
> States) can welcome a single partner whose trade is even larger than our

own – a partner no longer divided and dependent, but strong enough to
share with us the responsibilities of the free world. . .

   The success of our foreign policy depends in large measure upon the
success of our foreign trade, and our maintenance of western political
unity depends in equally large measure upon the degree of western
economic unity. An integrated Western Europe, joined in trading
partnership with the United States, will . . . further shift the world
balance of power to the side of freedom.[2]

The objective of negotiating a reduction in European tariffs was
successful, but the economic foundations for the European pillar of the
Atlantic alliance did not fully meet US expectations. While there was
initial success in creating a customs union, the West Europeans did not
yet emerge strongly enough to share fully the responsibilities and
initiatives of the free world. The end of the 1960s was characterised by
the debate over *le défi américain*, which expressed a widespread
concern that US investment was dominating Europe.

   Despite some tensions over the first enlargement of the Community,
US views remained positive. Indeed, as the 1970s progressed there was
a growing sense of disappointment that the process of integration was
moving more and more slowly. And, in the aftermath of the first oil
shock, the EC failed to make progress on Economic and Monetary
Union. Market integration also came to a halt in Europe as individual
governments responded to pressures created by the economic recession
of the mid-1970s by introducing national support programmes for
industries in difficulties. By the mid-1980s a tendency had emerged to
write off the Community. The United States was undergoing significant
change as a result of the deregulation initiated during the Carter
administration and pressed home during the first Reagan administration. In contrast, Western Europe was seen as suffering from Eurosclerosis, and US officials were prone to lecture their European
counterparts on the need for positive adjustment in order to revitalise
the European economy.

   The 1992 initiative, with its promise of a stronger, more dynamic
European Community, was therefore welcomed by the US administration, as were initiatives to create both European economic and
monetary union and a political union. In the background, however,
there were fears from the business community and Congress of
potential European protectionism. The United States is not relaxed
about the potential economic impact of European integration (see
below), but political reforms in the Soviet Union and Eastern Europe
have once again reinforced the strategic case for greater European
integration. When the Berlin Wall came down, the Bush administration was quick to recognise the importance of a strengthened European Community as a source of stability in a rapidly changing Europe.

For the US foreign policy establishment 1992 held out the prospect of Europe finally fulfilling earlier US expectations, as expressed by President Kennedy. It would mean adjustments in US attitudes, but the United States appeared willing to accept these. For example, in response to political and economic reform in Eastern Europe, the Western OECD countries (the G24) decided to initiate a programme of assistance for Hungary and Poland, which was later extended to other countries. The United States was happy to see the European Commission administer this programme.

In the post-cold war era it is generally assumed that economic relations will play a greater role than in the past. For example, European security will be influenced by the success or failure of the East European economies and above all the Soviet Union to achieve economic stability and prosperity. In this the European Community will also play a central role, such as through the negotiation of trade agreements and association agreements with the East European economies. There are few signs of tension between the EC and United States on this front. There is a common interest in promoting stability in Eastern Europe. Competition for markets in the East may not create as much tension as the divergence between the EC member states and the Reagan administration over the use of economic sanctions against the USSR, which was a source of major tension in the mid-1980s.

5.2 Growing economic interdependence

Over the years US–EC economic interdependence has continued to grow despite the threats of trade war and cyclical ups and downs. The EC today represents the United States' largest export market for visible trade – 24 per cent compared to 22 per cent for Canada. With a combined GDP of about the same size as the United States, it also has a relatively high income elasticity of demand for US exports.[3] As a result the United States has no structural trade deficit with the EC as it has with Japan. The trade deficit which had built up during the early 1980s was soon reduced as European growth picked up. Relative to Japan the EC is also an open market with few structural barriers (the CAP aside) against the export of US goods and services. Growth generated by the 1992 process could therefore be expected to benefit the United States.

The increase in investment in both directions has also contributed significantly to transatlantic economic interdependence. The EC accounted for 40 per cent of total US foreign investment ($127 billion) in 1988, and US investment has grown since the 1992 objective became credible in 1987/8. The sales by EC affiliates of US multinational companies totalled $620 billion in 1987 (US Department of Commerce). A great deal of transatlantic trade is also accounted for by multinational companies operating on both sides of the Atlantic, so there is a mutual interest in avoiding trade disputes. The removal of barriers within the EC, and any economic growth generated in the process, are therefore of direct benefit to many important US companies with a presence in Europe. The creation of a wider European market through, first, the European Economic Area and then enlargement of the EC could well benefit US affiliates based in Europe in the same way. Growth in Europe resulting from market integration in this wider Europe will benefit all companies including European affiliates of US firms. In the other direction the United States is even more important for EC foreign investment which totalled $194 billion in 1988. US sales by European multinationals totalled $606 billion.

5.3   The US constituencies

The fact that US multinational companies have an established presence in the EC means that they stand to gain from European growth, and that they have a clearer understanding of what 1992 means than smaller US companies or those with no manufacturing presence in the EC. This creates a difference between the 'insiders' and the 'outsiders'. The insiders are in principle very positive about 1992 and tend to have difficulties in only a number of limited areas. (The key areas of difficulty are discussed below.) Reciprocity was perhaps the most important, and it was US multinationals that led the charge on the EC's early approach to reciprocity. The outsiders have been consistently more sceptical if not negative about the 1992 process as a whole.

When in 1988 the debate on 'Fortress Europe' was engaged in the United States, a clear distinction could be seen between the 'insiders' and 'outsiders'. The former were well informed, and targeted their lobbying at specific pieces of legislation, such as the reciprocity provision in the Second Banking Directive. The outsiders were more likely to use the image of Fortress Europe as a means of pressing for Congressional action on unfair trade. Having completed the legislative work on the US–Canada Free Trade Agreement and the Omnibus Trade and Competitiveness Act, Congress was also ready for a new trade issue. Congress at first expressed general alarm about Fortress Europe and accused the US administration of failing to defend US interests adequately. After hearings and a number of voluminous reports,[4] not to mention a multitude of consultants' reports and newsletters, the mood changed. Now there is little talk of Fortress Europe, although the rhetoric of regional trading blocs is still used to justify US protectionism. Rather, the concern is more focused on a series of specific issues.

5.4 Reciprocity

The focus of US concerns about the reciprocity provisions of the 1992 programme was the debate over the Second Banking Coordination Directive (SBCD). The SBCD is a central element of the EC's 1992 programme for financial services. It implements the concept of home country control by enabling banks satisfying regulatory requirements in one member state to operate in other member states. As this means that a US or other non-EC bank once recognised in one member state can operate throughout the EC, a third country provision was introduced. This provided the opportunity of limiting access to the EC market unless certain conditions were fulfilled by the home country of the bank seeking EC recognition. The US banks and financial services companies feared that this third country provision would deny them access to the EC market, unless the United States introduced 'mirror image legislation'. US legislation, in the shape of the Glass–Steagall and McFadden Acts, is more restrictive than European regulations in two senses. First, it prohibits banks from offering other financial services such as dealing in securities. This means that it is not possible to develop universal banking, *Allfinance* or *banque-assurance* in the United States. Second, banks cannot branch in other states, although this aspect of US regulation is being progressively undermined by state legislation which permits banking across state boundaries. This legislation could only be changed with considerable difficulty, especially following the savings-and-loans débâcle in which the Federal government was obliged to bail out, at very great expense, savings-and-loans companies that had taken advantage of the deregulation of the sector and become overextended. US financial services companies therefore feared that reciprocity provisions in the SBCD could significantly damage US interests. Moreover, the United States saw the threat of restricted access to the EC market as an erosion of GATT provisions on national treatment. Article 3 of the General Agreement on Tariffs and Trade incorporates the so-called national treatment provision, which stipulates that foreign suppliers should be treated on the same terms as national (or EC) suppliers. Singling out foreign companies established in the EC would be inconsistent with this.

The EC revised and clarified its reciprocity provisions in the final version of the SBCD, which was adopted by the Council in December

1989. The provisions will not apply to subsidiaries of US banks established in the EC before 1 January 1993. And, while the EC will still seek *de facto* as well as *de jure* national treatment or 'effective access comparable to that granted by the Community', the Council of Ministers was given greater control over the application of the third country provisions. Approval to negotiate with the United States (or any other third country) will require a qualified majority of the Council, except in cases where 'national treatment offering the same competitive conditions' is denied to an EC bank, when the Commission can itself initiate negotiations. More importantly the Commission must seek approval from a committee of member states' representatives before asking member states to suspend authorisation of any banks from third countries which do not satisfy these conditions. If the committee (probably the Article 113 committee) does not support the Commission's proposal, the issue goes to the Council, which must then approve any such sanctions using a qualified majority vote.

These modifications to the SBCD reassured the United States that they would not face demands for mirror image legislation from the Commission. The need to secure qualified majority support from the Council before introducing any sanction also reduces the danger that the provision would be used in a protectionist fashion. The SBCD was seen by the United States as a test of EC intentions. It was also important because it clearly sets a precedent for directives on investment services and insurance. An easing of tensions on this issue has helped to defuse the fears of Fortress Europe.

5.5   Forced investment

The United States has also expressed concern about forced investment. As a result of the generally favourable treatment given to producers located in the Community, some US firms have felt under pressure to make forced investments in the EC when they would not otherwise have done so. For example, the fact that the third country or reciprocity provisions of the SBCD will apply from 1993 may be seen by some companies as a way of forcing them to invest in the EC. The issue is one that mainly concerns the 'outsiders', or US companies with no pre-existing presence in the EC.

The case that contributed most to US concern was the decision to change the rules of origin provisions for semi-conductors. Despite efforts dating back to the early 1950s, there is no agreed common rule for defining a product's origin. The EC, in line with provisions of the Customs Co-operation Council, uses *inter alia* the principle of 'last substantial transformation' to define the origin of a product. Origin is important in two general instances: to determine what products are eligible for preferential treatment, such as under the Generalised System of Preferences, which allows products from less developed countries access to the EC at low tariffs, or in implementing EC trade policy instruments. The Community maintains that it must be flexible in its interpretation of 'last substantial transformation'. In 1988 it changed its rules for determining the origin of semi-conductors to include in the definition of origin a specific production process. In other words, all semi-conductors had to have this process carried out in the EC if they were to qualify as EC origin. As a result, INTEL was obliged to invest in expensive plants within the EC in order to be able to satisfy the new rules. INTEL launched a highly effective lobbying campaign in Washington and was able to get the issue moved close to the top of the US agenda of 1992 concerns.

Although the basic approach to rules of origin in the Community is the same as that in the United States, that is the last substantial transformation, there is concern at the lack of transparency of European decisions on changes in the rules. US companies fear that decisions taken by the EC will be used as *de facto* trade policy instruments. In order to limit the scope for using rules of origin as an instrument of commercial policy, the United States has supported an initiative to negotiate agreed principles and standards for rules of origin in the GATT Uruguay Round. It seems likely that any agreement on the end of the Round will include common principles on rules of origin, such as transparency, but work on the vital common standards will take quite a lot longer. Such differences are not a major problem for US 'insiders', they can after all usually satisfy the origin tests. Future tensions are more likely to come from 'outsiders'' complaints or the exportation of products to the EC by Japanese companies based in the United States. Such Japanese 'transplants' are expected to grow during the 1990s, and the EC, under pressure from the French and Italians, could well argue that they are not US but Japanese in origin and thus subject to EC quantitative restrictions on Japanese exports into the EC.

5.6   Procurement

As with many 1992 initiatives there is support in the United States for the EC programme to open public procurement markets. The problems arise with the third-party provisions of the excluded sectors or utilities directive on which the Council agreed a common position in February 1990. The Community's measures aimed at opening procurement markets go some way beyond GATT. By the time the EC's programme of seven directives is implemented it will cover the purchase of supplies, works and services by national/federal and local government, as well as public and private utilities. There are also directives for all forms of purchasing.

In comparison the GATT Government Procurement Agreement covers only the purchase of supplies at national/federal level and has no effective compliance provisions. The EC argues that this difference justifies its third country provisions in the directive extending the EC regime to cover utilities. It argues that these are justified until such time as multinational or bilateral negotiations can offer the EC broadly equivalent benefits in other markets. The third country provisions, added to the utilities directive, take the form of a 50 per cent local content provision and a 3 per cent EC price preference. According to these a purchasing utility *may* decline to handle bids according to the criteria laid down in the directive, if the products concerned contain less than 50 per cent EC content. In order to ensure that this was used as a negotiating lever rather than a means of long-term protection, the Council decided to review this provision after the Uruguay Round negotiations and before the directive was implemented.

The United States, which has long argued that European markets for procurement have been closed when US markets are wide open, has targeted the sectors of telecommunications and power plants. US suppliers in these sectors have lobbied hard to block the local content provision, which they see as a means of keeping European markets for the Europeans. Again, there is something of a division between the 'insiders' and the 'outsiders'. In the absence of an agreement in the GATT negotiations, the pressure to threaten the use of unfair trade provisions of Section 301 of the US Trade Act to restrict EC exports to the United States has grown.[5]

The United States is in a difficult position in the GATT. It does not feel it can include state and local purchasing in an agreement, because of political and constitutional sensitivities about federal control over the states. Nor does the administration accept that private as well as public utilities should be covered.[6] Finally, compliance (or bid protest provisions) exist only at the federal level and in some but not all states. There is also a patchwork of national and local 'buy American' legislation.

In July 1990 the EC made some ambitious proposals aimed at extending EC market-opening measures to the multilateral level. The United States' difficulties in accepting the cover of state and private utility purchasing has prevented this going very far. In the absence of a GATT agreement the EC will implement its 50 per cent provision in January 1993, along with a 3 per cent price preference. This could precipitate trade tensions with the United States.

5.7 Standards and certification

Concerns about European standards-making procedures are also found mostly among smaller US-based companies. Those with a presence in Europe understand and are mostly actively involved in the European standards-making process. Some small US firms fear that 1992 will result in a 'harmonising up' of standards and thus make access harder. This seems to reflect a lack of understanding of European standards-making in general and the new approach to standards in the 1992 programme in particular. Mutual recognition would suggest that the reverse will happen. Indeed, countries with highly developed standards-making procedures, such as Germany, are concerned that the minimum requirements set by the EC may lead to 'harmonising down' rather than up.

The other fear has been that standards are set in Europe without US companies having a say in their content. The United States claims its standards-making process is open to anyone. This concern led the US Secretary of Commerce, Mosbacher, to ask for a US seat at the European standards-making table (CEN and CENELEC). The EC's response was that if the United States were interested in agreed standards, it should participate more actively in international standards-making bodies and implement more ISO standards.[7] European standards are in most cases consistent with ISO standards. The EC also argues that while US standards-making may, in theory, be open to anyone who wants to participate, the existence of a large number of private standards-making bodies makes this prohibitively expensive. There are about 250 active US standards-making bodies.

The claim that US firms find European standards-making difficult to follow is also strange, since the vast majority of national standards are drawn up by three standards-making institutions, DIN (Germany), AFNOR (France) and BSI (Britain). Notification measures introduced before the 1992 programme was launched, along with the existence of the CEN and CENELEC, also mean that there is a high degree of transparency in European standards-making.

The second fear of US-based companies is that they will face costlier testing and certification procedures than their EC competitors. While mutual recognition of testing and certification in Europe will reduce the US costs, because it will be necessary to have a product tested and certified in only one member state of the EC rather than numerous countries, the EC in its July 1989 proposals was not prepared to accept an extension of mutual recognition of testing and certification to the United States. The main issue is that mutual agreements between individual member states of the EC and the United States will not be automatically recognised by the EC as a whole. The 40,000 or so private US testing houses are also concerned that they will lose business.

In 1989 the EC agreed to strengthen consultations procedures with the United States on standards-making by providing information and receiving comments from the United States. But this has raised problems within the United States. Those who are active in the privately run and financed US system are unhappy about ANSI (the American National Standards Institution) assuming a central co-ordination function.

In the field of standards, as in other areas such as the regulation of financial services, the 1992 process has thus aroused concern in the United States not only because of its potential impact on US exports. In both of these areas, as well as in procurement, 1992 is also a challenge, because it demonstrates ways in which the existing US procedures make international agreement or co-operation difficult. It shows too that the regulatory approach adopted by the EC is better able than that of the United States to keep pace with the needs of businesses, which are now used to operating internationally.

5.8   The social dimension

One aspect of European integration of concern to the US multination-als but not the US-based exporters is the programme to implement the European Social Charter and the social dimension to the EC as set out in the social protocol in the Maastricht agreement. The main issue for the US companies is the one to which European companies, and notably the British CBI, are also most strongly opposed: namely consultation procedures for employees. During the 1980s US multina-tional companies formed a coalition to lobby against the Vredeling proposals on consultation which would have given European em-ployees of US companies consultation rights with their US-based employers. The US companies are now concerned that the provision on consultation in the Social Action Programme will have the same effect. This is an issue on which the EC affiliates of US companies will seek to co-operate with European business in order to modify or influence the form of any legislation rather than work through the US system.

5.9   Multilateralism versus regional blocs

One further concern voiced in Washington is that 1992 and the agreement with EFTA over the European Economic Area to be followed by EC enlargement may result in the creation of a (West) European regional bloc. This usually provides the background political rhetoric for efforts to achieve specific concessions as regards the 1992 programme. But the rhetoric is also used by US politicians seeking to strengthen US national trade legislation; if the EC is forming a wider bloc, then the United States must protect its own interests. The US position on regional blocs is also influenced by its desire to retain the option of negotiating bilateral free trade agreements. Following its agreement with Canada, agreement now seems to have been reached with Mexico. Unlike the Japanese the Americans are not particularly concerned about the effects of 1992 on the multilateral system as such. The United States has considerable leverage by virtue of its large market and tendency to run trade deficits on visible trade. There are also strong elements of support, both in Congress and business, for more use of bilateral market-opening policies. The use of section 301 as a threat to close the US market to products from a country is seen to be an effective means of forcing trading partners to open closed markets. Congress can also introduce its own trade legislation if it feels any US sector is suffering. With these sentiments in Congress the US administration and multinational companies (the insiders in Europe) have sought to head off protectionist pressure by promoting multilateral trade negotiations in the shape of the GATT Uruguay Round.

The Uruguay Round is seen by the United States as a litmus test of the EC's commitment to multilateralism. On this front the United States has accused the Community of foot dragging and preoccupation with 1992 at the expense of the multilateral talks. This view, however, owes as much to the US administration's sense of urgency about the Round, because of the need to prove to Congress that progress is being made, as to any preoccupation with 1992 on the part of the EC. Indeed, it is difficult to find anyone in Europe who challenges the principle of multilateralism in the same way that some people on Capitol Hill do.

The US administration's desire to satisfy its domestic lobbies has led it to raise expectations about the Round, and resulted in the United States adopting maximalist positions in a number of the negotiating groups. In agriculture the United States initially pressed for elimination of all support. This position was subsequently modified to one seeking a 70 per cent reduction, but the EC has had trouble agreeing on a much more modest package, initially aimed at 30 per cent. The political pressure has all been on the EC to make concessions, but this should not hide the fact that there are strong forces in Congress opposed to reductions in farm support. Nevertheless the inability of the EC to adopt a more positive position on agriculture has soured US–EC trade relations, despite some more recent concessions.

The US administration has pressed others to make major concessions in the Geneva talks in areas in which it has had difficulty delivering the US domestic constituencies. For example, in services it has consistently pressed for concrete results, but has been unable to deliver its own financial services, transport or telecommunications sectors. In each case the United States has sought exemption from the General Agreement on Trade in Services (GATS). In public procurement it wishes to see markets opened, but can do nothing to control state purchasing practices or 'buy American' legislation. It wishes to see industrial subsidies eliminated, but cannot act to discipline US state subsidy programmes. In the OECD the United States wanted to make the National Treatment Instrument more binding, but could not in the end sign an agreement that would bind the individual states. Although all federal governments have difficulty getting their constituent states to comply with international agreements, it is surprising that it is the United States' rather than the EC's inability to do so which has slowed negotiations.

The Community has, of course, adopted positions which militate against multilateral solutions, such as in agriculture and anti-dumping, but the US rhetoric suggesting that 1992 inhibits the EC from reaching multilateral agreements must be tested against the performance of both the United States and the EC in the GATT Round.

Finally, it is interesting to consider the issues conspicuous by their absence from the US debate about Europe. Perhaps the most interesting is that there is virtually no discussion of the potential impact on the United States of European moves towards economic and monetary union. Although this is not strictly part of the 1992 programme, Americans are ready enough to throw non-1992 issues, such as agriculture, into the same pot. European economic and monetary union could have considerable impact on the United States. For example, the creation of a European Central Bank to implement monetary policy and common decisions on the level of the ecu *vis-à-vis* the dollar will strengthen the European voice on monetary issues. To date the United States has been struggling to come to terms with the implications of interdependence in the field of trade and investment. If European decisions on monetary and economic policy also impinge on US domestic policy options, the adjustment will be that much greater. The lack of interest in this issue was probably due to the uncertainty surrounding the success of efforts to create economic and monetary union. There is also a history of dismissing efforts at European co-operation in economic and monetary policy. On this, as on many issues, the picture may be a little clearer once the issues of ratification of the Maastricht agreement and the Danish 'no' vote have been resolved.

Notes

1. This chapter draws on research work on *Europe as a Partner*, for which major funding has been provided by The Ford Foundation.
2. Special message to the Congress on Foreign Trade Policy, quoted in *Europe 1992, An American Perspective*, ed. G. Hufbauer (The Brookings Institution, 1990).
3. Hufbauer estimates 1.9 (see Hufbauer, *ibid.*).
4. See, for example, *The Effects of Greater Economic Integration within the European Community on the United States*, The US International Trade Commission (March 1990). Also 1989 first report.
5. These are not formally part of the Uruguay Round but are politically linked to it.
6. See USITC, *op. cit.*
7. The United States sees the ISO as biased towards European standards since the United States has one vote to the EC's twelve.

6

The effects of the Single Market on the pattern of Japanese investment

George N. Yannopoulos

6.1 Economic integration and foreign direct investment

The completion of the European Community's internal market will be achieved through the removal of a host of non-tariff barriers to trade and the mobility of factors of production and the liberalisation of the conditions for the provision of service activities inside the Single Market. This completion of the European Community's internal market will enhance the locational advantages of European markets.

The propensity of a firm to engage in foreign production is influenced by the combination of ownership-specific advantages, internalisation opportunities and locational advantages of the target market (Dunning 1981). Economic integration increases the locational advantages of the markets inside the trading bloc, and in this way it may increase the relative profitability of servicing these markets via local production facilities (direct investment) rather than through exports or licensing.

In addition, the process of economic integration may also affect the distribution of ownership advantages between firms of different origins. The Single European Market with its expanded size and the opportunities for scale economies that it offers is expected to stimulate innovative activity inside the European Community through the ability to sustain larger R&D expenditure. This increased innovative activity will offer opportunities for the accumulation of ownership-specific advantages by firms of European Community origin.

Economic integration brings about changes in the distribution of locational advantages across markets and in the distribution of ownership-specific advantages across international firms.

The extent of the global redistribution of locational advantages depends on the changes in the structure of effective protection of the integrated market and the growth-enhancing effects of market unification. These growth effects are both once-for-all changes and permanent additions to the Community's long-term growth (Baldwin 1989). The removal of the non-tariff barriers in intra-EC goods transactions and factor movements will produce complex changes in the relative degree of protection of Community producers compared to outsiders trading inside the Common Market. Much will depend on the forms the common commercial policy of the European Community will take as the various non-tariff barriers in intra-Community trade are removed.

It may be argued that the removal of many non-tariff barriers to intra-Community trade will bring about benefits (that is, resource cost savings) not only to producers trading inside the Common Market but also to firms exporting to the Single Market from outside locations. One can think of the elimination of such non-tariff barriers like contents, packaging and similar regulations in the food industry or the elimination of technical barriers to trade like differences in product specification and in the terms of product certification or the lifting of capital market controls. However, there are other non-tariff barriers whose removal does not have the characteristic of a semi-public good as is the case with the elimination of the type of non-tariff barriers just mentioned. Various market-entry barriers like public procurement or conditions for the provision of service activities can be eliminated by treating differentially insiders and outsiders given the lack of any binding GATT rules in such matters. In addition, the removal of many non-tariff barriers to internal trade often has implications for the common external commercial policy of the Community. The way these changes in the Community's external commercial policy are implemented will shape the structure of effective protection of Community production from outside competition.

Changes in the Community's common commercial policy which can directly affect the relative profitability of exporting to the Community in comparison to producing inside the Single Market include: quota reorganisation in replacing member state quotas on imports of particular products from specific countries, the future of specific rules of origin like those applicable to microchips or photocopiers, agreement on local content provisions to cope with the question of the 'screwdriver' plants and the procedures on the application of anti-dumping rules.

The uncertainty as to the final design of the European Community's common commercial policy and the fluidity of some of the rules proposed (for example, on local content) increase the attraction of producing inside the Single Market rather than exporting to it. Such uncertainties and policy ambiguities invite strategic responses by internal firms keen to maintain or expand their market share in the unified market of the Community.

6.2   Foreign direct investment responses

Foreign production through direct investment in the Single Market becomes the strategic response of firms in coping with changes in relative competitiveness, locational advantages and ownership strengths brought about through the removal of intra-Community barriers and the redesign of the common commercial policy of the Community.

Four types of investment responses by international firms can be identified: *defensive import-substituting investment* to cope with the trade diverting effects of integration; *offensive import-substituting investment* to take advantage of the opening up of the new markets and the expected expansion in their size; *reorganisation investment* to redistribute production already established inside the Community towards locations with more favourable cost conditions in the unified, Single Market; and *rationalised investment*, which is undertaken in response to the new international differences in production costs generated through the enhanced efficiency inside the Single Market following the removal of the various intra-EC non-tariff barriers to trade (Yannopoulos 1990). Though these four types of direct investment are responses to the trade effects of further European integration, nevertheless they are not necessarily trade replacing. Defensive import-substituting investment is certainly trade replacing while offensive import-substituting investment is likely to restrict opportunities for trade expansion. However, rationalised and reorganisation investments are likely to be complementary to trade, encouraging either more trade of the inter-industry type (in the case of rationalised investments) or of the intra-industry variety (in the case of reorganisation investments).

Changes in the configuration of ownership, location and internalisation advantages do not by themselves stimulate new foreign direct investment. Foreign direct investment will be the main instrument to service a foreign market if the firm has the capacity to exploit simultaneously all the three advantages: ownership, internalisation and location.

On the basis of the discussion in the first section, the process of further integration in the European Community has two effects on the configuration of ownership, internalisation and locational advantages affecting foreign direct investment decisions by non-Community multinational enterprises. On the one hand, the locational advantages of production sites inside the Community increase, making production in the Community a more attractive alternative to service the Community markets. On the other hand, the dynamic effects of further integration on R&D activities and innovation potential will strengthen the ownership-specific advantages of multinational firms of Community origin. If the second effect is more immediate and stronger then it may outweigh the attraction to foreign direct investment generated by the first effect. In any case, even if changes in locational advantages are preponderant, these will not bring foreign direct investment flows to the Community if outside firms do not possess adequate ownership-specific advantages.

In order to assess the potential response of Japanese multinational firms to the changes in locational advantages generated from further European integration we must now turn our attention to the technological and organisational strengths of Japanese firms. This will give us an indication of the sectors in which Japanese firms have strong ownership-specific advantages which they can combine with any emerging locational advantages of European production to engage in foreign direct investment.

6.3 Relative strengths

To assess the extent to which Japanese firms can take advantage of the benefits of the Single Market by investing in the Community it is not sufficient to look only at the revealed comparative advantages of Japanese firms through trade. A country's relative trade performance may not reveal the technological strength of its industries if exports and international production are more substitutable for one another, rather than complementary. Indeed, in countries like the United Kingdom and the United States, where their multinational firms are in the phase of maturity of their internationalisation history, there is strong evidence of substitutability. However, this does not appear to be the case with Japan as its firms are at a relatively early stage in their internationalisation growth (UNCTC 1990).

A good indication of the potential ownership-specific advantages enjoyed by firms is to look at their comparative advantage in innovative activity. Dunning and Cantwell (1989) derived a measure of revealed technological advantage to capture the firm's comparative advantage in innovative activity by using data on foreign patenting in the United States.

Comparing the technological and organisation strengths of Japanese firms in relation to their European rivals, one clearly sees the Japanese firms enjoy their technological strengths in the electrical equipment and motor vehicles sectors.

In Table 6.1 we summarise the findings from the Dunning and Cantwell study of comparative technological and trade advantages of Japanese firms *vis-à-vis* their European rivals. This table classifies the size of the comparative advantage (technological or trading) into three classes: S = small (up to 0.5), M = medium (0.5–0.99) and L = large (1.0 and above). In addition it shows whether the index of revealed comparative advantage, technological or trading, has been falling (F) or rising (R) between 1970 and 1986.

The index of revealed technology advantage is derived from data on US patents in industry i, granted to residents of a foreign country j, in period t, (P_{ijt}) compared to all foreign patents granted by US authorities to residents of all foreign countries seeking patent protection in the United States according to the following formula:

Index of revealed technological advantage:
$$(P_{ijt}/\Sigma_j P_{ijt})/(\Sigma_i P_{ijt}/\Sigma_i \Sigma_j P_{ijt})$$

The trend in comparative advantage in trade is assessed by the index of revealed comparative advantage which is calculated as follows:

$$(X_{ij}/\Sigma_j X_{ij})/(\Sigma_i X_{ij}/\Sigma_i \Sigma_j X_{ij})$$

where X_{ij} stands for the value of exports in industry i from country j in a given period.

Table 6.1   Classification of Japanese firms according to their revealed comparative advantages, 1970–86.

Sector	Trends in technological advantage	Trends in comparative advantage
Food products	MF	SF
Chemicals	MF	MF
Metals	MF	LF
Machinery	SR	MR
Electrical equipment	LF	LR
Motor vehicles	LR	LR
Other transport	LF	LF
Textiles	LF	MF
Rubber products	MR	LR
Non-metallic minerals	LF	MR

Source: tabulated from Dunning and Cantwell (1989).

The evidence summarised in Table 6.1 shows strong and rising technological advantages in motor vehicles, and strong but slightly falling technological advantages in electrical equipment, in other transport equipment, in textiles and in non-metallic minerals. The rate of decline of the index of technological advantage was not so significant as to bring the value of the index below the critical level of 1.00 at the end of the period.

It is interesting to note that the sectors where the Japanese firms have considerable technological advantages are precisely those where the uncertainties surrounding the future course of the common commercial policy and consequently the effective protection of European production are higher. This coincidence of Japanese technological advantages (and thus of potential ownership-specific advantages) and expected changes in the relative protection rates of European production in the unified Single Market will encourage Japanese foreign direct investment of the import-substituting type – both defensive and offensive. This coincidence is not of course unexplained. The move towards a more protectionist stance of the common commercial policy in the Single Market is encouraged by lobbies of industries threatened by the strength of Japanese competition. Indeed, it is in those sectors where Japanese direct investment in Europe is showing signs of acceleration.

Japanese direct investment abroad has been encouraged not just by their strengthened technological advantages but also by the rising value of the yen. The continuous appreciation of the yen in the 1980s has acted as an important factor facilitating the globalisation of Japanese industry.

6.4 Trends in Japanese investment in the Community

Data on Japanese direct investment abroad show that up to 1991 Europe (including the non-EC countries) accounted for approximately 20 per cent of the cumulative total of Japanese direct investment abroad. North America accounted for more than twice as much of Japanese direct investment abroad, while Asia amounted to 15 per cent and Latin America to only 12 per cent (Table 6.2). Since 1987 Europe's share has grown markedly from around 15 per cent, mainly at the expense of the last two groups.

The data in Table 6.2 show that Japanese 'non-manufacturing' investment in Europe was over three times as large as manufacturing investment. It is possible that part of the 'non-manufacturing' investment may indeed be manufacturing related and may have been

Table 6.2 Geographical distribution of Japanese direct investment abroad (cumulative to 31 March 1991; US$bn).

	Manufacturing	Non-manufacturing	Sales offices	Real estate	Total
Europe	15.2	51.1	2.3	0.04	68.6
North America	46.2	107.2	1.1	0.5	155.0
Latin America	6.6	37.1	0.05	0.02	43.8
Asia	21.6	31.0	0.9	0.04	53.5
Middle East	1.3	0.7	1.5	—	3.5
Africa	0.2	6.3	—	—	6.6
Oceania	2.7	18.5	0.1	—	21.4
All regions	93.9	251.9	5.9	0.6	352.4

Source: Japanese Ministry of Finance (1988, 1992).

classified as manufacturing if the services were provided on a unitary site.

During the 1980s the stock of Japanese direct investment in the European Community has grown in real terms at a rate of approximately 10 per cent per annum during 1980–5, and at an annual rate of over 12 per cent in 1985–7 (Table 6.3). Since then growth has been dramatically faster, with a five-fold nominal increase in just four years.

The changing position of the European Community in the strategies of Japanese multinationals can be seen from Table 6.4, which shows the share of the Japanese direct investment abroad channelled to the countries of the European Community.

Between 1973–7 and 1988–91 the share of the Japanese direct investment abroad located in European Community countries more than tripled from 6 per cent to 22.2 per cent. This big jump appears to have been taken since 1984–5, which coincides with the publication of the White Paper on the completion of the internal market and the start of the discussions on 'Fortress Europe'. This trend has continued as shown by the fact that in 1988 the number of Japanese manufacturing ventures in the Community increased to 392 from 282 a year earlier (UNCTC 1990). The growing importance of European Community locations in the global strategies of Japanese multinational firms seems to coincide with another change in the sectoral composition of Japanese direct investment in the Community. As one can see from the data in Table 6.5 the largest part, indeed at least 80 per cent of Japanese direct investment in the countries of the Community (with the exception of Italy and France), was concentrated in financial services and trade.

This pattern of foreign direct investment is partly explained by the early phase of the multinationalisation of the Japanese firms and the fact that during this early phase foreign direct investment was

Table 6.3 The stock of
Japanese direct investment in the
EC, 1980–91.

Fiscal year ending 31 March	$ billions	Rate of change (%)
1980–1	3.9	10.7
1981–2	4.5	10.0
1982–3	5.3	10.0
1983–4	6.2	10.1
1984–5	7.7	10.8
1985–6	10.0	12.0
1986–7	13.4	12.6
1988–9	40.0	n/a
1990–1	64.0	n/a

Source: Commission of the EC,
relations between the Community
and Japan.

Table 6.4 Shares of Japanese direct investment in the EC, 1973–91 (%).

Period	United Kingdom	West Germany	Belgium	France	Netherlands	Italy	EC
1973–7	1.9	1.1	0.7	0.9	1.2	—	6.0
1978–82	2.0	1.8	1.7	1.1	0.9	0.1	8.1
1983–7	3.9	1.5	4.5	0.9	3.3	0.2	14.5
1988–91	9.2	1.9	0.5	1.7	5.2	0.5	22.2

Source: Ministry of Finance, Financial Statistics of Japan (various issues).

Table 6.5 Sectoral distribution of Japanese direct investment in the EC, 1981–6 (US$m).

Country	Manufacturing	Commerce	Banking and insurance	Total
United Kingdom	356	394	1,158	2,117
West Germany	192	583	22	1,055
Belgium/Luxembourg	138	123	2,272	2,705
France	219	221	10	586
Netherlands	160	528	1,287	2,039
Italy	64	39	0	136

Source: Ministry of Finance, Monetary and Financial Statistics (various issues).

supportive of the export thrust of Japanese firms. Trading and financing activities were spreading globally to sustain and strengthen the export drive of Japan's manufacturing firms.

Changes in the locational advantages of European Community markets encouraged not only by the growth-enhancing effects of the internal market programme but by uncertainties regarding the future course of the Community's external commercial policy particularly on quota reorganisation (for example, motor vehicles) and rules of origin (for example, electronic products) have already induced new trends towards more investment in manufacturing. This is perhaps more noticeable in motor car production. Nissan, Toyota, Honda, Subaru, Suzuki and Hino have all established assembly, production and co-production operations in selected locations within the European Community. Their pattern of operations inside the European Community suggests that they act by considering the Single Market as having been established already, choosing locations offering the most advantageous cost for each specific production process.

Nissan, for example, has located its financial and regional headquarters in the Netherlands, its distribution centre in Belgium, its passenger car production in Britain and its commercial vehicles division in Spain. Toyota seems to have already adopted a similar pattern.

Japanese firms producing inside the European Community appear to seek ways of strengthening their ownership advantages against a potential encroachment by Community firms by mobilising their organisational capabilities to the full. One of the factors that contributes to strong ownership advantages by Japanese firms in electronics and in motor vehicles is their success in organising contractual networks. These contractual networks bring together diverse groups of small producers acting to supply sourcing and subcontracting services to the large firms. This ability to organise contractual networks will prove decisive in the internal market. It will be the instrument to exploit this market to the full and take advantage of any prevailing cost and skill differentials.

Similar patterns to those observed in motor vehicle production are emerging in the semi-conductor industry. The early establishment of test and assembly operations by Fujitsu, NEC and Hitachi has been followed by the setting up of fabrication facilities by these companies.

The strategy of the Japanese multinationals to treat the Community market as a unified entity, as a Single Market, is reflected in the concentration of Japanese direct investment in a few Community countries that offer the required cost advantages and in addition a more stable investment climate. As one can see from Table 6.6, two-thirds of the stock of Japanese direct investment in the Community in 1987 is found in three countries: the United Kingdom, the

Table 6.6 Regional distribution of Japanese direct investment in Europe (%).

Area	1970	1980	1987	1991
United Kingdom	85.1	44.9	31.1	38.2
West Germany	2.5	11.1	9.3	8.5
Belgium	3.1	6.5	4.1	2.8
Luxembourg	1.3	2.4	19.3	8.6
France	3.4	7.9	6.2	7.3
Netherlands	0.5	6.6	15.0	21.6
Italy	1.1	1.5	1.2	1.7
Spain	0.6	3.9	4.2	3.2
Ireland	0.2	3.3	1.9	1.0
Other EC	0.5	2.0	0.9	0.4
Total EC	98.3	90.2	93.5	93.3
Non-EC Europe	1.7	9.8	6.5	6.7

Source: Ministry of Finance, Financial Statistics of Japan (various issues).

Netherlands and Luxembourg. The Netherlands has shown the most dramatic increase, although Luxembourg was also rising rapidly until recent years.

The Fortress Europe worries have thus acted as European pull factors for Japanese direct investment in the Community. One should not forget, in interpreting these trends, that there are also Japanese push factors as well, generated both by the programme of exports, their successful penetration of the US market and the stage of their international involvement having reached a phase of some maturity, plus the sheer size of the Japanese investible funds requiring an outlet.

6.5 Conclusions

The global redistribution in locational and ownership-specific advantages enjoyed by multinational firms stimulated by the internal market programme of the Community has generated concrete strategic responses by Japanese firms previously servicing the markets of the Community primarily through exports. The response is in the form of direct investment in selected locations and the organisation of contractual networks Community-wide with the objective to supply from these locations the entire unified market. The direct investment response has been stronger in the sectors where the Japanese firms have considerable technological advantages such as motor vehicles, other transport equipment, electrical equipment, office equipment, and so on.

The further spread of Japanese direct investment in the European Community will depend on four major factors:

1. The final design of the common external commercial policy and especially the use of specific rules of origin, local content requirements and Community-wide quotas in place of member-state specific quotas.
2. The extent to which the attempts to forge strategic alliances with Community producers and to set up organisational, contractual, networks succeed.
3. The ability of the Japanese multinationals to sustain and enhance their ownership advantages in the face of the strengthened competitive position of the Community firms.
4. The future parity of the yen. The continuing appreciation of the yen has proved an important enabling factor in the drive of the Japanese firms towards multinationalisation.

References

Baldwin, R. (1989) 'The growth effects of 1992', *Economic Policy*, no. 9, October, pp. 248–81.

Dunning, J. H. (1981) *International Production and Multinational Enterprise* (London: Allen and Unwin).

Dunning, J. H. and Cantwell, J. A. (1989) 'Japanese manufacturing direct investment in the EEC, post 1992: some alternative scenarios', University of Reading discussion papers in International Investment and Business Studies, no. 132, September, p. 40.

UNCTC (United Nations Centre for Transnational Corporations) (1990) 'The implications of the completion of the single internal market of the EC for TNC activity'.

Yannopoulos, G. N. (1990) 'Foreign direct investment and European integration: the evidence from the formative years of the European Community', *Journal of Common Market Studies*, vol. 28, no. 3, pp. 235–59.

7

ASEAN and EC-1992

Jacques Pelkmans

ASEAN, the Association of South East Asian Nations, comprises the fastest growing countries of the world economy. Apart from including the only NIE (newly industrialising economy) not to have encountered domestic political or social growth constraints – Singapore, with 11 per cent real growth in 1988, 9.2 per cent in 1989, and 10 per cent first quarter 1990 – it consists of recent record-holders, Thailand (with growth rates above 10 per cent for three years), Malaysia (growth in the 7–9 per cent range), Indonesia (recent growth 6–7 per cent), Philippines (oscillating growth due to internal instability) and Brunei (an oil-exporting sultanate). The ASEAN countries do not owe their growth to the integration of ASEAN countries into a free trade area, a customs union or a common market. Intra-group trade liberalisation and economic co-operation are still modest. These growth marvels owe their performance to exports, especially to the OECD countries. The quality and very high growth rates of exports were and still are fostered by foreign investment and imports of intermediate inputs from the target markets.

It is important for the EC to strengthen its economic ties with this buoyant and promising region. ASEAN's import demand increasingly reflects rising income levels, providing great export opportunities for EC product and services suppliers. ASEAN's performance is itself a main factor in the development of intra-area trade in the Asia–Pacific region, by far the most dynamic area in the world economy.

The strength of ASEAN industry and services is already making itself felt in the European market, and the product range of their industrial export goods and the scope of their services is widening rapidly. Soon, ASEAN firms will begin to make direct investments in the EC, Eastern Europe and Turkey so as to benefit better from the promising decade Europe has before it.

It is in this light that the relation between European integration, especially 1992, and ASEAN should be viewed. This chapter discusses the likely impact of 1992 on ASEAN in agricultural food and industrial exports, services and direct investment. However, three basic ingredients for answering these questions are surveyed first: a bird's eye view of ASEAN–EC economic relations, a closer look at ASEAN's trade with the Community and an overview of the external dimension of 1992.

7.1 ASEAN–EC economic relations: a bird's eye view

Economic relations between EC and ASEAN are dominated by five aspects: trade in goods, trade in services, direct investment, development aid and efforts evolving from the EC–ASEAN Co-operation Agreement (signed in 1980, renewed and extended in 1986 and in 1990). By far the most important is goods trade, linked with business services (such as financial and shipping), air transport primarily linked to tourism and EC direct investment in the region.

In goods trade ASEAN has strengthened its position in the EC from a 1975 share in EC overall imports of 1.8 per cent to a 1989 share of 3.4 per cent. Since EC imports are dominated by EC and other OECD countries (EC and EFTA already provide roughly three-quarters of all EC imports), the relevant share to observe is that of ASEAN in the EC imports from all developing countries: this share has risen from 3.9 per cent in 1975 and 6.8 per cent in 1985 to 10.3 per cent in 1988. The competitive performance is impressive over a wide product range: the share increase is due just as much to products which are becoming relatively less important for overall ASEAN exports, such as food (ASEAN share of EC imports from developing countries rising from 10.1 per cent in 1975 to 13.8 per cent in 1988) and raw materials (from 23.4 per cent to 30.5 per cent), as it is to manufactures (up from 8.7 per cent to 14.8 per cent), which increasingly dominate overall ASEAN exports. It is also noteworthy that such increases in EC import shares took place despite ASEAN's export concentration in product categories encountering EC protection, such as agriculture/ food (the Common Agriculture Policy (CAP) in general; Voluntary Export Restraints (VERs) in agriculture), textiles and clothing (the MFA and its bilateral enforcement by EC member states), footwear and consumer electronics. Moreover, ASEAN does not enjoy special preferences like the ACP and non-EC Mediterranean countries do, except for GSP treatment. However, as Langhammer and Sapir (1987) have shown, the relatively modest opportunities that GSP might offer for ASEAN have largely remained unexploited due to a byzantine system of exceptions, tariff quotas and GSP alterations which the EC has imposed.

It would appear, from the scant data that are available, that ASEAN is showing quite a good performance in services trade with the Community. In the only recent empirical study, Langhammer (1989) finds that, in 1987, revenues for private non-factor services accounted for 24 per cent of total (goods and services) exports from ASEAN to West Germany and 19 per cent in the case of France. He also finds 10 per cent for the Netherlands, but this figure is perhaps not fully comparable. In the German case ASEAN holds higher shares in German imports of services (1987: 1.8 per cent) than in goods imports (1987: 1.5 per cent). The apparent lack of data on the United Kingdom's imports of services from ASEAN is a serious omission given the United Kingdom's position in services trade and its special relationship with ASEAN.

Direct investment from the EC is quite substantial and rising absolutely, but its share in the total inflow remains largely constant. The region is so buoyant that it attracts investment from the United States and Japan with very high annual increments. Apart from the attractiveness of ASEAN in terms of growth (and prospects), the division of labour in the Asia–Pacific region prompted Japan to be the first to invest heavily in ASEAN to exploit their comparative advantages for relatively labour-intensive products. The Japanese example has been followed recently by Taiwan, South Korea and even Hong Kong despite its emphasis on subcontracting in China. In addition, Japan traditionally invests in ASEAN to gain access to raw materials and fuels. Therefore, growth rates of EC direct investment in ASEAN pale compared to the large inflows of direct investment from other sources. Moreover, EC investors have made relatively modest use of 'outward processing' provisions in EC trade policy with respect to ASEAN (for instance, in textiles and clothing they have typically preferred Eastern Europe and Mediterranean countries) while showing a preference for direct investment in developing countries with large domestic markets (that is, for local output, often behind protection). This means that, compared to Japan and to some degree the United States, EC investments in ASEAN are not the source of ASEAN exports to the EC.[1]

Some ASEAN countries still receive substantial development aid, both from EC countries and from the EC as a group. The EC as a group has announced further increases in the aid, especially to Indonesia, the Philippines and Thailand. There is a direct connection with 1992 here since the doubling of the Community's Structural Funds under the 'cohesion' provisions of the Single European Act as well as the preparedness to step up aid to Eastern Europe had raised fears in ASEAN that the lesser developed countries of ASEAN would suffer as a result. EC Commissioner Matutes' medium-term development plan has put these fears to rest.[2]

Finally, the EC–ASEAN Co-operation Agreement provides a framework for political and economic consultation as well as technical assistance. The Agreement provides for neither trade preferences nor bilateral trade negotiations of any kind. Modest programmes of trade and development promotion have been initiated, as well as the 'Cheysson facility' for feasibility studies for EC–ASEAN joint ventures.

7.2 A closer look at ASEAN–EC trade

No attempt will be made to survey EC–ASEAN trade. The following will only provide some stylised facts about bilateral trade in a global context as a basis for a qualitative impact assessment of the impact of EC-1992.

The magnitude of product trade between the two groups is considerable but not large (see Table 7.1).

In 1989, the EC imported ecu 15 billion from ASEAN and exported ecu 14 billion to it, both shares of extra-EC trade being 3.4 per cent. Growth rates were high during the 1970s and again in the late 1980s. For ASEAN the EC is much more important as an outlet than ASEAN is to the EC: the EC takes a little over 15 per cent of all ASEAN exports, up from 10.2 per cent in 1984. This is almost as much as the United States (16 per cent) and little lower than Japan (20 per cent). The sharp increase of ASEAN exports to the EC is due to very high growth rates of manufactured exports, whilst agriculture/food and raw materials exports show comparatively modest growth rates (fuel exports to the EC are negligible).

This spectacular sectoral growth performance has dramatically altered the structure of ASEAN exports, notably to the EC and the United States, but less so those to Japan (Table 7.2).

There is a sharp reduction in ASEAN reliance on exports of food and raw materials, a selective reduction in the weight of ores, minerals and fuels and a phenomenal increase in the share of manufactures exports. Trade with Japan in non-manufactures is somewhat of an exception partly as a result of the pattern of direct investment. The share of manufactures in exports to the EC increased 2½-fold, the US share almost quadrupled and the Japanese share rose more than five-fold in a period of thirteen years, albeit from a small initial value.

Table 7.1   EC–ASEAN trade, 1975–89.

	EC imports from ASEAN		EC exports to ASEAN		Average % change	
	ECU	%[1]	ECU	%[1]	Imports	Exports
1970	1,066	1.7	1,264	2.3		
1980	7,201	2.5	5,486	2.5	21.0[2]	15.8[2]
1986	9,213		8,497			
1987	10,037		8,906		8.9[3]	4.8[3]
1988	12,203	3.2	10,688		21.6	20.0
1989	15,170	3.4	14,096	3.4	24.3	31.9

Notes:
1. Share of extra EC imports/exports.
2. From 1970 to 1980, annually.
3. Over 1986.

Source: Eurostat.

Table 7.2   Product composition of ASEAN exports, 1975–88.

Year	EC	United States	Japan
Food			
1975	42.5	19.8	19.2
1988	24.5	9.0	13.2
Raw materials			
1975	25.6	7.7	10.4
1988	13.0	5.1	14.8
Ores, minerals, fuels			
1975	8.4	52.2	67.5
1988	1.7	8.2	54.7
Manufactures			
1975	23.0	19.2	2.8
1988	59.1	75.9	15.8
Of which: Textiles/clothing			
1975	4.1	3.8	0.5
1988	13.9	13.2	1.5

Source: data from EC Commission (1990); calculated from import data.

Although these strong increases are more or less reflected in the textiles and clothing sector, it is obvious that the rapid export growth must have spread to several other industrial sectors since textiles and clothing only make up between 10 per cent and 22 per cent of the industrial exports, dependent on the target market.

Table 7.3 provides a snapshot of the product composition of ASEAN manufactured exports to the EC in 1987. Other important

Table 7.3   EC imports from ASEAN in 1987: product composition of manufactures.

	Value[1]	%[2]
Total EC imports from ASEAN	12,060	100
Of which:		
manufactures	6,641	54.9
SITC63 (wood products, cork, excluding furniture)	459	3.8
SITC65 (textiles)	385	3.2
SITC75 (office machinery)	704	5.8
SITC76 (telecom., audio, video)	760	6.3
SITC77 (appliances, etc.)	1,471	12.1
SITC84 (clothing)	1,188	9.9
Other manufactures	1,664	13.8

Notes:
1. In US dollars.
2. % denotes shares of all EC imports from ASEAN.

Source: OECD, Trade by commodities, C-Series.

export sectors – besides textiles and clothing – include wood and cork products other than furniture, office machinery and automatic data processing equipment (and components), telecom and audio/video apparatus and electrical machinery and appliances. The widening product scope is also apparent from the relatively high share of the category 'other manufactures', ranging from chemicals and non-ferrous metals to footwear. Hiemenz (1988) shows that, in the mid-1980s, ASEAN had achieved an export pattern remarkably similar to that of the non-ASEAN Asian NICs. As ASEAN is no longer relying on being a primary goods exporter its interest in the product market aspects of 1992 is significant. Even Indonesia and the Philippines have recently begun to implement long-run strategies of export-led growth by means of promotion of manufactured exports, facilitation of direct investment, competitiveness campaigns, deregulation and some liberalisation. This tends to raise the sensitivity in ASEAN about future restraints or rising costs of market access to the Community due to 1992.

At the aggregate sector level (one-digit SITC) the changing export composition of ASEAN would seem to indicate a gradual shift from *inter*-industry EC–ASEAN trade to *intra*-industry trade (ITT). As shown in Schmitt-Rink and Lilienbecker (1990), this apparent characteristic of the exchange vanishes at the three-digit SITC level more clearly for textiles and clothing than for electronics (electronics other than computers and audio-video may reach ITT ratios up to 0.44 for 1988). Specialisation between the EC and ASEAN is still largely 'vertical', and accords with what one would expect from a neo-factor proportions theoretical perspective of the international division of labour.

7.3   The external dimension of 1992: a confusing debate downplaying the benefits?

A general treatment of the 'external dimension' is beyond the scope of this chapter (see among others Beuter and Pelkmans 1989; Pelkmans 1990; Page 1990). This section will be limited to a few general, but frequently overlooked, points and a survey of the main issues.

A proper understanding of 1992 and its external dimension requires a clear distinction between existing trade policies of the Community and the external aspects of the 1992 programme. In formal terms there is no connection between the two. In material terms they may be related in two ways. First, and by far the most frequently encountered, third countries are interested in future access to the EC market, and it is immaterial for them to distinguish the policy origin of measures that may impede access or make it more costly. Of course, this is a valid instance of positioning from a third country's point of view. Nevertheless, it leads to discussions about '1992' which go beyond the well-defined purpose of the '1992' programme. It is not a primary aim of the White Paper nor the Single Act to alter trade policy as such.

Second, and little recognised, let alone given an adequate treatment in terms of political economy, 1992 is so sweeping and broad in (sectoral) scope that it is capable of loosening or undermining old coalitions – based on such factors as entrenched positions, regulation, other protection, even monopoly rights – which kept long-prevailing protection in place. In doing so, it unexpectedly contributes greatly to a new and more vigorous free(r) trade orientation of the Community, consistent with the pro-market and liberalising spirit of 1992 as a programme. Thus, the EC has (unilaterally) removed a large number of national quotas in three tranches in 1989 and 1990. The EC is pursuing a vigorous policy to employ world standards,[3] as the basis for the thousands of European standards to be agreed. Neither Japan nor the United States has ever seriously pursued this road, even though the GATT Code calls for it. Thus, in some sensitive dossiers such as telecom terminal equipment and cars, the EC has opted for free trade (subject to non-discriminatory certification, which in itself is also a gain), thereby breaking open the deeply entrenched positions of many national players. In the car case the surprise is not that previously protected producers attempt to prolong the transition period and stagger the opening up by arguing foɪ inclusion of the output of 'transplants' into the quota (or VERs) but that the national quantitative restrictions will have to go! Before the '1992' programme was embraced national quantitative car protection remained an untouchable taboo.

A survey of the external dimension rapidly becomes unmanageable in view of the very broad scope and technical detail of 1992. It is useful to concentrate on the products and services markets, but there is a cost to it: domains such as property rights, company law, merger control and some labour market issues as well as immigration and border checks on persons will be neglected.

Products and services markets are subjected to horizontal and vertical 1992 legislation. The major horizontal domains are border control issues, technical barriers, indirect taxes and public procurement. All these categories, however, have sector-specific aspects to them as well, which complicate the impact-assessment considerably. Examples include the specifics of border controls for the various modes of transport, the high specific nature of (the removal of) technical barriers even in the 'new approach', the excise taxes in the fiscal dossier and the 'excluded sectors' in public procurement.

The vertical measures are numerous. In product markets, agricultural products assume a special place due to the ambitious and technical programme to remove veterinary and phyto-sanitary barriers. Health issues are the most sensitive of all regulatory issues and hence the requirements that have to be met before removing intra-EC border controls altogether are severe. They include adequate, reliable and permanent controls in the country of origin and adequate financial compensation mechanisms for farmers when massive slaughtering is imposed by the EC. The upshot will be a rise in health standards in some EC countries, but it would be wrong to conclude that this will reduce the 'comparative advantages' of these countries in the common market. The *ex-ante* situation is simply that they cannot export, unless they guarantee the standards of the destination country. The assumption is that the health requirements are broadly supported by the population, and hence 'codify' the demand of the well-informed consumer; in other words, where health is important, well-informed consumers would not demand low standard plant or animal products. Therefore, after certification and inspection systems have become equally ambitious in the EC, they will facilitate intra-EC exports especially for those countries. To extend these control systems to third countries is demanding, but (as the US case demonstrates) is not impossible. However, it does require detailed and permanent co-operation (if not harmonisation) with respect to requirements, inspection and certification. A different question altogether is whether, in general, health requirements go up in the EC; this issue would seem to go beyond 1992 as such.

In industrial markets a useful distinction can be made between GATT-controlled issues and 'beyond-GATT' issues. The most important issue by far in the former group is that of national quantitative protection, especially in textiles and clothing, footwear, cars and consumer electronics. In addition, in so far as technical barriers fall under the GATT Code, the specific sectoral impact may be important for, say, ASEAN (for example, toys and jewellery; perhaps some machines; electrical/electronic equipment subject to 'electro-magnetic compatibility' because they might degrade performance or cause interference).

In the 'beyond-GATT' field the sectoral impact of public procurement in the 'excluded sectors', viz. public transport, supplies to utilities and to telecom administrations and the reciprocity provisions are a major issue. To the extent that the removal of technical barriers goes beyond the (very modest) GATT Code it would also have to be classified here.

GATT does not (yet) play any role with respect to services. The key areas to single out for an understanding of the external dimension include financial services (banking, insurance and securities), telecom services and all (six) modes of transport but especially maritime, road haulage and civil aviation.

Even if one excludes the 1992 measures in the factor markets, the impact on direct investment and various forms of inter-company collaboration ('alliances') between 'insiders' and 'outsiders' would appear to be too important to be ignored.

Beyond this question, one enters highly speculative issues such as the external effect of the greater competitiveness of EC firms in terms of costs, quality and innovation. The stylised simulation in the Cecchini Report (EC 1988), based on the realisation of cost savings, leads, *ceteris paribus*, to a reduction of extra-EC imports (of manufactures) up to 10 per cent. Clearly, if one is sceptical about the Cecchini results, then one can be less pessimistic about this import reduction caused by greater EC cost competitiveness. This chapter will not go into the calculations based on import demand elasticities and expectations of macroeconomic growth. It has been done elsewhere (Kol 1989; McAleese 1990; and so on). These simple calculations concur in that the EC's augmented import demand in the medium run, caused by 1992-induced growth, would more than compensate the expected fall in imports due to improved competitiveness. However, this aggregate effect should be verified for sectors and regions, such as ASEAN.

7.4   Agriculture and food products

The 1992 effects on access to the single food market are relatively small. First, the nature of the CAP is hardly touched by 1992, although the level of prices is. The February 1988 decisions to double the Structural Funds were made possible by a mini-reform of the CAP, which is expected to exert – and indeed has already exerted – downward pressures on the EC price level. Since a reduction in the guaranteed EC price level will diminish the export subsidies for CAP products dumped on the world market, it must imply (*ceteris paribus*) a rise in the level of world prices. Whereas the impact on EC imports is probably negligible given the nature of CAP protection, the effect on world markets will be positive for food exporters and local food suppliers competing against imports from the EC. ASEAN may therefore enjoy some modest benefits from a (*ceteris paribus*) less depressed world market in temperate zone products. Its agricultural and food exports are, however, overwhelmingly of the non-competing kind, that is, tropical products. Thailand and Indonesia also export cassava (tapioca) which is a grain substitute for animal feedstock, but the true competitor here is the United States with its exports of soy beans and corn gluten to the EC.[4]

Second, the monetary compensatory amounts (mcas) will be removed. According to Matthews and McAleese (1989) the switch-over system will gradually be abolished, which should decrease the level of protection in the medium term (if Germany is compensated temporarily).

Third, coffee and tea excise duties will have to go. ASEAN is a very modest exporter of coffee (Malaysia and Indonesia) and might benefit from an estimated increase in EC coffee imports of ecu 650 million (Davenport 1988) due to the removal of the high German coffee excise (41 per cent) as well as those of Denmark (15 per cent), Italy (9 per cent) and Belgium (6 per cent).

Fourth, some specific cases (such as bananas; seasonal quotas from Mediterranean countries on non-tropical products) will not affect ASEAN.

Fifth, the only major field where problems might perhaps arise is in the technical (health) regulations about food requirements and inspections. This field is not well surveyed from an economic point of view. For an appropriate evaluation – that is, not merely checking the few incidental complaints – enormous amounts of accessible information about health requirements in food are needed, as well as about their alternatives, costs and (social) benefits. Moreover, one should attempt to separate the '1992' effects from the very substantial regulatory provisions which existed already for processed agricultural products and food. All this is highly ambitious and, to my best knowledge, no such work would seem to be available. The key export products of ASEAN to pay attention to are vegetable oils (especially palm oil and coconut oil) and residues of such oil (such as bran and oil cake), processed vegetables, processed fruits and juices, canned pineapple and, less importantly, tobacco, dried fruits and nuts, cocoa, sugar and even cereals (Nieva and Faigal 1988). I suspect the 1992 impact to be marginal in processed agricultural products but not necessarily in fish and fish products (such as shrimps), where health problems arising from ASEAN imports have been observed repeatedly. One additional reason to expect no major changes is the prevailing case law on the mutual recognition of (non-essential) national provisions about food and drink. The Cassis-de-Dijon case law emerges from cases in food and many of its refinements.[5] The case law pre-dates the 1992 process, although 1992 has enhanced awareness, no doubt. Essential for ASEAN is the fact that Cassis-de-Dijon applies to ASEAN suppliers as well; were ASEAN to export beer to any EC country other than Germany, and legally market it there, it could then proceed to sell beer in Germany.

7.5 Industrial products

7.5.1 *GATT-controlled*

By far the most important issue here is quantitative protection. The problem having received most publicity is that of cars. ASEAN enjoys free access to the EC car market. Although Malaysia intends to boost its car exports, the volumes shipped hitherto are so small that this supply can be neglected for the next few years. This leaves textiles and clothing, footwear and consumer electronics.

ASEAN's interests in textiles and clothing exports to the EC are great. Detailed Commission proposals are not tabled yet because the MFA negotiations, tied this time to the Uruguay Round, are not complete. The 1992 requirement is clear: national quotas – and hence, Article 115, EC annual authorisations[6] – monitoring and statistical surveillance mechanisms for potentially sensitive MFA products at national level will have to be removed. There are in principle four possible solutions: (1) EC quotas (which do already exist and hence there should be no immediate fear of more restrictive joint quotas), (2) tariffication, (3) removal of national quotas without any substitution, and (4) VERs. Tariffication is considered too complex to negotiate. Also, one surmises that the protectionists like to cling to volume protection, given the at times extremely low cost levels of outside suppliers. Removal of quotas for categories, with consistent underutilisation of both national and EC quotas is feasible.[7] VERs are unlikely since the main reason for their frequent use – targeting one or only a few countries – is invalid in textiles and clothing. Moreover, compliance of VERs hinges on conditions which are not fulfilled in this sector: supplier companies are too numerous, the wholesale/retail linkages too flexible and off-shore processing rules too complicated. ASEAN should thus expect EC quotas for the sensitive categories.

If quotas remain as they are (ignoring here the traditional upward adjustment, usually 6 per cent a year, except for dominant suppliers), Davenport and Page (1989) expect EC imports to rise by perhaps 3.1 per cent to 5.2 per cent only on account of EC-1992. The reason is that the transfer restrictions for national quotas among EC countries fall away. Their simulation shows that Thailand and the Philippines would probably benefit most. The EC has already begun to reduce the restrictiveness of national quotas: in the case of dominant suppliers the permitted transfers for 1991 have gone up to 8 per cent; for other suppliers (like ASEAN) 16 per cent. Further augmenting these transfer possibilities would eventually remove the rationing effect and existing EC quotas would suffice.

Whether the EC will stop applying the MFA hinges first of all on the US position (which is more protectionist), and second, on the safeguard clause negotiations in the Uruguay Round. The internal EC problem is compounded by Iberian EC membership since this has dramatically reduced Spanish and Portuguese quantitative and tariff protection *vis-à-vis* third countries' textiles and clothing suppliers. Spain experienced increases of 82 per cent in 1987 and 75 per cent in 1988 of imports of clothing from non-EC sources; in textiles, the growth rates are 40 per cent and 30 per cent. The question is whether adjustment and improved competitiveness in the two countries may reduce these extreme import growth rates; if not, this would undoubtedly strain the liberalisation process.

The case of footwear is more simple. In the middle and lower market segments of leather footwear as well as all non-leather footwear EC industry is under heavy competitive pressure due to comparative disadvantages or (in the case of sports shoes, for example) late application of new technologies. Non-EC imports shot up by 69 per cent over the period 1985–8, with intra-EC imports stationary and consumption rising less than 2 per cent a year; hence the penetration rate (imports as a per cent of 'apparent consumption') rose very fast from 25.5 per cent (1985) to 42.8 per cent (1988). The inroads are especially made by China and East Asian NIEs. ASEAN's exports to the EC are still small (mostly Thailand), but Indonesia is currently investing heavily in the shoe industry for export purposes. It should not be forgotten, however, that in the upper leather segments the EC industry is an unchallenged market leader worldwide. EC producers increasingly turn to CAD-CAM and other results of the BRITE programme, as well as just-in-time methods in order to regain or maintain an edge over non-EC imports.

The threats for ASEAN would seem to be minor. If there is one, it would, curiously enough, arise from recent liberalisation by the EC! In footwear the EC traditionally maintained a large number of national quotas on imports from Eastern European countries, sometimes on all 'state-trading' ones. All quotas on Eastern Europe had been removed by mid-1990, which may soon lead to greater inroads of low value-added shoes from Eastern Europe, which may well further increase protectionist pressures. Eastern European export performance would certainly improve dramatically if joint ventures with or direct investment by EC firms would improve quality and marketing. The EC as a whole maintains VERs, with South Korea and Taiwan. Note however that Italy, France, Spain and Portugal maintain safeguard clauses, the application of which sometimes leads to Article 115 authorisations or VERs. The VERs in this splintered industry with its fragmented distribution are unstable, hard to monitor and generally short-lived. For this reason there is industry pressure for EC-wide quotas after 1992 but it is likely that the Community will prefer the VER method for dominant suppliers only. ASEAN is therefore unlikely to be hit. The problem for ASEAN might be a commercial one: as competition on the EC market heats up, making inroads will be harder.

In electronics three subsectors are of importance for ASEAN exports to the EC: semi-conductors, consumer electronics and telecom components (mostly) for terminal equipment. The first two subsectors are 'GATT-controlled', but in semi-conductors there are no aspects which properly apply to 1992 (origin rules are not related to the White Paper). Even in consumer electronics the few modest quota problems pale compared with other issues such as anti-dumping, (TV) standards and tariff reshufflings. The quotas (with occasional use of Article 115 authorisations) and VERs of Italy, France and Spain are all directed against Japan and the East Asian NIEs, not against ASEAN. The EC has already employed some common VERs *vis-à-vis* Japan and South Korea. The few national quotas left will probably be removed altogether as they have become irrelevant (for example, France on black and white TVs).

Other issues which are GATT-controlled include the application of the GATT standards code to the 'new approach' and other 1992 initiatives about technical barriers. Not only does this present few special problems, the cost savings and the liberalisation effects should be expected to be positive also for ASEAN.

7.5.2   Beyond GATT

Besides services – which are obviously 'beyond GATT' – the 'beyond GATT' items in the 1992 programme consist of public procurement in the 'excluded sectors' and a few issues in the field of technical barriers.

Public procurement among the previously excluded sectors is of importance for ASEAN with respect to telecom terminal equipment and components. For components there is free access since it is the suppliers[8] which source and purchase. The terminal equipment market falls outside the GATT Procurement Code. The 1992 programme has liberalised this market completely: since June 1990 an EC Directive has been in force requiring free competition in the sales of equipment to individual subscribers or companies, in installation and maintenance services. This applies to telephone sets, modems, telexes, data transmission terminals, PABX or branch exchanges, mobile phones and, if isolated, also to satellite receivers. Related Directives deal with the approximation of technical specifications of terminal equipment, including the mutual recognition of their conformity. ETSI (the European Telecommunications Standards Institute) will write the new EC-wide standards as well as the conformity testing requirements. The free competition in this huge and rapidly growing market extends fully to third countries. ASEAN could seize the opportunities here.

The remaining issues in technical barriers would seem to consist of two minor ones. First, the GATT Code has no provision on the harmonisation of the 'essential requirements' themselves. Thus, whenever the EC formulates Directives with 'essential requirements' there is little guarantee that they are not more demanding than the requirements that ASEAN exports might meet in the US or Japanese market. In the 1992 programme the EC has pledged to utilise world standards whenever they exist and conform to the 'essential health or safety requirements'. This may solve the issues of technical detail but not the more fundamental questions of harmonisation as reference-to-standards cannot supersede the obligation to adhere strictly to the 'essential requirements' in EC law. Whereas this is generally less of a problem in matters of safety (however, 'electro-magnetic compatibility' is a major exception), it is a major and perhaps increasing problem in matters of health as EC consumers and governments alike have become more and more critical of additives and other health issues. Second, higher standards may emerge, as a result of harmonising regulatory interventions in the context of 1992. Although this is not a systematic trend, some instances may cause problems for specific exporting countries. An example of great relevance to ASEAN is in jewellery.

The ASEAN interest is in 'real' jewellery (that is, with precious metals and precious stones), imitation jewellery and costume jewellery (the latter covers a larger spectrum of decorative items such as brooches and hairclips). For precious stones voluntary standards remain the unquestioned basis for trade; in costume jewellery there is a special problem of commercial property rights (marks and designs); both are not really affected by 1992. However, a 'new approach' draft directive is in the making, dealing with hallmarking, minimum gold carats requirements, test methods and advertising for jewellery. Moreover, an environmental draft directive on batteries will affect watches and the like. Finally, VAT rates on jewellery diverge enormously. The EC proposal will amount to self-hallmarking and a harmonised set of products for which this will be mandatory (non-compliance is fraud). Third countries will be treated identically but, since fraud must be effectively punishable, exporters will be required to appoint authorised representatives. Obviously this will inhibit small suppliers from ASEAN. Carat requirements would not seem to present problems for ASEAN (Asian traditions prescribe very high carats), rather for some EC countries. Test methods will be entirely based on ISO methods, although there is a sensitive issue of what precisely 'plating' is (3 microns of gold for jewellery and 5 microns for watches), which may affect competitiveness marginally.

The point is that the 'new approach' may sometimes raise average standards, although this does not necessarily have to mean a ban on imports (nor, incidentally, should it be condemned as such: an assessment of the information requirements for the consumer may justify minimum standards).

7.6 Services

Since services are 'beyond GATT' the key underlying issue is that of reciprocity. Giving 'national treatment' with respect to the right of establishment, ownership and the free provision of services is exceedingly rare in the world economy. Studying the examples of EFTA countries, Canada, Japan or Singapore which all pursue fairly restrictive services policies show the nature of the EC problem: liberalising far ahead of everybody else may lead to very unec ual possibilities for international expansion in services for EC-headquartered as compared to non-EC service providers. For certain modes of transport and financial services the discrepancy between the United States and 1992 is also considerable. In an age of globalisation of services, the sole granting of national treatment between the United States and the EC amounts to almost unrestricted access to the whole EC market for US service providers, without granting EC providers similar internationalisation opportunities in the US market.

The reciprocity debate has now passed the stage of Fortress Europe. In financial services reciprocity will not be applied retroactively, it will not mean mirror reciprocity but 'effective market access' and 'national treatment' together. For ASEAN two provisions are of importance: the degree of development will be taken into account and the removal of exchange controls will not be part of the assessment of 'effective market access'. The actual application of 'reciprocity' in financial services therefore will probably only hit Singapore as being (almost or fully?) developed. Singapore does restrict access in various ways and has been among the six countries mentioned by Sir Leon Brittan.[9] However, note that the presence of ASEAN's financial institutions in Europe is minimal at the moment.

Of the other services where 1992 plays a major role, by far the most important case for ASEAN is air transport (other ASEAN services will only marginally be affected by 1992). ASEAN airlines have emerged as major, low-cost, high-quality competitors to the larger OECD airlines. Their interest in the external dimension is three-fold:

1. the access to the internal market of scheduled services;
2. the impact of 1992 on the organisation of the world market for civil aviation;
3. the impact of the restructuring of EC (and EFTA) air transport on the competitiveness of EC airlines, and the emergence of Euro-mega-airlines.[10]

The external dimension will require renegotiation of Air Services Agreements (ASAs),[11] previously concluded between member states and third countries. Not counting Denmark, there are 609 such bilateral agreements. Moreover, other bilateral arrangements such as Memoranda of Understanding, Exchanges of Letters, Agreed Records, and such like also exist. Finally, almost all ASAs have confidential annexes on capacity and frequency, sometimes on tariffs and other aspects. At present the situation is merely being analysed and an internal EC debate has begun on the legal basis for external negotiations. It is therefore too early to foresee how these renegotiations will be conducted. In any event, one has to keep in mind that the main point for the Community will be – indeed 'must' be, from a Single Market point of view – to eliminate differences in access or competitive conditions between member states in their air transport with any particular third country X. In a number of cases, also – one presumes – in that of ASEAN, this will lead to adaptation of access, the introduction of 'gateways' to the EC and possibly the alterations of frequency and capacity specifications in existing bilateral agreements. Since air transport has extreme mercantilist traditions, one can understand the anxiety in ASEAN about the possibility of future power play by the EC when renegotiation begins. Moreover, there is a problem of competition policy and its extra-territoriality when intercontinental alliances of airlines are formed which may well create dominant positions on certain routes, or indeed major hubs, or with respect to distribution and marketing (for example, frequent-flyer tie-in arrangements; computer reservation systems).

7.7 Impact on direct investment

There is a well-established economics literature suggesting that successful market integration attracts direct investment (for a survey, see Balassa 1977). In ASEAN there is a fear that 1992 makes the Community so attractive to invest in that direct investment flows towards ASEAN will suffer. Some observers have even coined the term 'investment diversion', although this phrase may unfortunately suggest a parallel with trade diversion. Trade diversion, caused by regional integration, is welfare-decreasing for the world as a whole whereas 'investment diversion' has not been analysed in a theoretical framework, capable of showing welfare effects.

Five distinct arguments behind the fear for 'investment diversion' so often expressed in ASEAN can be identified:

1. *1992 will boost investment in Europe.* No doubt factually correct, it does not follow, however, that EC business will, or would need to, divert investible funds destined for ASEAN to Europe. If prospects are good in both regions – and they are – there should be no problem in financing sound projects in both regional markets. In the short run and only for firms beginning to reach beyond the EC, investment choices may be constrained by management and human resources bottlenecks as well as overall borrowing capacity: in such cases, if the EC option is chosen, the ASEAN one may temporarily be shelved. This assumes substitutability between the two investments. If local production in ASEAN is for ASEAN or Asia–Pacific market outlets, substitutability with an EC option tends to be low, irrespective of '1992'. If there are outward-processing or other intermediate exports back to Europe, substitutability is purely a matter of relative costs, but it is questionable whether this kind of investment is influenced by 1992.
2. *The EC-South, especially Spain and Portugal, compete with*

ASEAN for direct investment. Membership of Spain and Portugal was negotiated before the '1992' programme. Given relatively low wages and the prevailing industrial structure, Iberian exports are likely to compete with many manufactured export products from ASEAN. It is therefore possible that adjustment processes in the Community do not lead to exit from comparative disadvantage sectors but to relocation to Spain and Portugal, perhaps in some cases as an alternative to ASEAN. 1992 can augment this effect, especially because the doubling of the EC structural funds and their better management may improve the investment climate and infrastructure significantly. However, these intra-EC relocations constitute only a part of the spectacular increases in direct investment inflows into Spain and Portugal. In many instances the decisive motives for investment bear no relation to ASEAN: investors from EFTA, Japan, the United States and Canada, once having opted to invest in the EC because of 1992, frequently choose Iberia; EC investors expect sustained growth in the two countries for years to come and invest in marketing, distribution or local manufacturing if proximity to customers is critical; investment in the services sectors is strong and responds to the deregulation prompted by 1992 and opportunities arising therefrom. For all these reasons one would expect the possible substitution effect, if present at all, to be small for ASEAN. Finally, one should not forget that the rapid external liberalisation of Spain, as an EC member, has boosted imports from ASEAN and exerts great adjustment pressures: direct investment therefore will facilitate the necessary jumps up the ladder of higher value-added products, which are largely beyond the present export capacity of ASEAN, except for Singapore. In this sense the trade/liberalisation/investment nexus may actually benefit ASEAN as well as Spain and Portugal.

3. *Eastern Europe's opening will attract direct investments especially from the EC and EFTA.* The fear with respect to Eastern Europe is that the great needs for Western direct investment and technology can be equated with great opportunities. There is also a presumption that European business will be less interested in 'globalisation', which would reduce the interest in investing in ASEAN. Both fears cannot be taken for granted. EC business has been rather prudent about investing in Eastern Europe up to now and has certainly not diminished its interest in globalisation. 1992 has received strong business support precisely because it would improve home market conditions as well as competitiveness, with a view to better performance in global competition. Moreover, prospects for growth and profitability in Eastern Europe are

anything but bright in the short to medium run and highly uncertain in the longer run. Otherwise the points about substitutability mentioned before also apply here.

4. *The rapid* rapprochement *between the EC and the Mediterranean may also reduce the interest in investing in ASEAN.* Since the *rapprochement* is largely political and has not led to closer market integration, in the form of the free trade areas or (new) associations, this argument is far-fetched. What can be observed, however, is that Japanese and US firms invest in Mediterranean countries such as Turkey precisely because access to the EC is almost entirely free of barriers. The question is whether this investment is diverted from ASEAN.

5. *The Community has sometimes given the impression that 1992 might lead to a Fortress Europe in some sectors.* The main purpose would be to attract local manufacturing investment substituting for imports from NIEs and, of course, Japan. If this argument were correct, 'investment diversion' would indeed assume a meaning comparable to trade diversion: it would be welfare-decreasing for the world. Yet, the argument has probably no validity in the case of ASEAN. First, Fortress Europe is not caused by 1992. There are instances of prevailing EC trade policies (for example, specific origin rules; anti-dumping) which might have prompted Japanese and Korean firms to invest in the EC. On the other hand, 1992 tends to reduce EC protection in a number of important product markets and opens up the EC in services markets and public procurement, albeit that in the latter cases the access of outsiders may be improved less than that of insiders, due to reciprocity provisions. Second, even if there were instances of investment prompted by fears that 1992 would turn the Community into a Fortress, ASEAN would only lose out if US and Japanese production in ASEAN generates export flows to Europe which could be substituted by investment in Europe. However, this is typically not the case: US and Japanese multinationals in ASEAN export almost entirely to neighbouring Asian countries and to the home countries, frequently as intra-firm trade.

Therefore the assertion about investment diversion caused by EC-1992 or the transformation of Europe more generally is weak and largely unfounded. Apart from the specific reasons advanced earlier, two general arguments underscore this. First, direct investment depends on business prospects and profit expectations and they are excellent in ASEAN. Investible sums are not fixed, except in the very short run, hence business plans in ASEAN can be financed irrespective of 1992. Second, EC business has regained confidence and initiative and can be expected to grow more competitive worldwide. This development will accentuate tendencies of 'globalisation', which brightens the position of ASEAN for attracting direct investment from Europe.

The sensitivity to a reduction of EC direct investments in ASEAN has deep-seated reasons. Prominent among the anxieties is the domination of Japan in the region. With very rapid increases in trade among Pacific Rim countries, fuelled by large inflows of direct investment from Japan and a growing dependence on intra-firm trade between Japan and ASEAN, there is a fear of becoming a backyard of Japan which is ill-received for both political and economic reasons. Up to a point this dominance is a natural development. US direct investment is dominant compared to Japanese and European investment in Mexico and Canada; the EC is dominant in EFTA and the Mediterranean, and eventually will be in Eastern Europe. The ASEAN desire for 'balancing' has non-economic motives which may generate dissatisfaction if the objective is set at an unrealistic level, such as 'equality' of stocks of direct investment from the three main OECD markets.

7.8   A final word

There are several traditional trade policy issues which strain the relation of ASEAN with the Community such as the CAP, GSP – especially its complexity and exceptions – and the MFA. Anti-dumping cases *vis-à-vis* ASEAN countries have been rare up to now although there is concern about the EC's attitudes once export successes affect local business in the Community.

Compared to these major issues, 1992 is to be seen as a very positive development with great opportunities for ASEAN in some product markets as well as in air transport. The uncertainties about the precise restrictions in textiles and clothing and in footwear, as well as the uncertainty about standards in general create some anxiety however. In air transport, this anxiety is even greater as neither tradition nor the Chicago Convention (regulating air transport relations among nations) provides any guarantee for an open and liberal treatment. Since one cannot speak of one 'ASEAN air space' in any operational sense of the word, and since national 'hubs' and airline interests are not only complementary but also conflicting, it might prove very difficult for ASEAN to team up in the future negotiations with the EC.

Most important for ASEAN is that the EC becomes more open generally, especially since EC growth prospects are good compared to the past and better than those of the United States in the next few years. The 1992 processes contribute to these bright prospects which is crucial for the market opportunities ASEAN will wish to exploit.

Notes

1. Wagner (1990) reiterates the serious data problems leading to a misleadingly high share of EC investors in overall foreign direct investment in ASEAN: the great discrepancies between the widely published data on 'approved foreign investments' in the various ASEAN countries and the amounts actually realised later, with the realisation rates always below 50 per cent. Based on source country statistics the (incomplete) picture of EC direct investment shows that it lay far behind Japan and the US up to 1986/7. Later data are exclusively on an approval basis and show a rise in the EC share.
2. Issues relating to aid are not dealt with in this chapter.
3. Since the stock of world standards is decidedly incomplete for the purposes of 1992 and since they often contain compromise formulae, the adoption of world standards as EC standards can only take place where they exist and where their quality is sufficient for the 'new approach', that is for the 'presumption' to live up to the 'essential health and safety requirements' which allow the free movement of goods in the internal market.
4. Thailand is subject to a VER imposed by the EC since 1982 which, given the gap between EC grain prices and US substitutes on the one hand and the cost competitiveness of cassava on the other hand, provides room for large rents for Thai business; nobody else in the world imports cassava on a large scale.
5. For a survey, see Wyatt and Dashwood (1990, chapter 10).
6. See various essays in Volker (1987) for detailed explanations. The essence is that the authorisations to apply intra-EC border controls so as to enforce national quotas will no longer be given.
7. As early as 1986, during the MFA-IV negotiations, the EC launched this idea but failed to get it accepted by other importing countries in MFA.
8. Not the Telecom Administrations, except for servicing.
9. In a speech to the Bankers' Association in London in June 1990.
10. The paper limits itself to a few notes on the first question.
11. This must take place since access to bilateral routes is restricted to airlines from the EC country which have concluded the bilateral agreement. In a Single Market, however, every EC airline must in principle enjoy access to any route originating in the EC if it would wish to offer such services. Since the bilateral agreements prevent this access they must be renegotiated.

References

Balassa, B. (1977) 'Effects of commercial policy on international trade, the location of production and factor movements', in B. Ohlin *et al.*, *The International Allocation of Economic Activity* (5th edition, London: Macmillan).

Beuter, R. and Pelkmans, J. (1989) 'The external dimension of the internal market, a survey', Paper presented to EC–ASEAN Conference on 1992, Kuala Lumpur, July.

Davenport, M. (1988) 'EC trade barriers to tropical agricultural products', ODI Working Paper, 27 (London: Overseas Development Institute).

Davenport, M. and Page, S. (1989) 'Regional trading agreements: the impact of the implementation of the single European market on developing countries', Report to UNCTAD (London: ODI).

EC (1988) 'The economics of 1992', *European Economy*, no. 35, March.

Hiemenz, U. (1988) 'Expansion of ASEAN–EC trade in manufactures: pertinent issues and recent developments', *The Developing Economies*, vol. 26, 4, December.

Kol, J. (1989) 'The EC after 1992 and the developing countries' (in Dutch), *Economisch–Statistische Berichten*, 26 July.

Langhammer, R. (1989) 'The EC internal market and ASEAN–EC trade in services', in N. Wagner (ed.), *ASEAN and the EC, the Impact of 1992*, Singapore, ISEAS.

Matthews, A. and McAleese, D. (1989) 'LDC primary exports to the EC: prospects post 1992', Paper for The Hague Conference of Dutch Ministry of Foreign Affairs, October.

McAleese, D. (1990) 'The EC internal market programme: implications for the external trade', in N. Wagner (ed.), *ASEAN and the EC, the Impact of 1992*, Singapore, ISEAS.

Nieva, C. and Faigal, G. (1988) 'Processed agricultural products: issues for negotiation between ASEAN and the EC' in R. Langhammer and H. C. Rieger (eds), *ASEAN and the EC, Trade in Tropical Agricultural Products*, Singapore, ISEAS.

Page, S. (1990) 'Some implications of Europe 1992 for developing countries', paper presented at the OECD Development Centre, Paris, June.

Pelkmans, J. (1990) 'Completing the EC internal market: an update and problems ahead' in N. Wagner (ed.), *ASEAN and the EC, the Impact of 1992*, Singapore, ISEAS.

Schmitt-Rink, G. and Lilienbecker, T. (1990) 'An analysis of EC–ASEAN trade in textiles and electronics, 1980–8' in N. Wagner (ed.), *ASEAN and the EC, the Impact of 1992*, Singapore, ISEAS.

Volker, E. (ed.) (1987) *Protectionism and the EC* (revised edition, Deventer: Kluwer).

Wyatt, D. and Dashwood, A. (1990) *The Substantive Law of the EEC* (London: Sweet and Maxwell).

8

The implications of closer European integration for Australia and New Zealand[1]

David G. Mayes

8.1 Australia and New Zealand and their links with the European Community

The European Community is an important trade partner for Australia and New Zealand, taking 15 per cent of Australian exports and 18.5 per cent of New Zealand exports, while supplying 23.5 per cent and 18 per cent respectively of their imports. However, there has been a dramatic transformation during the 1950s, 1960s and 1970s away from the United Kingdom as the dominant partner (Tables 8.1 and 8.2) especially in the case of New Zealand where the United Kingdom's share of exports went from 66 per cent in 1950 to 13 per cent in 1980.

Japan is now the most important trading partner in both cases and the United States also has a substantial trade share. Trade between the two countries is also important for New Zealand, forming a fifth of the total (but only 5 per cent for Australia, reflecting the disparity in size of the two countries).[2] There is thus no dominant role for a single country in these trade flows although the rapid rise of Japan including associated direct investment does pose problems of absorption.

However, this trade pattern is not the result of the free play of market forces. The EC would form a much larger share of exports (and probably imports) if major exports were not subject to quota and tariff restraints. A third of Australian exports are manufactured products (Table 8.3) but two thirds are agricultural products or raw materials. Even within manufacturing, most of the products are processed foods or fairly simple products of the raw material (Figure 8.1). Only a little over 10% are manufacturers in the complex sense of the word. EC restrictions on agricultural products are even more important in the case of New Zealand.

Table 8.1   Australia: shares in total trade by country.

	Exports						Imports					
	United Kingdom	Rest EC	Japan	United States	New Zealand	Other	United Kingdom	Rest EC	Japan	United States	New Zealand	Other
1950	33.0	—	6.0	15.0	5.0	41.0[1]	48.0	—	2.0	8.0	—	42.0[2]
1960	19.0	—	17.0	10.0	6.0	48.0[1]	30.0	—	6.0	20.0	—	44.0[2]
1970	11.0	—	27.0	12.0	5.0	45.0[1]	21.0	—	14.0	25.0	—	40.0[2]
1980	4.7	8.7	26.6	11.7	4.7	43.6	9.3	12.9	17.1	21.8	3.4	35.5
1987	4.3	11.5	25.6	11.3	5.7	41.6	7.2	16.5	19.7	21.4	4.1	31.1
1988	3.6	11.1	27.1	10.7	5.0	42.5	7.4	16.1	20.1	21.7	4.4	30.3

Notes:
1. Includes 'rest of EC'.
2. Includes 'rest of EC' and New Zealand.

Sources: IMF, Direction of Trade Statistics. Vernon Report, vol. 2. Appendix K; Commonwealth Bureau of Census and Statistics. Overseas Trade.

Table 8.2 New Zealand: shares in total trade by country.

	Exports						Imports					
	United Kingdom	Rest EC	Japan	United States	Australia	Other	United Kingdom	Rest EC	Japan	United States	Australia	Other
1950	66.0	—	1.0	10.0	2.0	21.0	61.0	—	—	7.0	12.0	20.0[1]
1960	53.0	—	3.0	13.0	4.0	27.0	44.0	—	3.0	10.0	18.0	25.0[2]
1970	36.0	—	10.0	16.0	8.0	30.0	30.0	—	8.0	13.0	21.0	28.0[2]
1980	13.2	10.3	12.6	13.3	13.2	37.4	11.7	11.6	14.3	14.0	18.5	29.9
1987	9.5	12.4	16.2	15.0	15.7	31.2	9.8	13.3	18.7	15.6	20.3	22.3
1988	7.2	11.3	17.7	13.7	17.4	32.8	8.8	12.0	17.0	16.6	21.5	24.1

Notes:
1. Includes rest of EC and Japan.
2. Includes rest of EC.

Sources: New Zealand, Department of Trade and Industry and Department of Statistics; IMF, Direction of Trade Statistics.

A$bn, 1987

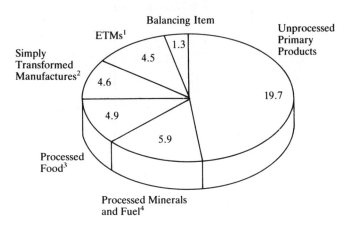

Total = A$40.9bn

Notes:
1. Elaborately transformed manufactures.
2. 48 per cent aluminium, 28 per cent other non-ferrous metals, 8 per cent chemicals, 8 per cent skins, tops = 90 per cent.
3. 47 per cent frozen/chilled meat, 15 per cent bulk raw sugar, 10 per cent dairy products = 72 per cent.
4. 46 per cent gold, 30 per cent alumina, 20 per cent refined petroleum = 96 per cent.

Source: PCEK/Telesis analysis of DFAT data. (Reproduced from Australian Manufacturing Council (1990).)

Figure 8.1 Composition of Australian goods exports.

The two countries are by no means the same in structure. Australia has the benefit of vast mineral wealth. New Zealand by contrast, although it has been extremely successful in diversifying its markets as shown in Table 8.2,[3] has been far less successful in diversifying its product range (with the possible exception of forest products) (Table 8.4). Thus we observe a highly specialised pattern of exports from Australia and New Zealand to the EC, largely based on the agricultural and raw material resources of the two countries and a series of niches which have been developed in particular areas of manufacturing (Tables 8.5 and 8.6).

Services trade is equally focused. Almost 80% of Australia's exports of services are transport and travel related, compared with 55% for OECD countries as a whole. This reflects the geographical isolation requiring heavier shipping costs to reach markets and a greater need for self-reliance on other services. It is important to recall the geographical structure of Australia itself: although 5–6 times the size of

Table 8.3   Australia: shares in total trade by commodity.

	Exports[1]				Imports[1]			
	0 + 1	2 + 4	3	5–9	0 + 1	2 + 4	3	5–9
1960					5.4[2]	8.1[2]	9.9[2]	76.6[2]
1970	30.1	34.4	4.8	30.7	4.8	6.8	6.6	81.8
1980	33.8	29.2	11.1	25.9	4.9	4.6	4.4	86.1
1987					4.8	3.8	4.0	87.4
1988	19.5	31.9	15.5	33.1	4.5	3.4	5.1	87.0
1989	20.8	30.7	14.8	33.7				

Notes:
1. SITC classification:
   0 Food and live animals.
   1 Beverages and tobacco.
   2 Crude materials, inedible, except fuels.
   3 Mineral fuels, lubricants and related materials.
   4 Animal and vegetable oils, fats and waxes.
   5 Chemicals and related products, not elsewhere specified.
   6 Manufactured goods classified chiefly by materials.
   7 Machinery and transport equipment.
   8 Miscellaneous manufactured articles.
   9 Commodities and transactions, not elsewhere specified.
2. 1963.

Sources: OECD, *Economic Surveys Australia*; OECD, *Foreign Trade*, Series A; Reserve Bank of Australia.

Table 8.4   New Zealand: shares in total trade by commodity.

	Exports[1]				Imports[1]			
	0 + 1	2 + 4	3	5–9	0 + 1	2 + 4	3	5–9
1980	46.7	28.1	1.2	24.0	5.4	5.7	22.6	66.3
1987	46.3	25.3	0.9	27.5	6.3	4.1	6.7	82.9
1988	43.9	26.6	1.4	28.1	7.2	4.7	5.4	82.7

Note:
1. SITC classification (for definitions see Table 8.3).

New Zealand in terms of GDP (194US$bn compared with 45US$bn in 1987), in many respects it is represented by the capital cities of the main states. In these terms New Zealand, with its concentration on Auckland, is not so unbalanced a competitor and transport costs from New Zealand to many Australian locations are actually lower than transport costs within Australia (Table 8.7). Hence, the basic market for which any Australasian firm produces is smaller in purchasing power than any of the member states except Luxembourg and yet the

Table 8.5 Australia: shares of trade with EC by commodity, 1988 (SITC classification).

	Total	0	2	5	6	7	8	Rest
Exports								
EC as % of total	15	5	22	4	11	20	16	15
category as % of								
total trade with EC	100	8	47	1	9	6	2	28
Imports								
EC as % of total	24	16	7	37	24	24	29	22
category as % of								
total trade with EC	100	3	1	13	15	40	18	11

Notes:
See notes to Table 8.3 for definitions.
Exports to EC in the category labelled 'rest' are mainly fuels (coal).

Source: OECD *Foreign Trade*, Series C.

Table 8.6 New Zealand: shares of trade with EC by commodity, 1988 (SITC classification).

	Total	0	2	5	6	7	8	Rest
Exports								
EC as % of total	19	21	29	12	5	7	8	4
category as % of								
total trade with EC	100	49	40	3	4	2	1	1
Imports								
EC as % of total	21	7	7	33	20	21	23	10
category as % of								
total trade with EC	100	2	2	21	19	39	15	3

Notes:
See notes to Table 8.3 for definitions.
A quarter of manufactured exports to the EC are leather, leather manufactures and dressed furskins.

geographical area as a whole is larger than the whole of Europe, including European Russia, put together. There is no hope that Australasian firms could gain the benefits of economies of scale from local markets that applied anywhere in Europe even before the 1992 programme. However, for most products transport costs are a fairly small percentage of the total cost so the absence of other barriers to trade within Australia means that the degree fragmentation is by no means complete.

Table 8.7 Index of freight rates between Australasian cities.

From/to	Dunedin	Christchurch	Wellington	Auckland	Hobart	Sydney	Melbourne	Brisbane	Adelaide	Perth
Dunedin	—	69–80	123–124	222–223	128–281	109–144	109–144	130–186	125–163	177–870
Christchurch	69–73	—	88–89	188–189	128–281	109–144	109–144	130–186	125–163	177–870
Wellington	126–127	62–92	—	100	128–281	109–144	109–144	130–186	125–163	177–870
Auckland	226–227	192	100	—	128–281	109–144	109–144	130–186	125–163	177–870
Hobart	141–374	141–374	141–474	141–374	—	126–217	89–158	140–231	121–196	160–230
Sydney	121–212	121–212	121–212	121–212	126–216	—	141–358	157–412	157–404	380–800
Melbourne	121–212	121–212	121–212	121–212	89–150	141–358	—	205–508	102–289	314–785
Brisbane	138–223	138–223	138–223	138–223	141–231	157–412	204–508	—	290–635	762–1010
Adelaide	136–223	136–223	136–223	136–223	122–196	157–404	102–289	291–635	—	280–510
Perth	144–238	144–238	144–238	144–238	159–219	377–796	314–785	760–1008	286–508	—

Butcher, G., 'Relative Transport Costs and CER', *Quarterly Predictions*, no. 77, March 1984, pp. 49–52. The index base is Auckland–Wellington = 100. It is computed on the basis of a load of 100 kg – one container. The interpretation is that to send freight from Dunedin to Sydney costs between 1.09 and 1.44 as much as the cost of sending the same load Auckland to Wellington. Note that a partial update of this table (1985) suggests that internal costs may be relatively higher and trans-Tasman costs relatively lower than in this 1983 table.

Source: Reproduced from *Closer Economic Relations*, Institute of Economic Research and Committee for Economic Development of Australia, 1985.

8.2   Routes of impact for Australia and New Zealand

In Chapter 1 we noted that both governments and firms in third
countries can play a role in the development of integration in the EC.
However, for governments to have much say they need bargaining
power and that is very limited for Australia and New Zealand, outside
the United Kingdom. It is not surprising, therefore, that they have
sought strength from combining with others, particularly through the
Cairns Group in the Uruguay Round negotiations and also with
discussions about wider arrangements round the Pacific Rim. They
have, of course, steadily developed their own closer relations, having
had a single labour market for a long time, developing a free trade
area and moving on to Closer Economic relations (CER), which are
now in their second phase.[4]

Firms also attain bargaining power from size, either from world size
or from being an important firm within the EC as a result of direct
investment. Australia has several such players, particularly in brewing,
with, for example, Elders, and in banking, with National Australia
Bank having a significant retail presence in the United Kingdom,
following the purchase of the Yorkshire Bank and Clydesdale Bank.
However, in general Australasian companies lack power in Europe.
Thus, as a result of this lack of national and firm bargaining power
their response must be largely reactive, taking the opportunities in
Europe as they see them and anticipating any increased competitiveness of European firms in Australasian and third country markets.
There also, of course, companies have the opportunity to gain market
share both by exporting and by direct investment.

There are clearly opportunities both for traders and investors but
given the remarks about lack of bargaining strength it is no surprise
that there have been some striking steps forward in the European
market by Australasian companies. Elders, AMP and National Australia Bank, for example, have proceeded by outright acquisition and
Brierley's IEP more by portfolio investment. However, such attempts
to enter the market are subject to control by European competition
authorities, in these cases those in the United Kingdom. Not all such
attempts are successful, that by Goodman Fielder Waltie to take over
Rank Hovis MacDougall failing when it was referred to the Monopo-
lies and Mergers Commission.[5]

In Chapter 1 the results quoted from Stoeckel *et al.* (1990) suggested
that gains for Australia and New Zealand from trade (investment was
not included) were likely to be small and that their sign was
ambiguous, the ambiguity depending upon the extent to which
European integration increased the size and growth of the EC market.

The greater that increase then the greater the chance of a favourable outcome. Investments in Australia which bring new technologies with them are explicitly welcomed in Australian industry policy.

Given this structural pattern, it is not surprising to see the conclusion that even if Australia and the EC were to go far further than the 1992 programme and both actually abolish all remaining tariffs on manufactures the calculated gains for Australian manufacturers would, according to Higgs (1990), amount to only A$35m (0.01 per cent of GDP). (It would only amount to A$100mn if Australia and the EC formed a free trade area and all other countries were excluded.)[6]

If Australia and New Zealand's major export categories are not included in any agreement then the 'benefits' from European integration largely pass them by. There may be some gain for the EC from substitution against other sources of manufactured imports in Australia and New Zealand. If agriculture is included in the tariff and quota removal Higgs's results change dramatically. The effect from increased Australian exports would be A$2bn (and between A$4.5bn and A$18.5bn in the implausible case of a free trade area) and a further A$4bn if coal[7] were also added. (More controversially, Higgs (1990) estimates a $A2.5bn gain to agriculture and resource exports from the unilateral removal of Australian tariffs and other protection on manufacturers.)

Since none of the proposed steps in European integration includes agriculture or coal,[8] then the only vestige of hope for Australia and New Zealand in getting an improvement in the impact of European integration lies in the increasing pressure on EC funds, which may emerge within the EC to offset the problems of convergence, forcing a relaxation of the CAP.

In Chapter 1 the following groups of measures in the 1992 programme were identified which can have an impact on third countries.

Frontier restrictions
    single country quotas
    voluntary restriction agreements
    removal of formalities
Technical barriers
    common standards
    single certification and testing
Market entry
    public procurement
    right of establishment
    takeover/merger

Freedom of movement of persons
Other market regulations
  e.g. transport, financial services
Fiscal (VAT, Corporation Tax, etc.)
Financial (state aids, capital markets, etc.)

On the whole these do not have a special impact for Australasian firms, although it was noted that the setting of health and phytosanitary standards could act as an effective means of protection where similar products were not grown or produced on a wide scale in Europe.

It is easy to consider these issues from only one direction. Once the concept of 'reciprocity' is raised then the bargaining position of Australia and New Zealand becomes more difficult because trade and other regulatory barriers have characterised their economies.

In particular, openness of public procurement – and indeed markets in general – is a rather sensitive point for Australia and New Zealand. They have been among the most restrictive of all the OECD countries[9] (Figure 8.2), but the trend has been steadily downwards during a period when the trend has been upwards elsewhere in the world (Figure 8.3). Nevertheless, granting reciprocity would pose considerable problems for both countries. Public procurement restrictions run deep in Australia, particularly with the activities of the states. New Zealand has abandoned a wide range of these restrictions and not having a federal structure might find reciprocity easier to apply.

Reciprocity over competitive conditions within Australia and New Zealand is rather easier to offer as both countries have strong legislation (the New Zealand Commerce Act and the Australian Trade Practices Act) and a leaning towards the active promotion of competition associated with the United States. Their companies are, therefore, open to foreign investment although the degree of involvement may be limited. Even in the case of the sale of New Zealand's state-owned enterprises there have been substantial foreign involvements.[10]

The second area of possible benefit comes in the form of state aids, which are heavily restricted in the Single Market to ensure equal treatment of companies from all member states. No such restrictions apply to third countries except those which might be caught under anti-dumping rules of the GATT. Although such aids have been widespread in Australia and New Zealand they are being rapidly reduced. Indeed, New Zealand is clearly the most rapidly 'deregulating' country in OECD and little now remains of the previous intervention. Thus, if anything, its companies lose support relative to those in the EC rather than vice versa as could be the case. (Of course, the whole point of deregulation is to increase economic efficiency and

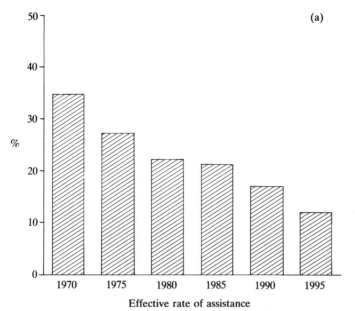

Effective rate of assistance

Source: IAC (1988); Bates and White (1988) (reproduced from Stoeckel *et al.* 1990).

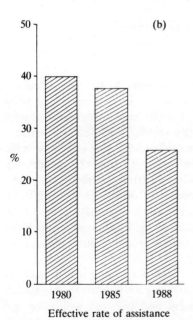

Effective rate of assistance

Source: IAC (1988); Bates and White (1988) (reproduced from Stoeckel *et al.* 1990).

Figure 8.2 (a)   Australia's declining industry assistance, including non-tariff. (b) New Zealand's declining industry assistance, including non-tariff.

1981 = 100

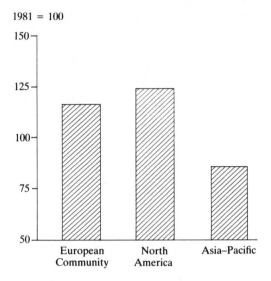

Source: UNCTAD (1989); World Bank (various publications); Centre for International Economics estimates based on extrapolation of known changes for countries cited in the text (reproduced from Stoeckel *et al.* 1990).

Figure 8.3   Trends in non-tariff barriers in the three regions.

if successful this will be of far greater benefit to New Zealand exporters. This gain is qualified because it is not yet clear what non-traditional activities which do not benefit from a degree of natural monopoly can be undertaken efficiently within New Zealand because of its small size. There have been notable success stories in specific areas, such as vegetable-peelers and scissors, but the productive economy only now appears to be picking up from the recession of the second half of the 1980s. The unpopularity of the results of these policies was undoubtedly a major factor in the government's loss of the 1990 general election, although its successor has continued in much the same vein, extending action to the labour market and tighter (and equally unpopular) budgetary controls.)

Adding these various factors together, the net competitiveness effect of the Internal Market seems to be clearly negative for most Australian companies, although some like insurers and brewers will have improved access and those whose business is transport and distribution can benefit from market growth. In so far as reciprocal removal of restrictions cuts costs and removes distortions there will be further gains. The crucial question, however, is the extent to which the

European market expands as it is this which provides the possibility of a clear net gain to third countries.

Further steps in widening the EC or indeed in assisting problems of convergence of member states under Economic and Monetary Union could provide problems for Australia and New Zealand in so far as they assist yet further countries to compete in their traditional product markets. The more direct the help and the more it is focused on agriculture then the greater the possible problem.

8.3 Concluding remarks

So what does this imply for Australia and New Zealand? What trade strategies should they follow? How should the EC react?

The current steps in closer European integration – the completion of the internal market, economic and monetary union and the broadening of the European Community to include members of EFTA and Eastern/Central European countries – are widely presented as an opportunity for all to gain. For major trade partners, those enjoying favourable treatment or having strong bargaining power this may well be true. But for Australia and New Zealand this is largely an irrelevance. A few, principally larger, firms may have an opportunity to expand but the net effect is likely to be small and it depends very much on the success of the European Community in increasing its growth rate. With its small domestic markets, developed economies and remoteness from Europe Australasia is worst placed to benefit.

In many respects it is investment which offers the way forward as much as trade, aided by the fact that the liberalisation of capital flows under the terms of the Single Market applies to all flows and not just those within the EC. Australasian investment in Europe will permit participation in the growth potential of Europe in the 1990s, while return investment would help develop the competitive industries that those countries need to continue to prosper in a discriminatory world.

However, from the point of view of Australia and New Zealand Europe is not tackling the relevant trade barriers which it has erected, namely those relating to agriculture and other resource-based products. Indeed, widening of the Community may make matters worse. The extent of the harm these barriers have caused in Australasia and the welfare losses they also cause within the EC have featured little in the discussion of the external impact in the development of the EC in Europe.

There is one source of hope in that closer integration of existing members and widening to include Eastern European countries involves considerable use of structural and regional funds within the EC. Given a reluctance to increase the overall size of the Community Budget this will put increasing pressure on the CAP, as the major expenditure, to ease the problem. However, it is unlikely that any such steps will unwind more than a small proportion of the registrations. Progress so far in the GATT negotiations on agriculture under the Uruguay Round has been limited although the EC does appear to have eased its position somewhat. Agreement, if it does occur, usually tends to come with a rush at the end of the negotiating timetable so there may be some hope.

In turn Australia and New Zealand have highly protected manufacturing sectors. Indeed, both governments have realised that much of this protection has been excessive and are in the middle of a programme of reduction. There is, however, very considerable controversy over how far the reductions should go because many industries may not be viable in open competition and it is not clear where alternative sources of employment could come from. However, the main argument that has been used in New Zealand against continuing the programme of protection reduction is not lack of viability of New Zealand industries but the observation that this process does not occur in competitor countries.[11] Since exports of the main products in which Australia and New Zealand have a comparative advantage are both price and quantity constrained there is limited scope for substitution. Nevertheless, there are industries for which small size and distance are not a great disadvantage, particularly those which involve substantial human skills and a high value to weight ratio. Both countries are in a good position to develop those skills.

The Australian Manufacturing Council (1990) has recently proposed a balanced programme of reduced protection, encouragement of efficient production and change and the fostering of industries which could become internationally competitive. All this argument over the particular inefficient second-best solutions could be largely set aside if the main distortion were removed namely, the discrimination against Australian and New Zealand's main exports by the world's richest countries in Europe, North America and Japan.

In the meantime, it is clearly a sensible strategy to continue to develop the Closer Economic Relations between the two countries to eliminate unnecessary barriers in their own markets and exploit what local economies of scale and cost reductions they can. It is also sensible for them to continue to seek international support for their trading interests from countries round the Pacific as those countries together form an economic force that even an enlarged European Community has to take notice of. Whether such agreements will also lead directly to great gains for Australia and New Zealand from intra-area trade is more debatable. It is their external impact which is of prime importance, particularly if the Uruguay Round achieves little to help and there is a move back towards the bilateral deals between the major trading areas which became increasingly popular in the late 1980s.

Notes

1. I am grateful to Albert Meyer for research assistance and to Alan Bollard, Andrew Britton, Geoff Mason, Jon Stanford and Bob Webb for comments and advice.
2. The combination of difference in product structure and the much greater importance of the Australian market to New Zealand than vice versa has a consequent impact on trade policy.
3. It was smart enough to anticipate the highly adverse impact of UK membership of the EC on its agricultural exports and sought new markets in the 1960s, not just in the 1970s when change was forced upon it.
4. These arrangements are discussed in detail in Mayes and Bollard (1992). They represent more than a free trade area in manufactures but fall a long way short of the degree of integration proposed in Europe. Attempts to extend CER into services have been difficult, non-tariff barriers abound and although currency union has been raised as an issue it is a long way off serious negotiation.
5. This emphasis on the United Kingdom is not, of course, coincidental and represents a sensible strategy because entry is easiest in the United Kingdom, first because of the openness of the system, which makes acquisition of companies rather easier but second, because the use of English in running the company which is acquired means that the most appropriate staff can be sent from head office or other operations to run the new enterprise, without regard to language. It also tends to reduce the degree of culture clash between the two parties.
6. Our own simulations with the Oxford Economic Forecasting model of the Australian economy (Burridge *et al.* 1991) suggest that the Australian economy is much more sensitive to changes in EC manufacturing demand and competitiveness. Nevertheless, the changes involved at around A$1bn are well short of the shifts quoted for agriculture.
7. These gains come entirely from ending protection for German and UK coal suppliers.
8. It remains to be seen how much privatisation of the UK electricity industry is going to affect imports of coal into the United Kingdom. Currently National Power and PowerGen have agreed contracts with British Coal over the next three years but the position could change thereafter as imported coal can not only be cheaper but of a lower sulphur content, thus enabling emissions targets to be met with less need for expensive investment in desulphurisation equipment. However, this is all largely separate from the main thrust of European integration.
9. The protection is heavily concentrated in Australia, with effective rates of 190 per cent on motor vehicles, 168 per cent on clothing and footwear and 74 per cent on textiles, compared with nearer 15 per cent as an average (AMC 1990). The figures shown in Figure 8.2(b) for New Zealand refer just to manufacturing and to trade barriers alone. Other forms of industry assistance are not included so the effective rates were actually higher than those shown.

10. For example, Telecom has been sold to American interests, around half the forests to Japanese, Hong Kong and Malaysian interests, State Insurance to British, the Post Office Savings Bank and New Zealand Steel to Australian and Air New Zealand to a consortium including Australian, American and Japanese owners.
11. This may not of course be logical as unilateral tariff reduction may still be the optimal policy from the point of view of resource allocation.

References

Australian Manufacturing Council (1990) *The Global Challenge: Australian Manufacturing in the 1990s* (Melbourne).

Bates, W. and White, E. (1988) *Industry Assistance Reform in New Zealand* (Wellington).

Burridge, M. *et al.* (1991) 'Oxford Economics Forecasting's System of Models,' *Economic Modelling*, July.

Cecchini, P. (1988) *The European Challenge 1992: The Benefits of a Single Market* (Aldershot: Wildwood House).

Higgs, P. J. (1990) 'Australia's Foreign Trade Strategy', Working Paper 12, University of Melbourne School of Management.

Industries Assistance Commission (1988) *Annual Report* (Canberra).

Stoeckel, A., Pearce, D. and Banks, G. (1990) *Western Trade Blocs* (Canberra: Centre for International Economics).

9

The implications of the EC for Australian trade and industrial policy in the 1990s

Jon Stanford

Once upon a time, Australia was very much an ex-colonial power whose foreign and economic policies were dominated by the influence of Britain. Australia could produce food much more cheaply than Britain, and so her export base was heavily biased towards agricultural products and the British market. Britain, on the other hand, special-ised in manufactured exports, and Australia and other countries of the Empire gave preferential access to British products. Both Britain and Australia benefited from this Ricardian approach. Britain gained cheap food and a market for its exports, while Australia was allowed to specialise in line with its comparative advantage in a world where trade in agricultural products was heavily circumscribed by restrictions. This halcyon time ended, at least as far as Australia was concerned, when Britain decided its future lay in Europe. On Britain's accession to the EC in 1973 barriers to Australia's agricultural exports were erected. The provisions of the Common Agricultural Policy led to Australia's efficient production of meat, cereals and most dairy products being virtually excluded from the European market.

In the 1970s and 1980s various EC missions visited Australia and generally gave short shrift to the complaints about their protectionist policies. They had two stock replies. The first of these was that Australia should accept protection of agricultural industries as an unfortunate fact of life and that we should 'find other markets'. Of course, Australian farmers had worked this out for themselves and were quite successful at finding other markets, in Asia and the Middle East. While 33 per cent of Australia's merchandise exports went to the United Kingdom in 1950, by 1990 this figure had fallen to 3.5 per cent.[1] Unfortunately, the playing-field in these new markets did not remain level for long. Not surprisingly, the CAP's system of subsidies led to overproduction, and the EC began a massive programme of export subsidies to dispose of the agricultural surpluses it had created. As well as excluding Australian produce from its domestic market, therefore, the EC proceeded to undercut Australia in the new markets it had developed by dumping its surpluses. Although it was a much more efficient producer than the EC, Australia then found itself unable to compete in many of the world's agricultural markets.

The second riposte from the EC was nearer the bone. It asserted that Australia, with one of the highest levels of industrial protection in the OECD, should not throw stones at other glasshouses. The message was: 'When you reduce your protectionist barriers to our industrial products we may start talking about agriculture.' Australia had not generally participated in the various postwar 'rounds' of multilateral tariff cuts, because of the exclusion of agriculture, and as is shown below it had one of the highest levels of industrial protection in the OECD by the early 1970s. Australian governments have recognised in recent years, however, that protection was retarding rather than enhancing industrial development. As a consequence, some very substantial reductions in barrier protection have occurred, commencing with the 25 per cent general tariff cut in 1973. While Australia announced unilateral cuts in protection of 60 per cent between 1988 and 1991, however, the EC has increased protection to its agriculture in recent years.

This summary of trade relations between the EC and Australia is admittedly oversimplified and it fails to acknowledge the multifaceted nature of the trade and investment relationship. Nevertheless, it illustrates the importance of the economic and trade policies of the European Community for Australia's welfare. EC protectionism in the past has led to Australians (as well as Europeans, of course) enjoying a lower standard of living than they otherwise would have done. The future direction of EC economic policies is of vital importance to other trading nations, and particularly to nations such as Australia, which depend less on manufactured exports (where EC trade barriers are lower) than most other developed countries.

If taken literally, the title of this chapter requires the author to make a number of predictions about future events in both of the world's hemispheres. This is clearly a menu for an indigestible repast for a paper of this nature, so it must be broken down into more manageable courses. A brief description of Australia's present economic situation and trade orientation is contained in section 9.1. The next section addresses some of the possible developments in Europe in the present decade which are important to Australia's well-being. These include not only 1992 and the Single Market, but also trade and competition policies and the implications of the changes in Eastern Europe. Section

9.3 discusses how Australian trade and industrial policy is likely to respond to the changes in Europe in the next few years in the context of recent policy developments.

9.1   Australia's economic situation and trade orientation

9.1.1   *Current account and foreign debt*

Since the mid-1980s, Australia's economic policy has been dominated by the weakness of its current account and the consequent accumulation of foreign debt. Between 1981–2 and 1990–1, the current account deficit averaged 4.8 per cent of GDP, far higher than the figure for any other OECD country. In the first half of the 1980s this deficit was associated with a rapid build-up in foreign indebtedness, with net foreign debt being equivalent to 31.5 per cent of GDP in 1985–6. It was widely expected in the mid-1980s that unless the deficit was rapidly reduced, the debt ratio would be over 50 per cent by the early 1990s. In fact this has not occurred, and the net debt to GDP ratio was 34.5 per cent in 1990–1. The debt-servicing ratio has increased, however, from 16 per cent of export income in 1985–6 to 20.2 per cent in 1989–90, before falling back under the 20 per cent mark in 1990–1.[2]

Although the debt is predominantly private – which raises some interesting economic issues as to whether it is a question for public policy at all – the government has taken the view that policy needs to recognise that the current account deficit is not sustainable at present levels. Unless some action is taken to reduce it, the eventual adjustment when imposed by the markets is likely to be even less pleasant than the life of Hobbes's ancient man – nasty and brutish, but also uncomfortably lengthy. All arms of economic policy have therefore been directed in varying degrees to the debt-stabilisation goal. The objective of macroeconomic policy has been to tread a delicate path between providing a sound environment for investment without increasing consumption to the extent of compromising the external balance. The loosening of monetary policy which followed the Crash of 1987 (as in many other countries) tended to upset this balancing act, with the result that merchandise imports increased by 23.5 per cent (constant prices) in 1988–9.[3]

One aim of policy is to increase exports both absolutely and in terms of their share of GDP. Associated with this is the desire to place a lesser reliance for export income on raw commodities, which are subject to large price fluctuations, and a greater emphasis on exports of both services and manufactured goods. Particular emphasis is placed on complex, or elaborately transformed, manufactures, which constitute the fastest growing area of world merchandise trade. What has been the outcome? As is shown in Figure 9.1, manufactures (using a balance of payments definition which excludes, for example, slightly processed minerals) have increased their share of exports from around 12 per cent to 16 per cent in a decade. While this may not seem significant, it does represent an increase in share of around one third over that period. Exports of agricultural commodities fell from commanding a 43 per cent share of total exports at the beginning of the 1980s to a little over 30 per cent one decade later.[4] It needs to be pointed out that this decline may overstate any underlying shift in comparative advantage because of the great increase in the barriers to agricultural trade in the 1980s.

Together with the greater emphasis on increasing exports in recent years and on achieving some change in their composition has gone a recognition that the greatest trade opportunities may lie in Australia's own region, which is, after all, the fastest growing and most dynamic in the world. In the context of the discussion of Australia's relations with the EC and its effect on her domestic policies, it is interesting to note how various trends in Australia's level and pattern of trade have developed.

Despite the rapid growth in Australia's trade with its regional trading partners (see below), Australia is still less of a trading force in

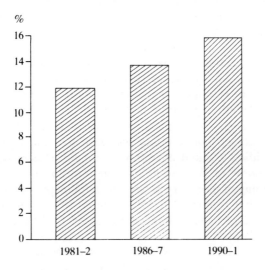

Source: Australian Bureau of Statistics (1991, Table 3.3).

Figure 9.1 Australia: manufactured exports as per cent of total exports, 1981–2 to 1990–1.

the Asia–Pacific region than would be expected, given her relative size and GDP. As may be seen in Figure 9.2, which provides data for 1989, several smaller economies than Australia account for a higher proportion of regional trade, particularly Hong Kong (which with approximately a quarter Australia's GDP accounts for a regional trade share over twice as large), Taiwan, South Korea and Singapore. This relatively low share of regional trade is likely to reflect to a large degree Australia's low share of trade generally in GDP, rather than any bias against trading in the region, although it is true that many Australian companies still feel more comfortable trading in the traditional anglophone markets of Britain and the United States. Nevertheless, the ASEAN countries as a bloc, and indeed several of them in their own right, constitute a much more powerful regional trading entity than Australia.

Another question to be addressed is the extent to which Australia has redirected its exports away from traditional markets and towards the rapidly expanding economies in its region. By the beginning of the 1970s, Japan had become Australia's major trading partner, taking 28

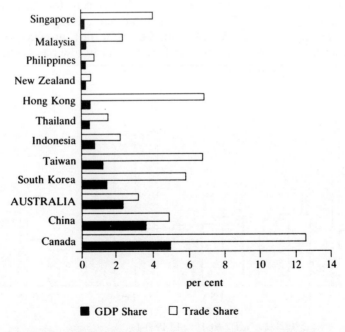

■ GDP Share   □ Trade Share

Source: Bollard and Mayes (1991, pp. 4 and 37). The United States and Japan have been excluded. Canada's trade share is boosted by its trade with the United States.

Figure 9.2 Share of Asia–Pacific trade and GDP.

per cent of exports. The countries which now make up the EC12 together accounted for one-fifth of Australian exports, while the ASEAN countries purchased less than 7 per cent (Figure 9.3). In 1990–1, Japan's share was very much the same as two decades earlier and the United States had declined only marginally in importance. The biggest change was that the EC's share of Australian exports had fallen markedly. To a large extent, however, this was a one-off phenomenon due in no small part to the United Kingdom's accession to the Community in 1973. During the 1980s the EC's share of Australian exports was maintained.

The other interesting feature of Figure 9.3 is the increasing importance of the ASEAN market. Within Australia's top twenty export markets (by value) in 1990–1, the six fastest growing markets over the last five years are shown in Table 9.1. Although Switzerland takes first place in this table, the growth is deceptive to the extent that it occurred from a very low base. Apart from Switzerland, therefore, the ASEAN countries provided the fastest growing export markets for Australia. Over the same five-year period, export growth to EC countries was relatively slow, for example, 5.1 per cent for the United Kingdom, 0.2 per cent for Germany, 1.8 per cent for Italy and −4.0 per cent for France. Of course, this trend may be slightly deceptive to the extent that the ASEAN market is a fast growing one, and Australia's exports again took off from a fairly low base. The EC by contrast constitutes a very mature market.

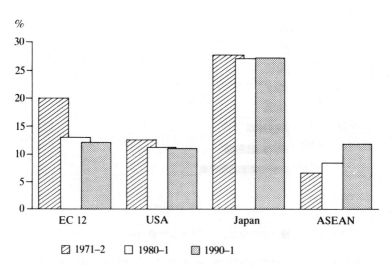

Source: Australian Bureau of Statistics, Cat. No. 5424.0.

Figure 9.3   Australia's main export market.

Table 9.1 Six fastest growing
Australian export markets
(five years to 1990–1).

Country	Average annual % growth
Switzerland	39.8
Singapore	35.8
Thailand	32.0
Indonesia	29.1
South Korea	21.7
Philippines	18.4

Source: Australia, Department of
Foreign Affairs and Trade (1991,
p. 21).

Nevertheless, the recent trend is clear. In 1990–1 Australia's exports to the EC fell by 8 per cent to a total of A$6.3 billion in current values. Exports to the ASEAN 6, however, rose by 27 per cent to the same total, A$6.3 billion.[5] The relative importance of imports from the two regions tells a different story, however, with Australia importing A$10.7 billion of merchandise from the EC in 1990–1, but only A$3.5 billion from ASEAN. Australia therefore has a very large trade deficit with the EC as a whole, and indeed a deficit with every individual EC country except for Benelux.

A somewhat similar pattern can be observed in Australia's trade in tourism services. In 1975, 20 per cent of Australian tourists went to Asian destinations and 33 per cent to European ones. By 1990 these percentages had changed to 35 and 23 respectively.[6] Tourism has been one of Australia's growth industries in recent years, and the data on inward tourism show that the greatest growth has been recorded in inbound tourism from Asia. This is shown in Figure 9.4.

The shift in trade emphasis away from Europe and in favour of Asia is mirrored to some degree in the data for investment flows. Britain has traditionally provided the bulk of foreign investment in Australia. In 1973, for example, the EC (including Britain) accounted for 45 per cent of Australia's inward investment flows (equity plus debt), compared to 34 per cent for the United States and only 2.5 per cent for Japan. ASEAN's contribution in those times was too low to be separately recorded. By 1990 these proportions had changed to 27 per cent for the EC and 18 per cent each for the United States and Japan. ASEAN accounted for 3 per cent of the total. These figures are dominated by lending, including short-term debt, however. In terms of equity investment, the EC accounted for 47 per cent in 1990,

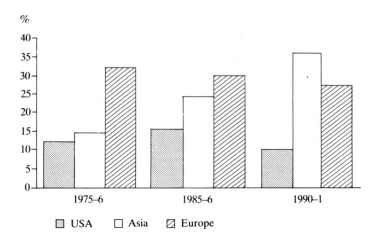

Source: Australian Bureau of Statistics (unpublished data).

Figure 9.4   Source of tourists to Australia.

compared with 52 per cent in 1973. Japan and ASEAN together accounted for only 7.5 per cent of inward equity investment in 1990.[7]

If we consider direct equity investment, the United Kingdom remains the main source of foreign capital for Australia. It is interesting that while the significance of the United Kingdom as an export market has declined markedly since her accession to the EC in 1973, Britain's paramount importance as a source of investment capital for Australia has not changed. Perhaps the reason for this is that the international capital markets are not nearly as distorted as the markets for trade in the products which Australia exports. Interestingly, this bias to the United Kingdom is reciprocated in terms of Australia's direct investment, one third of which went to the United Kingdom in 1990.

Inward flows of human capital show a much more marked trend away from Europe and in favour of Asia. A high level of immigration has been maintained by Australia since the Second World War. Until the 1970s an informal 'White Australia' policy was maintained, with the overwhelming majority of migrants being drawn from Britain, Ireland and Southern European countries, particularly Italy and Greece. The extent to which this policy has changed may be seen in Figure 9.5. Whereas half Australia's immigrants came from Europe in 1975–6 and only a quarter from Asia, this situation had been exactly reversed by 1990–1.

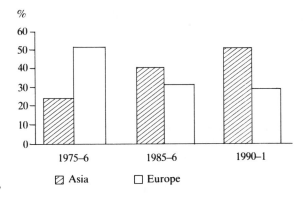

Source: Australian Bureau of Statistics (unpublished data).

Figure 9.5 Sources of immigrants to Australia.

9.2 Australia's concerns with EC policies

The above discussion suggests that while the Asian countries are of increasing significance as economic partners for Australia, the EC remains a major export market and source of investment capital. Australia has a number of concerns with likely economic developments in Europe in the 1990s. These are by no means restricted to the Single European Market of 1992. Given, indeed, that Australia's main concerns relate to market access, it is not clear that the 1992 process will have a great influence on Australia, and the major focus will remain on the traditional areas of conflict, namely the Common Agricultural Policy and EC countries' protection of other activities in which Australia has a comparative advantage (e.g. coal). The various areas of concern are outlined below.

9.2.1 *Single European Market*

The implications of the Single European Market for third countries must remain unclear until we see how the 1992 process works out in practice. To the extent that the 1992 reforms cause the Community to grow faster than it otherwise would have done, even if barriers to external suppliers remain at their present level, there will be beneficial trade creation effects for third countries. Where internal barriers are removed but external ones are not, however, there may be trade diversion effects, which will disadvantage other countries. In this case it is necessary to evaluate the probable balance between the trade creation gains and the losses from diversion. Davenport and Page (1991) have attempted this for the developing countries and found that under a fairly optimistic view of how the Single Market will operate in practice, the gains for the developing world just outstrip the losses. Some individual countries, however, are likely to face net losses. The more pessimistic scenario is the Fortress Europe outcome, under which internal barriers are lowered but the wall against outside traders is heightened. Under this scenario many outside players would be likely to lose more from trade diversion than from trade creation.

Of course, it is impossible to tell at this stage how 1992 will eventuate in practice, and much rests on the outcome of the Uruguay Round. In any move towards further integration balances will have to be struck between the countries that broadly follow liberal economic policies (such as Britain and the Netherlands) and those that are more interventionist (primarily France, Ireland, Italy, Greece and the Iberian economies). Because of the need for compromise, it seems likely that the EC market will be, in the words of Jacques Delors, 'ni fortresse, ni passoire'.[8] Much remains to be achieved in terms of market liberalisation.[9] Some of the more recent decisions and debates give little cause for confidence. For example, the recent decision on motor vehicle protection, which was greeted in some quarters as a victory for the economic liberals, provides for strict restrictions on Japanese imports until the end of the century. Britain, which considers itself to be one of the leading non-interventionist countries, no doubt went along with this because of the perceived national benefits arising from growth in its Japanese transplant manufacturers. Another issue among many is the EC policy on high-definition television (HDTV). The decision-making process on HDTV standards was recently summarised as the Commission attempting 'a delicate trade-off between the interests of broadcasters and manufacturers'.[10] As is often the case in the EC, the consumer does not merit any role in the 'trade-off', nor indeed any mention at all. These cases and others reinforce the suspicion that while *Festung Europa* may be an exaggeration, we will at least be confronting *dirigisme sans frontières* in the new Europe.

Published work on the likely implications of 1992 for Australia suggests that the gains from trade creation are likely to be small, and could be outweighed by losses from diversion.[11] Undoubtedly, Australian companies will find some benefits in the 1992 process. Firms intending to do business in the EC will no longer have to confront a variety of regulations, standards and legal requirements in the various countries, as they have done until now. As a consequence, marketing a product throughout the Community should become a less daunting (and less expensive) process. Hopefully, more uniform competition policies should make it easier for Australian corporations to merge with or take over European ones. This optimism must be tempered by the fact that Britain has one of the most relaxed attitudes to foreign takeovers of any country in the Community and yet has failed to allow a number of major Australian takeover attempts (for example, by Goodman Fielder Wattie and Elders). In principle, also, the breaking-down of national preference policies when it comes to tendering for public contracts should benefit Australian concerns such as Telecom and transport companies. Again, however, it is necessary to see how the reforms work out in practice since competition may well be more imagined than real. Indeed, public procurement policy is likely to contain an inbuilt 3 per cent European preference margin in some industries, arguably in contravention of GATT.[12]

Not unnaturally, the architects of the 1992 process place more emphasis on improving the Community's welfare than that of the rest of the world. The problem is that in their eyes the welfare of the Community is not always equated with purchasing goods and services from the cheapest sources when these happen to be external ones. As was suggested above, while the EC is keen to regulate the quality and standards of the products consumers buy, it is less concerned about the price. Consumers have often received short shrift at the hands of national governments because of their lack of lobbying power, but at least they have the ultimate ability to vote governments out of office. The lack of this discipline on the institutions in Brussels implies that the consumer has much less influence at the supra-national level. This has unfortunate implications for the conduct of industrial and micro-economic policy generally.

9.2.2 *Common Agricultural Policy*

One of the French arguments against allowing the Uruguay Round to become 'bogged down' in arguments over agricultural protectionism was that trade in farm products was not worth worrying about since it accounted for only a relatively small proportion of world trade. Of course, one reason for the fact that agriculture only accounts for around 13 per cent of global merchandise trade[13] is that huge barriers to such trade exist, not least those erected at the behest of the French. Also, while trade in farm products may not matter very much to France, agricultural exports still account for around one third of Australia's merchandise exports (down from 43 per cent at the beginning of the 1980s),[14] and food exports represent around 15 per cent of the total.

Yet food exports accounted for only 6 per cent of Australia's exports to the EC in 1990–1, compared with 24 per cent of exports to the United States and 16 per cent to North Asia (see Figure 9.6). The Cairns Group countries are, almost by definition, economies with a comparative advantage in farm products, whereas the EC clearly has an advantage in industrial products. Yet Australia's exports to the Cairns Group were twice as intensive in farm products than her exports to the EC in 1990–1. Either we have discovered a new manifestation of the Leontief Paradox, or the EC's agricultural policies both reduce and distort Australia's trade with the Community. In 1990–1 Australia's imports from the EC12 were 68 per cent greater than her exports to the Community.[15] While not suggesting for a moment that balanced bilateral trade should be an objective of policy, it is surprising that trade with such a large trade bloc should be so one-sided. It is probable that the CAP has been a major contributory factor to the acute imbalance of trade between Australia and the EC.

The CAP remains the *bête noire* of Australo-European economic relations, and the subject of an unrelenting Australian education campaign directed towards EC taxpayers and consumers. The Australian Bureau of Agricultural and Resource Economics (ABARE) has produced a cascade of statistics to demonstrate the iniquity of the policy. We are told that the annual costs of agricultural protection to consumers and taxpayers in industrialised countries amounted to over

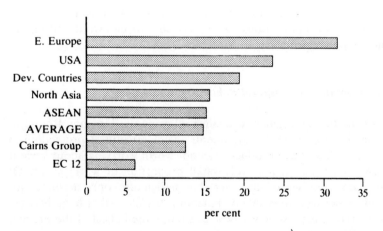

Source: Australia, Department of Foreign Affairs and Trade (1991, section 2).

Figure 9.6   Australia: food exports as per cent of total exports, by market, 1990–1.

$200 billion by the end of the 1980s. The annual cost of the CAP to EC consumers and taxpayers was estimated at 60–70 billion ecu at 1984 prices.[16] The Australian government finds that many food prices in the EC are at least double what they are in Australia, and that the CAP adds between 32 and 52 per cent to food bills in low-income households in the Community.[17] Income distribution anomalies are further evidenced by the fact that poorer countries in the south, such as Spain (average GDP per head less than 75 per cent of the EC average) find themselves as net contributors to the EC budget, while richer countries, such as the Netherlands, are net beneficiaries. One reason for this is that the costs of the CAP now account for over half of the EC's budget outlays, and the most assistance goes to cool temperate products, which are grown in the original six signatories of the Treaty of Rome.[18]

Anderson and Tyers (1991) suggest that complete global farm trade liberalisation in the 1990s would result in Western Europe importing an extra 37 million tonnes of grain annually by the end of the century, plus 17 million tonnes of meat, 67 million tonnes of dairy products and 8 million tonnes of sugar. Australian farmers would gain a high proportion of these additional exports, and the price of agricultural commodities would rise. Each non-farm household in the EC would gain US$1,500 at 1985 prices, and $3,000 in the rest of Western Europe and Japan.

The cost of the CAP to Australia's farmers is not merely that resulting from import barriers to the EC. The effects of the EC's export subsidies on third markets and the impact of the CAP and export subsidisation on prices of agricultural products must also be accounted for. During a period of acute slump in Australia's rural industries, these costs become all the more resented. It is a considerable understatement to say that the success of the Uruguay Round is of great importance to Australia.

9.2.3 *Coal*

Minerals now challenge agricultural products as the mainstay of Australia's trade. As the world's largest coal exporter, Australia has been concerned at the lack of access to EC markets. In fact, coal exports to the EC12 exceeded A$1 billion in 1990–1 for the first time and accounted for over 16 per cent of Australia's exports to the EC. (This compares with a 20 per cent share of exports to North Asia – mainly Japan – but this trade is facilitated by relative propinquity among other things.)[19] Nevertheless, much of EC coal production is inefficient by world standards and some countries in the Community have protected their domestic industries heavily. In 1986, for example, coal prices before subsidies in the major protected European markets were often more than twice the landed price of imports from outside the EC (see Table 9.2).

The level of assistance to the industry in some EC countries has been very high. For example, total subsidies to the German coal industry were estimated at A$8.5 billion in 1987 compared with total export revenues by Australia's coal industry (the largest exporter in the world) of only A$4.8 billion in 1987–8.[20] Britain and France have severely restricted imports in order to protect their domestic industries. Although this situation is gradually changing, there is clearly considerable scope for Australia to increase its coal exports to the EC. Protection of the coal industry, and of miners' jobs, is an emotive political issue in many countries. A change of government in Britain, for example, could conceivably reverse the move to lower protection. It is also possible that EC preference could be given to imports of coal from Eastern Europe at the expense of countries such as Australia and South Africa. Despite the recent moves in the right direction, this is likely to remain an area of concern for Australia during the 1990s.

9.2.4 Manufacturing industry assistance

Although Australia is not a major exporter of elaborately transformed manufactures (i.e. complex products as opposed to slightly transformed minerals, for example), exports of these goods to the EC12 constituted 16 per cent of total exports to the Community in 1990–1. When taken together with the percentage accounted for by food exports (around 6 per cent) this provides another indication of the distorted pattern of Australia's exports to the Community.

Table 9.2 Pit-head steaming-coal prices (before subsidies), and import prices, 1986 (US$/t).

	Indigenous production	Imports from non-EC countries
France	96.86	43.20
Germany (FR)	128.60	48.63
United Kingdom	96.77	54.67
Japan	118.50	44.85

Source: Australian Bureau of Agricultural and Resource Economics (1990b, p. 9).

As was discussed above, one of the objectives of Australia's industry policy is to increase the level of complex manufactures exports so as to be able to reduce its dependence on commodities and take advantage of the fact that the price of manufactures on world markets has tended to rise relative to raw materials. Australia's basic approach to this has been to level the domestic playing-field via tariff cuts and microeconomic reform, together with some limited measures to attract foreign investment in certain industries. *Dirigiste* measures in other countries, particularly major economies, will tend to reduce Australia's chances of competing internationally in these activities and attracting foreign investment.

While the Community has maintained a commendably low level of barrier protection against imports of industrial products, some countries have used less transparent measures to provide high levels of assistance to their national industries. In addition, the level of budgetary assistance to industry in the Community has been relatively high in recent years as is shown in Table 9.3.

These figures must be considered high, particularly when it is appreciated that they represent only assistance provided to 'favour certain undertakings' at the *national* level. As well as excluding difficult to measure areas, such as purchasing preferences, therefore, they exclude support given by way of general Community measures such as the structural readjustment funds and regional measures. These interventions are by no means insignificant, and it is particularly

Table 9.3 State aid to manufacturing average, 1986–8, EC countries.

	Percentage of gross value added	Ecu per employee
Belgium	4.4	1,601
Denmark	2.0	770
France	3.7	1,456
Germany	2.7	1,135
Greece	15.5	3,545
Ireland	6.1	2,504
Italy	6.7	3,077
Luxembourg	2.3	956
Netherlands	3.3	1,458
Portugal	8.3	701
Spain	5.3	1,528
United Kingdom	2.7	806
EC12	4.0	1,515

Source: Commission of the European Communities (1990a, p.10).

notable that the amount provided under the Structural Readjustment Fund will nearly double from £5.1 billion to £9.2 billion between 1987 and 1992.[21]

Although the EC's industrial policy, as spelled out in the so-called Bangemann Report of 1991,[22] leans on free market principles in theory, there must be some concern that the practice diverges from the theory quite considerably. While there is some pressure to reduce state aids, there have been few signs of a decline in recent years, except in Britain, among the major EC countries. New pressures have built up and given rise to additional assistance. Intensified Japanese competition, for example, has led the French government to provide a substantial cash injection into Groupe Bull and Thomson. The integration of the old DDR has led Germany to pursue a highly interventionist policy in the east. Where national aids are not used other measures sometimes are. We have already discussed the examples of the motor vehicle industry and high-definition television, which represent protection at the Community level. The EC's anti-dumping policy has also been used as a protectionist tool in recent years, in a way which may often disadvantage European industry rather than assist it. For example, it is estimated that the anti-dumping action against Japanese photocopiers has resulted in a cost to consumers of £297 million a year. The nominal level of protection has escalated four-fold to 20 per cent, and the level of effective protection (assistance to value added) could be considerably higher.[23]

Some governments in the EC have historically followed a planned approach to economic development and are strong believers in an interventionist industrial policy. There must be grounds for concern that the way in which compromises are reached over wider issues of political and monetary union in the Community could lead to free market principles being sacrificed in areas such as industrial policy which may seem relatively less important. An example of this is provided in the run-up to the Maastricht Summit in December 1991. One draft clause on industrial policy, known as the 'Cresson Clause', invited countries to support an approach under which the European Council may 'decide on specific measures, in particular in favour of the industries of the future'.[24] Although this clause was not supported, the *dirigiste* forces in the Community remain strong, and little has yet been done to reduce intervention in many of the national economies.

9.2.5 *Eastern Europe*

The developments in Eastern Europe in the last two years have raised some new problems for policy-makers in other countries. The EC, preoccupied as it has been with absorbing some new member countries during the 1980s and with its moves towards a single market, has had to contemplate opening its borders to trade with the east and accepting some countries, notably Czechoslovakia, Hungary and Poland, as eventual members of the Community. Paradoxically, however, the collapse of the Soviet Union in the east has given an impetus to the deepening, rather than the widening, of the Community as a result of the resurgence of German power following reunification. In addition, while accepting the desirability of assisting the Eastern European countries to move successfully towards market economies, some EC countries have been reluctant to expose their domestic industries to this new source of competition. The Eastern bloc, whose comparative advantage may well lie in many of the same industries as Australia's, has undergone the similar experience of seeing its legitimate aspirations for economic welfare via trade subordinated to the paramount interests of the EC's small farmers.

Ultimately, however, it is possible that much of the east will be absorbed into the Community, and the dream of a united Europe stretching from the Atlantic to the Urals may become a reality. Third countries such as Australia will accept the development of this new economic force and will learn to compete with it, not only for markets but for investment resources. The capital requirements of the eastern bloc will be prodigious over the next few years. Some estimates have suggested that if the Eastern European countries, including the ex-Soviet republics, are to catch up with the West in terms of living standards, within ten years they will require additional investment of up to $1.5 trillion a year. Unless global savings increase, it has been suggested that interest rates will have to rise by up to three percentage points or investment in other countries will fall by over 2 per cent of GDP.

Clearly this poses a threat to a country like Australia with its traditional reliance on an inflow of foreign capital and its medium-term problem of financing a large current account deficit. Nevertheless, as long as the competition for resources is on equal terms there can be no grounds for complaint. The playing-field in East Germany, however, has not been level. The German government has provided large subsidies to investment in the east, both by means of the tax system and through the *Treuhand*. If that approach were applied more widely in the ex-Comecon countries, there could be profound implications for less favoured countries seeking to develop their industrial base in a manner not too different from those in Eastern Europe. A similar argument applies to trade. If the Community decided to allow privileged access to agricultural products from Eastern Europe, while still maintaining substantial barriers to Australia's primary exports, there would be a very justified cause for complaint. By all means remove barriers to Eastern European exports, but provide a similar benefit to the rest of the world (and European consumers) at the same time.

9.3 Australia's policy response

As discussed above, in the last decade Australia has been forced, by its current account and foreign debt problems, to face some fundamental structural problems. Economic policy has been directed towards creating a more efficient industrial base, mainly by opening up the economy to competition and via other aspects of microeconomic reform. The basic thrust of this policy has been determined by the fundamentals of Australia's economic situation, and by a realisation that defensive industrial development policies and the acceptance of highly restrictive practices in a wide range of service and infrastructural industries have retarded growth in Australia's living standards. It must be stated at the outset that the approach followed by the EC has not had a substantial impact on Australia's policy thrust in the past, nor is it likely to be a dominant force in the future. Nevertheless, the EC is a very significant trading partner and source of investment for Australia, and if Europe were to become a fortress in trade and investment terms this could influence Australia's industrial and trade policies in particular.

9.3.1 *Industrial policy*

Recent trends in industrial policy

Industrial policy has undergone a deep-seated change in direction under the Hawke Labor government since 1983. Previously, and indeed since Federation in 1901, the stance of policy was almost purely defensive with a heavy reliance on tariff protection. A substantial manufacturing sector developed under this umbrella, accounting for around 27 per cent of GDP at its apogee in the late 1960s. It was inherently weak, however, because its orientation was directed inwards, towards a small local market. To be sure, foreign companies invested in Australia to jump the tariff wall, but they tended not to export from there. High tariffs weighed heavily on more efficient Australian industries, particularly in the agricultural and mining sectors, thereby restricting Australia's ability to participate in the rapid growth in world trade during the last forty years. By 1970 Australia had the second-highest level of tariff protection in the OECD (Figure 9.7), and until the mid-1980s remained the only developed country which had not seen its foreign trade increase as a percentage of GDP in the period since the Second World War.[25]

The Whitlam government was the first to attack the icon of protectionism with its 25 per cent across the board tariff cut in July 1973. Subsequently, the oil price shocks and associated recessions put a halt to further significant breaches in the tariff wall for a decade or more, and in fact protection was increased substantially to the two 'problem children' – the motor vehicles and textiles, clothing and footwear industries. In 1988, however, the government announced that all tariffs above 15 per cent would be cut to that level over three years, and all tariffs between 10 and 15 per cent would be reduced to the lower figure. The exceptions were motor vehicles and textiles, clothing and footwear, but very large cuts in protection were also announced for those two sectors. Overall, this represented a reduction of around 30 per cent and one which was made unilaterally. While the decision was taken in the context of the Uruguay Round and would be used as 'coin' in the negotiations, the cuts would be executed for domestic reasons irrespective of the outcome of the Round.

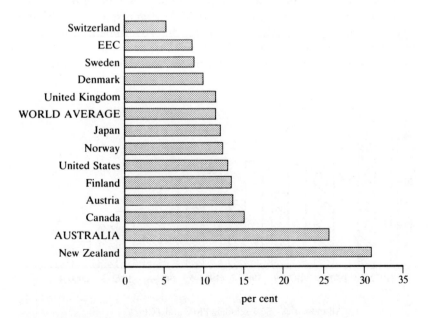

Source: GATT, *Basic Documentation for the Tariff Study* (Geneva, 1972).

Figure 9.7 Average tariffs on dutiable imports, 1970.

This trend to much lower levels of protection was reinforced in March 1991 when further reductions to the year 2000 were announced. A striking feature of this announcement was not only that it took place during a period of weakness in the current account, as did the 1988 statement, but that it also occurred in the middle of an exceptionally deep recession. Under the terms of this recent announcement, all tariffs will be reduced to 5 per cent by the end of the decade, except those on motor vehicles (15 per cent) and textiles, clothing and footwear (25 per cent or less, with many rates in the 10–15 per cent range).[26] The last quantitative import restrictions will be abolished in the early 1990s. These changes, which are more substantial than any other OECD country has undertaken unilaterally, represent a reduction in barrier protection of 80 per cent between 1983, when the present government took office, and the year 2000 (Figure 9.8).

The reductions in protection have been complemented by some 'positive adjustment' measures. In particular, support has been given to industrial R&D, both through a tax concession and a grant scheme for companies which are unlikely to be able to benefit from the tax deduction. Tax relief has also been available to assist the establishment of a venture capital industry, and export market development assistance has been provided. Some specific industries and activities have also been supported, mainly in areas such as aerospace, information industries and pharmaceuticals, where the government can use its purchasing 'muscle' to persuade foreign-owned multinationals to undertake more value-adding operations in Australia. These program-

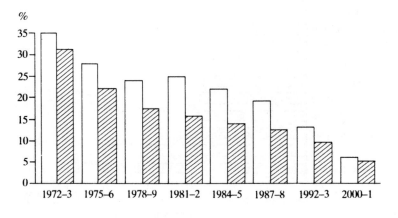

□ All industries ▨ Excluding PMV and TCF

Source: Data provided by the Industry Commission, Canberra.

Figure 9.8 Australia: average rate of effective protection, 1972–2000.

mes, while valuable to industry, are very small beer in financial terms compared to the enormous reduction in the subsidy equivalent of tariff protection. Budgetary assistance to Australian industry amounted to less than 3 per cent of manufacturing gross product in 1990–1. While this figure is only slightly lower than the EC state aids average (see Table 9.3 above), it should be remembered that the European figure includes only national programmes and omits EC assistance.

Effect of EC on future industrial policy

Overall, therefore, the thrust of Australia's industrial policy since the mid-1980s has been one of reduced protection, deregulation and non-interventionism. The question to be addressed is whether any conceivable change in EC policies, or developments in Europe generally, would be likely to induce Australia to move to a more *dirigiste* approach. The short answer is that a fundamental reversal in the direction of policy is most unlikely, but that there could under certain circumstances be a change in emphasis in favour of some measures to stimulate investment in export-oriented manufacturing operations. Much would depend on two issues, namely the outcome of the Uruguay Round in regard to agricultural trade and the extent of European interventionism in respect of stimulating investment in European (including East European) projects.

Taking the thorny issue of agricultural protectionism first, we have seen that Australia's level of food exports to the EC is much lower than could be expected if the European market were more open. This contributes to a large trade deficit with the EC, and to Australia's current account problems. Australia's food exports to other markets are also constrained by EC export subsidies. If it became likely that these conditions would continue to apply to those products in which Australia has a natural comparative advantage, one option for Australia would be to take measures actively to develop a comparative advantage in other products, namely advanced manufactures, in which trade is more liberal.

The development of new areas of comparative advantage could be attempted by methods which are not frowned upon, such as improving education and training and providing world-class infrastructure. An alternative approach would be to follow the same course as many European and Asian countries, namely to encourage investment in new 'desirable' activities by means of subsidies, development grants or favourable taxation arrangements. Australians have tended to label this approach 'new protectionism', and for a number of reasons have eschewed it to date. The belief has been that 'winner picking' is a risky business and that the dangers of resource misallocation have been evidenced by the results of previous high tariff policies. There is also widespread support for the view that, if there is a current account 'problem', the exchange rate will provide the means of restoring equilibrium. Equally, according to this view, if other countries shut their borders to Australia's exports, the answer is not in tit-for-tat protectionism, but rather to let the market, via the exchange rate, reallocate factors of production to other activities.

The same arguments may also be applied to the other contingency mentioned above, namely measures taken by other countries to attract investment to their domestic economies at the expense of others. Again, the neo-classicists would assert that the market would solve the problem by virtue of the fact that (eventually) the non-subsidised returns on investment projects in Australia will exceed subsidised returns elsewhere. While this process may take some time, and be accompanied by some pain in terms of reduced output and employment in the interim, it could be argued that it was likely to lead to less diminution of the community's welfare than misplaced intervention.

This neo-classical *Weltanschauung*, in its essentials, represents the dominant paradigm in Australian policy formulation at present, although it may be fair to say that it is advanced with less confidence now than was the case in the late 1980s. On the opposite side two main points should be made. First, in a world where comparative advantage may be much less easy to identify than in Adam Smith's day, Australia faces some significant disadvantages in attracting investment in manufacturing and advanced value-adding projects generally. Second, it is not at all clear that the market's resource-allocating mechanisms, namely the exchange rate, always operate in the manner the neoclassicists feel they should. These points are discussed in turn.

One of the characteristics of global investment by transnational corporations in recent years has been that many projects, probably the majority, are essentially footloose between a number of alternative locations. In a distortion-free world they could be undertaken equally profitably in any one of several countries. In Australia, many foreign corporations in recent years have appraised our attributes as a base for investment required to service Asia–Pacific markets, but all too often they have decided eventually in favour of other countries such as Singapore, Malaysia or Thailand. Australia possesses many advantages, such as political stability, a skilled workforce, a sophisticated international capital market and a congenial environment. Various avoidable disadvantages also exist, however, including inefficiencies in transport and other infrastructural industries, higher than world prices for some goods because of tariffs, and restrictive practices in the labour force. These problems are all being addressed vigorously at present, and substantial improvements in many of these areas suggest that they may not be a major deterrent to investment in the future.

The problem for policy-makers is that Australia faces a number of other disadvantages, which are not susceptible in any comprehensive way to remedial action. These include the following two major difficulties.

1. Despite its location in the dynamic and populous Asia–Pacific region, the Australian market is both geographically isolated and small:
   (a) Melbourne is little closer to Tokyo than is San Francisco;
   (b) the domestic market comprises only 22 million people even when New Zealand is included.
2. The exchange rate of the Australian dollar is more volatile and subject to greater fluctuations than the exchange rates for most major currencies because of Australia's reliance on trade in commodities. The value of the A$ is highly correlated with commodity prices, creating uncertainty for manufacturing investment: for example, between September 1986 and March 1989, when commodity prices rose strongly, the *real* effective exchange rate for the A$ appreciated by over 30 per cent at a time when Australia's inflation was higher than the average for her trading partners.

Of course, the disadvantages identified above do not necessarily imply market failure in the technical sense, and would not therefore constitute any neo-classical argument for intervention. They may be inalienable features of the natural environment which conditions the determination of Australia's comparative advantage. Nevertheless, they create impediments to investment in Australia. One manifestation of the increased riskiness of such investment is that the hurdle rate of return tends to be considerably higher for a project in Australia than for similar projects in other countries.[27] This problem is exacerbated in the Asia–Pacific region by the fact that while Australia models its taxation policies on the economically rationalist approach of other anglophone countries, most of its neighbours, who compete with Australia for regional projects, do not. A plethora of tax holiday schemes and other incentives to inward foreign investment exist in the region, and have the effect of increasing the after-tax return on projects in these countries compared to Australia.

These issues would be less important if the economy were able to adjust readily to these factors and allow equilibrium to be restored. The second issue relates to the efficiency of the market equilibrating mechanisms when structural adjustment is required following the exclusion from, say, European markets of products in which Australia has a comparative advantage. In the eyes of many such a 'shock' would lead to a current account deficit and thus to a currency depreciation, after which exports would increase and the return on Australian investment projects would rise thereby restoring equilibrium. Unfortunately, the experience of the last decade does not support this simplistic view of how the exchange rate works. While we may not know exactly what does determine the exchange rate, it is at least clear that a number of factors are important, including relative interest rates, inflation, commodity prices, 'news' and last, and sometimes least, the current account deficit. Australia's deficit has been running for over a decade at a level which cannot be sustained indefinitely, and while the A$ has become the fifth or sixth most frequently traded currency in the world over that period, the deficit does not appear to have played a major role in determining the direction of the trade.

What, then, are Australia's industry policy-makers likely to do if Europe displays a preference for its own products and seeks to bias investment towards itself and away from other countries? They will be operating in a situation in which Australia has to broaden its export base, or accept deep cuts in living standards (*à la* New Zealand), where Australia faces severe natural disadvantages in attracting investment, and where market-based mechanisms seem to work only imperfectly and slowly at best in restoring equilibrium.

The most likely outcome, it seems to me, is that Australia will persist with its liberal policies of reductions in protection, deregulation and microeconomic reform. The free operation of market forces will provide the main influence on the allocation of resources between competing activities. The progress with the microeconomic reform agenda will make Australia more attractive to global investors.

Nevertheless, it may be deemed desirable to take action to improve the environment for investment in new activities. While the strategic trade theorists may not have provided many clues as to when and how to intervene, they have at least demonstrated that in a world of intervention, the country that chooses to level its own playing-field may not necessarily maximise the welfare of its community. An approach based on liberalising markets is not necessarily inconsistent with taking some general measures to compete with the tax policies of other countries so as to increase the after-tax returns on investment. True, many studies have suggested that investment incentives do not, in the longer term, increase the *quantity* of investment. But they can influence the *timing* of the investment. In a situation where the exchange rate works at best imperfectly and slowly to restore equilibrium, measures which acted to pull investment forward could be seen as desirable.

9.3.2   *Trade policy*

Historically, Australia's trade policy has exhibited certain consistent characteristics. First, at least since the weakening of the British connection, it has always had a multilateral rather than bilateral emphasis. With the exception of the customs union with New Zealand, Australia has not been enthusiastic about trade blocs. Second, its advocates and representatives have tended to preach the virtues of free trade abroad, which has not always sat easily with Australia's tariff levels and lack of bindings. Third, it has almost always adhered strictly to the terms of the GATT and exhibited a relatively high degree of transparency in its instruments. Fourth, it has tended to avoid the postwar tariff cutting 'rounds' on the grounds that agriculture has been excluded.

The second of these tendencies has been facilitated in recent years by Australia's commendable record in cutting its industrial protection unilaterally, by its adherence to the GATT and by the fact that the positive adjustment measures it has employed have by and large been both modest and transparent. The most interesting of these characteristics is the first one, namely the determination to take a multilateral approach to freeing up trade. This has been displayed to good effect in the leading role Australia has played both in establishing the Cairns Group of agricultural exporting countries and in prosecuting its agenda in world councils. The establishment of the Cairns Group was a major breakthrough in terms of Australia's long-lived attempt to confront agricultural protectionism, and a reduction in EC, Japanese and US barriers to trade in these products arguably would benefit Australia more than any other conceivable development on the international trade scene.

Nevertheless, Australia has not neglected its own backyard in recent times and has placed an increasing emphasis on trade and foreign policy in its own region. The reorganisation of the Australian Trade Commission (Austrade) has seen a major shift of resources away from Europe and the USA and in favour of the Asia–Pacific region. Australia played a major role in establishing the Asia–Pacific Economic Co-operation group (APEC), whose members between them account for over half of world trade.[28] But while trade partners in ASEAN may have some sympathy with Australia's attempts to improve market access for its industrial and agricultural products,

Australia's apparent preoccupation with EC and US trade matters could reinforce the views held by some that Australia is a non-Asian power located there via a geographical accident. This may have implications for Australia's capacity to participate in a regional trade bloc if the opportunity were to arise.

Effects of EC on future trade policy

The main way in which developments in the EC are likely to affect Australia during the 1990s is in the field of trade policy rather than industrial policy. Again, this is highly dependent on the outcome of the Uruguay Round. The main issue, of course, is that of trade blocs. The increasing integration of the twelve EC economies, together with fears on the part of some that a Fortress Europe may be in the making, has led other countries to look to the possibility of forming trade blocs of their own. This is most evident in North America at present, but there has also been some discussion of the possibility of forming an Asia–Pacific trade bloc. What, then, are the prospects for such a bloc, and is it likely that Australia would seek to join such a body?

In practical terms, while APEC is most unlikely to develop into a trade bloc, it is not beyond the bounds of possibility that the ASEAN countries could form such a bloc in the foreseeable future. The issue has been discussed by the countries concerned and has not been dismissed out of hand. The individual economies have roughly similar levels of economic power (although some are markedly more success-ful than others), many cultural similarities, a good record in economic growth and development and are relatively free of economic ideolo-gies. Apart from Singapore, which has little agriculture, the structures of the six economies display more similarities than differences, although tariff levels differ markedly. Importantly, each country has identi-fied itself as a member of a political and economic bloc for some time, and they have become used to acting in a collective way. Measured steps towards forming a customs union and then a more comprehen-sive economic union would appear to be a logical progression.

The likely attitude of the ASEAN countries to forming a trade bloc with other powers, such as Australia, New Zealand and Japan, is uncertain. Malaysia has been seeking support for a regional grouping, known as the East Asian Economic Caucus, but it has been suggested that it would specifically exclude Australia and New Zealand (together with the United States and Canada on the other side of the Pacific). ASEAN might not welcome the inclusion of Japan in a trade bloc because of concerns about economic and political domination. It is clear that the United States, which saw its trans-Pacific trade pass its transatlantic trade in the 1980s, would oppose the formation of a powerful Asian trade bloc. Because of the importance of the US market for all the countries concerned this objection is likely to have a substantial influence.[29]

What would Australia's attitude be to the possibility of participating in a trade bloc in the Asia–Pacific region? It is useful to examine some of the pros and cons from Australia's point of view before assessing what particular circumstance, if any, would make it beneficial to Australia to join such a grouping. On the plus side, membership of a customs union which extended to primary commodities would give Australia assured market access for the products in which it has a comparative advantage. This would clearly be the major potential advantage, but the scale of the benefit to Australia would, of course, depend on the degree to which barriers to these exports existed in the rest of the world economy. Second, with a common external tariff Australia's manufactured goods could be given advantageous access to a larger market than at present, and have to face less intense competition than at present from rival firms in Europe, the United States and Japan (assuming Japan was not a member of the bloc). Third, a number of political advantages could accrue to Australia as a result of being a member of a more powerful bloc of countries.

On the negative side, in a world which was not erecting notably higher barriers to trade, membership of an Asia–Pacific trade bloc could retard Australia's economic development. A common external tariff, in particular for a bloc which excluded Japan, could divert consumption to inferior and more expensive goods produced within the bloc, and on the production side could divert Australian resources into activities which were not competitive on a global scale. This would reduce Australia's welfare. Turning to the first advantage cited above, Australia at present faces few barriers to its trade in minerals, and is unlikely to face many in the future. The benefits to the mineral industry of membership of a trade bloc, therefore, may be non-existent. On the agriculture side, while the potential market for Australian produce in the region is very large, it remains questionable whether Asian countries which entered into a customs union would be willing to open their agricultural markets to a world-scale competitor such as Australia. The political advantages identified above also may be a double-edged sword. We have seen at Maastricht how relatively slight cultural and economic differences between countries can make integration difficult even between Western democracies. The differences between Australia and many of her regional neighbours, in areas such as economic policy, trade unions and general political and social philosophies, are of a much greater magnitude.

Overall, the benefits to Australia of joining a regional trade bloc, on the somewhat heroic assumption that her regional neighbours would invite her to join such a grouping, are dubious. It might be beneficial under a scenario where two conditions applied. First, where the Uruguay Round talks failed and the world divided up into trade blocs, probably based on the 'Triad' economies, with only limited trade between them. This would clearly heavily restrict Australia's ability to improve its living standards via trade growth. Second, if the bloc which Australia joined included one of the major industrial powers, namely Japan or the United States, this would drastically reduce the potential losses from resource misallocation outlined above. It must be said that neither of these conditions is likely to be fulfilled. While the Uruguay Round may break down over agricultural and services trade, there is little likelihood that the world will return to 1930s-style protectionism as a result. It is widely recognised that the great increase in wealth experienced by developed and many less developed economies since the Second World War has been built on growth in world trade. As for the second condition, under a protectionist scenario it is hard to see why Japan would benefit from entering into a trade bloc with Australia. Japan would still expect to obtain unrestricted access to Australia's minerals irrespective of whether a trade bloc was formed, while it might not relish exposing its inefficient agricultural industries to Australian competition.

9.4 Conclusions

Although Australia's economic centre of gravity has shifted towards the Asia–Pacific region in recent years, the European Community is one of the 'Triad' of global economic powers and as such is an important trading partner for Australia. It is notable that since Britain joined the Community the strong investment links have been maintained between the two countries, but the trade links have been substantially eroded. The United Kingdom now takes less than 4 per cent of Australia's exports (down from one third forty years ago), and exports to the EC as a whole are now only as great as Australia's exports to the ASEAN countries. Australia records a very large trade deficit with the European Community.

Much of the 'blame' for this, if blame there be, may be laid at the door of the EC's Common Agricultural Policy. The CAP has not only severely restricted Australia's exports of agricultural products to the Community but, via the export subsidy programme associated with it, has also undermined Australia's ability to sell in third markets those products in which it has a clear comparative advantage. This is evidenced by the fact that Australia's food exports to the Community account for a much lesser share of total exports than to any other major market.

The CAP remains by far the major concern in Australia's economic relationship with the Community. It is not the only concern, however. Australia is the leading world exporter of coal, and this is an industry which is highly protected in some EC countries. There are also some signs that the increasing integration of the EC countries may lead, if not to a Fortress Europe, at least to *dirigisme sans frontières*. To outsiders it often appears as if the Community's concerns are more with its own producers, even the inefficient ones, than consumers, and that many countries within it fail to recognise the benefits of liberalising world trade. Assistance to a number of industries, including electronics and motor vehicles in particular, together with the constant emphasis on reciprocity whenever trade liberalisation is mooted, provides some evidence of this.

For more than a decade, Australia has faced a persistent and fundamental disequilibrium in its balance of payments. A build-up of foreign debt has resulted from the need to finance a current account deficit, which has averaged just under 5 per cent of GDP since 1980. To maintain its living standards in the longer term, Australia is confronted with the necessity of increasing its exports. The Australian government has addressed this problem with a programme of substantial unilateral cuts in industry protection, together with the liberalisation of internal markets via microeconomic reform. Because major markets, particularly the EC, are virtually closed off to many of the products in which Australia has a comparative advantage, one objective of these policies is to broaden Australia's export base while maintaining the pressure to achieve lower protection in agricultural markets.

Should the Uruguay Round fail because of intransigence over agricultural and/or services trade, and should the world then become a more protectionist place with a division into regional trading blocs, the implications for a middle-rank, geographically isolated, primary producing country like Australia would be severe. Would developments in the EC then be likely to induce Australia to change its liberal industrial and trade policies? The answer seems to be 'Not really'. If other countries choose to reduce their living standards by producing the wrong goods and services, the neo-classicist would assert that there is no reason to follow suit.

The presence of market failures, however, and the lessons of the theory of the second best and the strategic trade theorists, suggests that the answer is not as simple as that. Australia might decide to complement its 'level playing-field' policies with, for example, some incentives to attract foreign investment and support for major projects. It might also need to examine the possible benefits of joining a regional trading bloc. But the crisis in world trade would have to be severe indeed if Australia were to gain more from joining a regional bloc than from continuing its traditional multilateral trading policies. The Asia–Pacific region will continue to grow relatively more important than Europe as an economic partner for Australia, but the possibility of Australia participating in a bloc along the lines of the EC seems remote.

Notes

This chapter was written while the author was on secondment to the University of London from the Department of Industry, Technology and Commerce in Canberra. The views expressed are those of the author, and are not necessarily shared by the Department. Thanks are due to the Bureau of Industry Economics in Canberra for assistance with some of the data used in this chapter.

1. Bollard and Mayes (1991, p. 33).
2. These figures are taken from Australian Bureau of Statistics (1991, Tables 3.11 and 3.12).
3. *Ibid.*, Table 3.2.
4. *Ibid.*, Table 3.3.
5. This figure may be slightly overstated due to entrepôt trade in Singapore. Australia, Department of Foreign Affairs and Trade (1991), pp. x–xi.
6. Australian Bureau of Statistics, cat. no. 3404.0.
7. Australian Bureau of Statistics, cat. no. 5305.0, 1991.
8. Quoted in Davenport and Page (1991, p. 3).
9. See, for example, Pelkmans (1991).
10. *Financial Times*, 2 December 1991, p. 2.
11. See, for example, Stoeckel, Pearce and Banks (1990), Mayes (1990).
12. Montagnon (1990, p. 87).
13. GATT figures, quoted in *Financial Times*, 1 November 1991.
14. Australian Bureau of Statistics (1991), Table 3.2.
15. Australia, Department of Foreign Affairs and Trade (1991), section 2.
16. Australian Bureau of Agricultural and Resource Economics (1990a).
17. Australian Government (1991, p. 1).
18. *Financial Times*, 5 December 1991, p. 20.
19. Australia, Department of Foreign Affairs and Trade (1991), section 2.
20. Jones and Savage (1989, p. 182).
21. Cook (1989, p. 71).
22. Commission of the European Communities (1990b).
23. Messerlin and Noguchi (1991).
24. *Financial Times*, 2 December 1991, p. 14.
25. There have been some signs of an increase in Australia's exports/GDP ratio in recent years. It rose from an average of 14.8 per cent in the three years 1981–2 to 1983–4 to an average of 18.0 per cent in the three years to 1990–1.
26. Ministerial Statements (1991).

27. These issues are discussed at length in Stanford (1992). See also Australian Manufacturing Council (1990).
28. See Ridding (1991).
29. See Ridding (1991).

References

Anderson, K. and Tyers, R. (1991) *Global Effects of Liberalising Trade in Farm Products* (London: Trade Policy Research Centre).

Australia, Department of Foreign Affairs and Trade (1991) *Composition of Trade, Australia, 1990–91* (Canberra).

Australian Bureau of Agricultural and Resource Economics (1990a) *Proposed Strategies for Reducing Agricultural Protection in the GATT Uruguay Round*, Discussion Paper 90–6 (Canberra: AGPS).

Australian Bureau of Agricultural and Resource Economics (1990b) *Reform of International Coal Protection: Implications for Australia and World Trade*, Discussion Paper 90–1 (Canberra: AGPS).

Australian Bureau of Statistics (1991) *Australian Economic Indicators* (Canberra), October.

Australian Government (1991) *Are You Paying Too Much?* (Canberra).

Australian Manufacturing Council (1990) *The Global Challenge: Australian Manufacturing in the 1990s* (Melbourne).

Bollard, A. and Mayes, D. (1991) 'Regionalism and the Pacific Rim', paper presented to a conference on *Regionalism and the World Economy*, University of Nottingham, September.

Calingaert, M. (1989) *The 1992 Challenge from Europe* (Washington: National Planning Association).

Cecchini, P. (1988) *The European Challenge 1992: The Benefits of a Single Market* (Aldershot: Wildwood House).

Commission of the European Communities (1990a) *Second Survey of State Aids in the European Community* (Brussels), July.

Commission of the European Communities (1990b), *Industrial Policy in an Open and Competitive Environment* (Brussels), November.

Cook, G. (ed.) (1989) *Australia and 1992 – The Nature and Implications of a Single European Market*, Sir Robert Menzies Centre for Australian Studies (Canberra: AGPS).

Davenport, M. and Page, S. (1991) *Europe: 1992 and the Developing World* (London: ODI).

Jones, S. and Savage, E. (1989) 'Protection of the German coal industry', *Agriculture and Resources Quarterly*, 1(2), pp. 182–90.

Mayes, D. G. (1990) 'The implications of closer European integration for Australia and New Zealand', *National Institute Economic Review*, 4/90, pp. 110–16.

Messerlin, P. A. and Noguchi, Y. (1991) 'EC industrial policy: worse than before', *Financial Times*, 26 July.

Ministerial Statements (1991) *Building a Competitive Australia* (Canberra), March.

Montagnon, P. (ed.) (1990) *European Competition Policy* (London: Royal Institute of International Affairs).

Pelkmans, J. (1991) 'Towards economic union', in *Setting European Community Priorities, 1991–92* (Brussels: Centre for European Policy Studies), pp. 39–95.

Ridding, J. (1991) 'Asia–Pacific trade bloc struggles for identity', *Financial Times*, 12 November.
Stanford, J. (ed.) (1992) *Industrial Policy in Australia and Europe*, Sir Robert Menzies Centre for Australian Studies (Canberra: AGPS).
Stoeckel, A., Pearce, D. and Banks, G. (1990) *Western Trade Blocs* (Canberra: Centre for International Economics).

10

Policy responses and conclusions

David G. Mayes

A recurrent theme in the previous chapters is that it is widely accepted that the Single European Market will boost incomes and trade in the European economic area and that as a consequence most third countries will benefit to a smaller or larger extent.[1] McAleese and Pelkmans both show that evidence from other trading agreements, in so far as it is comparable, indicates that market expansion effects tend to outweigh any losses in market share. However, the extent of that benefit will vary both by product area and by country. To quite a large extent the generally favourable outcome is not merely the result of the originally planned measures, but also the consequence of successful pressure by third countries and their firms, principally the United States, to reduce the Fortress Europe element to relatively minor proportions.

The response of third countries to European proposals is thus crucial in determining their external impact. As Woolcock clearly points out, two sets of distinctions must be made in exploring that response. First, there is that between government and business. Governments and other public authorities can make a policy response, but it is the individual firms as producers and purchasers who will determine much of the actual outcome. Second, we can distinguish within the firm sector between those firms that already operate in Europe or intend to do so, and those that face European competitors either in their home markets only or as exporters. The form of response even within the field of direct investment in Europe, for example, depends very much on a firm's current and future production strategy. Those strategies have both offensive and defensive elements, as Yannopoulos explains, and as a consequence governments find themselves facing a difficult balance of interests between those who see the opportunities offered by the development of Europe and want policies to assist them, and those that see the threats it poses to their own businesses and wish the government to take a defensive stance. The first concern in external policy has thus been to try to create a Europe where opportunities are as large as possible, but offered on terms where all can compete on an equal basis irrespective of the nationality of their ultimate ownership.

The ability to influence the EC depends on the ability to bargain. At the macroeconomic level, only the United States and, to a lesser extent, Japan are able to offer a real threat of retaliation so that the EC responds. Other groupings, such as those formed to get the Uruguay Round in motion, have been rather less successful. However, such influence occurs at the detailed level as well, where lobbying and research studies can be much more effective in influencing opinion because the political stakes are lower. However, by the same token, it is at this detailed level that the most effective protectionist measures can be implemented, whether through anti-dumping duties or specification or health requirements. Here countries with a rather narrow export product range can find themselves adversely affected.

However, there are two aspects of the process of integration which are less benign. First, there are major areas of existing protection, such as in agriculture and coal, which are not affected directly by the current process of integration. Second, the steps beyond the Single Market may have a more specific effect. The transition to EMU means that several member states have to undertake fairly substantial deflationary programmes. These have two consequences: they depress demand in the EC and drive up interest rates, where monetary policy is used as the major instrument of deflation. Furthermore, the dramatic turnround in Central and Eastern Europe means that the balance of trading structures is changing. The CMEA countries had relatively little external trade relations with third countries, and those they did have were dominated by extensive reciprocal agreements, including counter-trade, which meant that external imbalances did not emerge as the natural corollary of the internal distortions.

Now that the distortions and controls are being eased, the full consequences of the previous pent-up imbalances can be observed. In the effort to import so much Western investment and consumer goods, exchange rates have been driven to very low levels to make the less sophisticated Eastern products and services competitive. This will impact on those third country producers that are also trying to produce in those same industry sectors. Agriculture is the obvious worry. Not only is it an area where many Eastern countries can provide products of a competitive quality, but the scope exists for selective benefits to be offered by the Community. Textiles, clothing, footwear and furniture provide further examples. Agricultural producers like Australia and New Zealand may find themselves squeezed on world markets as production from the former CMEA comes on stream.

There are thus both threats and opportunities for third countries to deal with, and their policy response is crucial in determining the effect on their economies. The sectors facing what they perceive to be adverse effects tend to respond by demanding protection, and to some extent this was adopted by the Democrats in the 1992 presidential electoral campaign in the United States. However, the beneficiaries do not put up a corresponding cry that their relative benefits should also be cut.[2] Their concerns are (1) that support for the disadvantaged should not harm them; (2) that the general principle of market openness be maintained; and (3) that any threat of retaliation should be avoided. The problem of retaliation is that often it cannot be in the same product area but affects an unrelated one, adding both a second distortion to the first and a new 'unfairness' to the one that generated the response in the first place.[3] Thus such schemes tend to escalate as one inequitable measure is matched by another.

The appropriate solution is to remove the distortions. However, what the Single Market and indeed the wider negotiations through the GATT and the SII have revealed is that the sources of distortion are often fairly far removed from the trade itself. Technical and fiscal differences can act as effective barriers. Although there is growing pressure towards international standards, the world is a long way from accepting other countries' testing procedures. The process of negotiating such changes, even within the EC, has been long drawn out and at times rather acrimonious, and the prospect of putting these changes on a multilateral basis is formidable. As a generalisation, it is a natural reaction to want others to change to one's own standard of behaviour. Unless there are very widespread codes in force internationally this inevitably means that most countries have to change, thus spreading the discontent very widely. Long-run benefits, often of uncertain size, are always very difficult political incentives when compared with large and fairly certain short-run costs.[4]

The arguments in favour of freer trade are widely known and well understood, so there is little need to repeat them here. The relevant question is whether the moves towards closer European integration affect the arguments which are used in third countries against those moves to freer trade, either positively or negatively. By the same token the arguments in favour of limited protection, either for strategic reasons or because changes take time to put in place and sunk costs need to be offset, or even the more modern arguments about the achievement of dynamic advantages that can be sustained through a virtuous cycle of innovation and R&D from higher profitability, do not need restating. We need to ask how they are altered by the likely circumstances.

10.1   The policy options

One of the great difficulties in describing what is open to third countries is that the process of European integration is not simply a matter of the formation or extension of a trading area or even the development of a wider set or non-discriminatory economic arrangements. It involves a list of more extensive political and social agreements as well. To some extent this is a greater emphasis on the positive rather than the purely negative measures of integration. (Early steps in integration, as in the NAFTA negotiations which have recently been concluded, involve the ending of discrimination by removing tariffs and quantitative restrictions. It is only later that countries agree to common methods of operation, through harmonised standards, similar fiscal systems, etc.) Some of the changes, particularly those embodied in the Maastricht Treaty, relate to improved methods of decision-making – more effective enforcement of decisions, a greater role for direct democracy through the European Parliament, for example. The appropriate response by third countries is then much more difficult. Much of the logic of the European Community is generated through economic geography. The option of joining such an arrangement, or even emulating it through similar arrangements of their own, is not open to the countries of the Pacific. However, in many respects they do not have to join to benefit. In so far as the measures of integration do make the market more homogeneous and do improve the speed of decision-making, this will benefit their companies, either as traders or as investors. Joining the Community will be exemplified by having the benefits of national treatment extended to those of their companies which seek to do business within the EC.

There is therefore a fairly traditional list of non-exclusive options available to third countries both individually and jointly in response to the process of European integration. These are shown in Table 10.1. However, the most obvious strategic response is to try to make sure that their companies, whether as investors or exporters, have the maximum opportunity to benefit from access to EC markets. In a negative sense this implies the avoidance of measures which inhibit outward trade and investment but it also implies avoiding structures which generate issues of reciprocity (for example, avoiding exclusion from the ability to bid for public sector contracts).

Table 10.1   Responses available for third countries to closer European integration.

---

1. Seek improvements.
2. Retaliate against adverse effects.
3. Adopt alternative regional trading arrangements.
4. Try to extend the European approach multilaterally.
5. Try to establish bilateral agreements.
6. Change unilaterally to get the best out of the external environment.

10.1.1   *Seek improvements*

Trying to persuade the Europeans to follow the path of agreement that is of greatest value to third countries is the most obvious approach. The other strategies are good examples of what to do when this first approach does not succeed. It is not a matter of concluding external agreements with the EC but of ensuring that the internal agreements within Europe are not unnecessarily adverse. The process of persuasion is not just a matter of threats but in many cases one of information and the provision of alternative ways forward. The implied severity of the original provisions of the second banking directive for American banks was clearly not properly appreciated by those who drafted it. They had in mind the removal of technical restrictions, which make it difficult for EC banks to operate in foreign markets. However, it is has been difficult to decide where to draw the line between permitting home country control, so that institutions operating under different rules can operate in the same market, and national treatment, whereby host country rules apply, but those rules are operated without regard to the nationality of the company to which they are applied.

In practice, the decision has been largely pragmatic, assessing the consequences of competition among rules. In the case of insurance, for example, there has been a distinction in the case of non-life insurance between 'large' risks, which are risks normally encountered only by companies and larger organisations, and 'mass' risks, which are general-run risks encountered by individuals and small enterprises. In the former case a European market can operate, first, because the purchaser is capable of shopping around across borders and second because the purchaser is also able to make a judgement between the merits of offers emanating from companies operating under the different national systems. In the case of mass risks, however, the individual is deemed not to be able to distinguish in that sort of way and hence host country control has become the method of approach. However, it is combined with the ability of foreign companies to set up in other member states on the same terms as national companies, and for there to be a considerable easing of the restraints on assets and terms, which previously made operating across borders difficult.

Thus there is now a clear way forward for third country companies, whether they want to operate in the large risk, reinsurance or mass risk areas. Natural barriers to entry still exist in the sense that it is easier to sell mass risks if one has a distribution network, say through a bank or a building society – hence the rise of *Allfinanz* and *banque-assurance* bringing these various financial services together.[5]

As in other services the way in which the final system will work is still evolving. It seems probable that all but a very small number of dossiers among the original 280 or so will be completed before 1 January 1993, so that in practice the Single Market still has a long way to go before it becomes fully operational even in the elementary sense, of 'all the measures coming into force'.

Much of the detail of implementation has not yet taken place. Measures in areas such as pharmaceuticals are not due to take effect until 1995 (Hart 1992b). Technical harmonisation in particular is a matter for negotiation within the European standards bodies in many instances, with Brussels taking a lower profile in setting minimum requirements relating to health, safety and the environment. In these instances standards are bargained among knowledgeable representatives and experts from the member states. Major third country firms can have an appreciable impact on that process, particularly when they have been long-established in Europe, like Ford and other US multinationals set up before the Second World War.

Even more newly arrived multinationals, like those from Japan, can start to have a major influence on how the European market develops. As Mayes and Ogiwara (1992) have indicated for the United Kingdom, and Langhammer (1991) has demonstrated more substantially for the Asian Pacific Rim, a Japanese-style culture for doing business can be inculcated among suppliers and downstream distributors. Thus as the markets of the member states become more open and more integrated, they do not necessarily adopt some new, peculiarly European character, but become internationalised, adopting major non-European characteristics as well. This is not just a one-way street with external ideas brought in by non-European companies operating in the European market, but by European multinationals adopting non-European approaches from their own experience in selling and producing in markets outside Europe. Given that the Single Market is intended to improve the competitiveness of Europe *vis-à-vis* the rest of the world, as well as improving internal efficiency, this form of business globalisation is to be expected. What Europe is doing is advancing the pace of confrontation between national systems, which is taking place on the international stage anyway, both through the increased scope of the current GATT round and through the Strategic Impediments Initiative of the United States and Japan.

Third countries thus have an interest in the opening-up of the European system to competition between rules, if they believe that their own products are superior and the services they can offer better tailored to customer needs. The more the European market remains under host country control, the more the domestic firms of that particular country have an advantage; although, of course, even that advantage can be bought through merger and acquisition if the market for corporate control is sufficiently open.

Each third country will have its own shopping list of improvements at the detailed level as these are both related to the product composition of trade and the importance of European production facilities which its companies own. In the case of the United States and Japan, companies are keen to ensure that strategic support through EC technology policy for advanced, high value-added products does not add to what are already high levels of protection compared to the EC average. Furthermore, these companies want to be on the inside, being a partner in the development of European technology rather than simply a rival for the sales in the final product market. International collaboration is normal, and local partnership is likely to be a considerable help both where there is a large public sector element to the purchasing or where local distribution channels are important.

Second, countries with large numbers of multinational companies will be very concerned about the way that competition policy and other rules governing company behaviour actually operate. In general, it will be domestic companies that tend to fall foul of market share or collusive/restrictive practice restraints, so third countries have an interest in a strong competition policy that prevents the emergence of 'European champions' and the effective closure of markets. Transparency in the application of the policy and the avoidance of multi-tier authorities and considerable variance across the member states will also make life easier for third country companies.

The ASEAN countries in the main are still in a phase of rapidly growing exports although the East Asian NIEs have now gone beyond this in some product areas and are seeking investment and partnership opportunities in order to increase their market share further. Their interests lie in the avoidance of restrictive measures on trade generated by the sheer rate of their success, whether these are generated through anti-dumping actions or other forms of *ad hoc*, 'temporary' restriction. To some considerable extent the Single Market assists them because it largely eliminates the 'voluntary' restrictions which can be imposed by individual member states. However, whatever the economic rights and wrongs of the case, these suppliers have to be sensitive to the impact they have, and 'orderly marketing policies' may be a means of defusing some of the tensions they generate. However, such behaviour requires either a monopoly or considerable collusion among the suppliers from the region, whether tacitly or explicitly, so it may be impossible to apply. On the whole ASEAN stands to gain most from the continued expansion and application of the multilateral trading system as it can currently expand successfully in open world markets despite the need to pay tariffs.

In the case of Australia and New Zealand much of the emphasis in seeking improvements lies in trying to extend the agenda, particularly to agriculture and, in the case of Australia, to coal. However, although external pressure may be of some help in encouraging change the greater change comes from internal pressures, through demands on the restricted Community budget, for example. Only by packaging together a lot of disparate issues has it been possible to put any pressure on the EC through the Uruguay Round. Here too the market will continue to evolve and the need to maintain pressure will continue. However, in these particular instances the position may get worse rather than better, if further preferential agreements are signed with Central and East European countries. These could not only restrict market access in themselves, but also increase the surpluses that might be dumped on the world markets that are still open.

10.1.2　Retaliate against adverse effects

One of the most taxing elements of international commercial policy is establishing what constitutes 'fairness'. In an ideal world of free trade, investment and payments it is not a relevant question as freedom is normally thought to constitute fairness. But even after all the Single Market measures are complete the world will be a long way from free trade. There is therefore the problem of a balanced approach to the distortions which inevitably exist. The Uruguay Round has been trying to move towards some co-ordinated approach to restrictions so that they can at least make their unfairness obvious.

'Tariffication' or quotas and other quantitative restrictions at least makes the competition to overcome the barrier rather fairer, as does increasing the 'transparency' of other non-tariff barriers so that one can see how they operate. However, there is the inevitable problem of whether to compensate the losers. Targeted measures are difficult to apply and can only be implemented under the terms of the GATT if the country concerned is shown to be violating GATT principles. Such measures are usually only effective against firms that are exporting to you. It is much more difficult to provide offsetting measures to support one's own exporters when they are being discriminated against. Hence the tendency for tit-for-tat measures, hitting the other country where it has an impact rather than solving the direct problem.

The tit-for-tat process is likely to be counter-productive and is a high-risk strategy. Even matching forms of market support can be counter-productive if it is merely a zero-sum game where each party has to keep increasing support if it wants to stay ahead. More productive is likely to be generic strategies, which support innovation, improvement of the skills base or infrastructure, as these are less likely to introduce further distortions to the system and themselves tend to facilitate the ability of the economy to change rather than inhibit it.

Retaliation is only really helpful as a tactical weapon, particularly in the form of a threat rather than actual exercise of the countermeasure as it tends to lead to a general reduction in welfare. On the whole such retaliation is used for a combination of internal and external motives. It may be intended to encourage the other country to change its policy, but it is also likely to be intended as a political gesture at home to show affected groups that some action is being taken. This tendency is particularly clear in the United States. However, in the past Australia and New Zealand have both maintained high levels of protection in order to keep their domestic manufacturing industries, largely because they saw little hope of reducing the barriers imposed on their own exports. Reduction of tariffs on manufacturing in those circumstances was thought merely to result in the demise of much of the industry without generating any alternative forms of activity to replace it. This strategy has been followed in New Zealand and is being followed more slowly by Australia. It remains to be seen which new industries will be established and which old ones will survive at world prices. Thus far New Zealand has merely experienced a prolonged recession and a reduction in the value of many of the sources of domestic wealth, but this may be more a result of the way in which the various parts of a dramatic turnround in the policy stance have been sequenced, leaving mechanisms to encourage change like labour market deregulation to late in the day.[6]

10.1.3 *Adopt alternative regional trading arrangements*

Perhaps the most attractive policy response for third countries to make is to say that if they cannot be fully a part of the EC market, and yet if the steps of integration currently being implemented are clearly so beneficial, they should form a similar grouping of their own. This is undoubtedly a persuasive argument, and one that led to the

Canada–US free trade agreement and the more recent NAFTA agreement, which is still to be ratified, which includes Mexico as well, with the clear intention of admitting other American countries should they wish to join under similar terms.

Much of the initial publicity for NAFTA has been at pains to show that although a little smaller than the new European Economic Area it is of relatively similar GDP and population. However, the comparisons are not as great as these statistics might suggest, both because of the great disparity among NAFTA's members and also because of its more restricted scope. The particular advantage of the EC stemmed, first, from the small size of all of its member states, when compared with the EC's major rivals, the United States and Japan, and second, the extent of the differences between them. Despite the federal structure of the United States and Canada their markets were already a great deal more homogeneous than the EC hopes to become before the end of the century.

This is not to say that the gains from NAFTA may not be considerable compared with the trade flows involved, but that in terms of world trade and intra-European trade it is relatively small. However, it is clearly an attempt to set up an alternative trade grouping and a means of mobilising joint interest in negotiations with the EC. By comparison with the EC it is organisationally very light (comparable to EFTA in this regard) and an interesting test case of how far integration has to go before many of the major benefits can be reached.

However, it is not a Pacific Rim Free Trade Area, nor is one in prospect, largely because of the role of Japan (Bollard and Mayes 1992a). US–Japanese trade relations are not at a point where such an agreement could be considered; while Japan is economically so large compared with the other countries of the western Pacific that they would have well-founded fears of economic domination through such an agreement. ASEAN itself is not a trading arrangement as such, although it is now proposed to implement one by 2005. Such a free trade area will be of only limited benefit as it is in sales to the main world markets that the greatest prospects lie, rather than some rationalisation of production among them – or indeed with the East Asian NIEs. Obviously, the more the process of development continues in the region, the greater the prospect for gain from a regional grouping.

There is also the Pacific Economic Co-operation Council (PECC) and its component organisations,[7] but although this covers a much larger number of countries it is not at present contemplating such an arrangement. However, when APEC was formed in 1989 it was thought of very much as a potential Pacific OECD and, if world trade negotiations were to go seriously awry, it could become the basis for further regional developments.

The major remaining trade grouping in the region is the Australia and New Zealand Closer Economic Relations Trade Agreement (ANZCERTA, usually referred to as CER). This already goes rather further than a straightforward trading area, with extensions into several areas, including business law, technical harmonisation, public purchasing and services. Currency union has been discussed but no plans are apparently in hand. The possibilities for further integration of the two economies, given that they already have integrated labour markets to an extent only matched by Ireland and the United Kingdom within Europe and considerable capital mobility, are distinctly limited. There are no obvious candidates for further members. All their immediate neighbours have very different economic structures. Indeed, there has been serious discussion of Australia applying for membership of the EC (Higgs 1990). Admittedly, there is some extension of the links to the Pacific islands through the SPARTECA agreement (South Pacific Regional Trade and Economic Co-operation Agreement),[8] but Indonesia, the next neighbour to the North, is seven times bigger, in terms of population, than the whole of SPARTECA including Australia and New Zealand.

Outside the Americas, therefore, regionalism does not look a very promising response to closer European integration, although regional agreements are likely to increase as are regional trading ties, especially as China takes a more open stance and the economic zones in the eastern part of the Russian Federation begin to develop.

10.1.4 Try to extend the European approach multilaterally

There is always an argument with regional trading agreements about whether they are a step towards or away from multilateral agreement. In the case of the EC this question has a finely balanced answer. The Community was very keen to make sure that it had got the deepening of integration established through the Maastricht Treaty before proceeding to negotiations with EFTA countries. Future agreements were seen very much as a matter of sorting out how other countries could accede to the existing *acquis communitaire*, and not as an actual negotiation over the *acquis* itself.

Technically speaking, there are problems about extending the Community beyond what could even elastically be described as 'Europe'. However, putting some of the Community's Single Market moves into a multilateral framework might be possible, for example, by extending standards-setting to the ISO, by concluding general agreements on the treatment of state aids, by opening public procurement, etc. Some of these could be accepted even without joining the Common Market and being inside the Common External Tariff. Similarly, agreements over competition policy and treatment of financial institutions and the right of establishment of other services could be extended.[9] Steps such as these would be the logical extension of multilateral negotiations after the GATT round has been digested, so it is probably an agenda for the second half of the 1990s. Rollo (1992) suggests that environmental agreements could be added to this agenda of competition policy and the international treatment of services (particularly financial services).

However, if the existing GATT round is anything to go by, future progress will be long and slow, and many recent memories will need to be forgotten before the willingness to undertake a further multilateral round emerges. The temptation will be to conclude more limited agreements.

10.1.5 Try to establish bilateral agreements

One such form that agreements outside the multilateral framework could take is through bilateral or possibly trilateral arrangements among the three main trading blocs, Europe, NAFTA and Japan. This could take the form of an extension of the SII talks or simply a constructive approach to dispute resolution among those groups. While this is anathema to the proponents of the multilateral approach and likely to generate ill-feeling among the NIEs and LDCs, it might nevertheless be a means of making progress in the major markets, which would spread the type of benefits being agreed within the European Economic Area.

Much less scope exists for such bilateral arrangements involving ASEAN or Australasia. For them multilateral arrangements remain the most plausible way to getting substantial changes in commercial relations with the EC.

10.1.6 Change unilaterally to get the best out of the external environment

A question remains over the extent to which countries should ignore international agreements and act unilaterally to get the most out of the changes in the international scene posed by European integration. Australia and New Zealand have separately come to this decision, rather more drastically in the latter case, and there are signs that some of the NIEs are thinking along the same lines. Here we are discussing not just commercial policy but the whole way in which industrial and macroeconomic policy should be framed in order to achieve the best prospects for international competitiveness. A similar set of suggestions tend to be put forward by the IMF and the World Bank in restructuring packages for LDCs.

Jon Stanford's chapter provides the only substantial discussion of this form of response.

There are two aspects to the policy, on the one hand the reduction in protection to low levels and on the other the introduction of positive measures to encourage structural adjustment. These positive measures do not have a particular sectoral focus but are intended to improve infrastructure, human capital and innovation. Additionally, the environment is being made more attractive both to domestic and foreign investment through deregulation and what is described as microeconomic reform – the improvement in labour market flexibility, for example. Stanford says relatively little about the importance of the provision of a non-inflationary environment through 'sound' fiscal and monetary policy but this is usually part of the whole package.

The major distinction between Australia and New Zealand over these policies is the question of speed. New Zealand has moved much faster; the protection has been removed before the new industries have been established. Two arguments are advanced for this greater speed. The first is that the change is politically difficult to sustain so unless it is done quickly the political backing will disappear before it is complete and the process will be reversed, engendering another costly cycle of support and then reduction in barriers, as has been the case in a number of South American countries. The second argument is that businesses and employees are reluctant to change and so will only respond rapidly to the shock treatment of the more rapid route.

However, in both cases new industries are slow to emerge and the base on which it is argued they can be built is relatively narrow. Both countries have a good endowment of skills and traditions of ingenuity. They have a strong agricultural base and, in the case of Australia, a strong resource base as well. Exploiting comparative advantage could come from pursuing these avenues and trying to increase the value added in the less produced exports – increasing the quality of wool, producing more processed products and so on (Australian Manufacturing Council 1990).

These policies seem necessary, whatever the commercial policies practised elsewhere. If agricultural exporting is more difficult then the need for change is increased. Even if it is eased, then it is still necessary for the countries to move to a higher value-added base if they want to increase their standard of living. An even faster exploitation of non-renewable raw materials is not a satisfactory long-run strategy even when those materials are as abundant as they are in Australia. For sustainability wasting assets need to be converted into permanent assets which can generate an enduring flow of foreign exchange to pay for the inflow of goods and services which it is not economic to produce domestically.

Although these issues are most acutely faced in Australia and New Zealand, it is arguable that similar strategies could usefully be pursued elsewhere round the Pacific Rim where the trading pattern is unfavourable. NAFTA is lowering the barriers in North America. Currently Japan, the East Asian NIEs and ASEAN are still able to develop rapidly on the basis of a trade surplus. But the macroeconomic and microeconomic conditions for growth need to be present. What is clear is that while European integration may have acted as the necessary stimulus, the response was needed anyway and needs to be maintained even if European integration falters.

Notes

1. However, the results of Stoeckel *et al.* (1990) show that it does not require extreme circumstances for some countries to lose out. Furthermore they also show that the gains are much lower than from a multilateral extension of the benefits.
2. The net result is that response is biased towards assisting the needs of those who might be disadvantaged. This not only tends to slow rather than accelerate the process of adjustment to the new competitive circumstances but results in a rather myopic assessment of costs and benefits rather than looking at the wider gains and penalties. Thus a subsidy for coal production has an immediate impact on the coal industry and those that depend on it, whereas the increase in interest rates caused by the greater demand for funds or the losses from those who would probably have been the alternative beneficiaries are not so well counted.
3. Take the example of bananas. The EC itself grows very little in the way of bananas but it favours imports from former colonies. Other banana producers cannot retaliate by restricting EC banana exports because there are none to restrict. They therefore have to pick a product area in which the EC will be sensitive. For developing countries it may be very difficult to find such a product and successful pressure can only come either through strategic raw materials like oil or the support of a much wider alliance.
4. An argument which is being put with some force in the context of monetary union.
5. Similar divisions and opportunities exist in the life market although the future for insurance is still believed by many to lie in a multi-domestic system rather than a fully fledged 'single' market (Hart 1992a).
6. See Bollard and Mayes (1992b, 1993) for further assessments of these policies and their lessons for the EC.

References 207

7. PBEC the Pacific Basin Economic Council – the business arm.
   PAFTAD the Pacific Trade and Development Conference – an academic organisation.
   APEC the Asia–Pacific Economic Council – the governmental arrangement.
8. The other members of SPARTECA are: Cook Islands, Federated States of Micronesia, Fiji, KiriBati, Marshall Islands, Nauru, Niue, Papua New Guinea, Solomon Islands, Tonga, Tuvalu, Vanuatu, Western Samoa.
9. There is a good discussion of these possibilities in Rollo (1992).

References

Australian Manufacturing Council (1990) *The Global Challenge: Australian Manufacturing in the 1990s* (Melbourne).
Bollard, A. E. and Mayes, D. G. (1992a) 'Regionalism and the Pacific Rim', *Journal of Common Market Studies*, vol. 30, no. 2, pp. 195–209.
Bollard, A. E. and Mayes, D. G. (1992b) 'Corporatisation and Privatisation in New Zealand', paper presented at University of St Andrews, forthcoming in conference proceedings.
Bollard, A. E. and Mayes, D. G. (1993) 'Lessons for Europe from the New Zealand Experience', *National Institute Economic Review*, January.
Hart, P. E. (1992a) 'The effects of 1992 on the insurance industry in Britain and Germany', National Institute Discussion Paper.
Hart, P. E. (1992b) 'The effects of 1992 on the pharmaceutical industry in Britain and Germany', National Institute Discussion Paper.
Higgs, P. J. (1990) 'Australia's foreign trade strategy', Working Paper 12, University of Melbourne School of Management.
Langhammer, R. (1991) 'Towards Regional Entities in Asia-Pacific', *ASEAN Economic Bulletin*, vol. 7, no. 3, pp. 277–89.
Mayes, D. G. and Ogiwara, Y. (1992) 'Transplanting Japanese Success in the UK', *National Institute Economic Review*, November.
Rollo, J. M. C. (1992) *Multilateral Trade and Commercial Policy: Notes on an Agenda for the 1990s* (Chatham House).
Stoeckel, A., Pearce, D. and Banks, G. (1990) *Western Trade Blocs* (Canberra: Centre for International Economics).

Index

208